Comprehensive Te[illegible]e for Jazz Musicians

2ND EDITION

by Bert Ligon

ISBN-13: 978-0-634-00176-5

Exclusively Distributed By

7777 W. Bluemound Rd. P.O. Box 13819 Milwaukee, WI 53213

Visit Hal Leonard Online at
www.halleonard.com

CONTENTS

INTRODUCTION

TECHNIQUE

Part of a musician's development is the building of technique necessary to execute musical ideas. For each instrument the list of obstacles is different and the subject of much debate around the practice rooms as to whose instrument is the hardest to learn to play. Playing music will develop some musical technique. However, learning to play certain things before hand gives the musician a better chance at creating a musical performance that transcends the technical difficulties of the piece. A major part of what we practice as musicians is control. This is no different from an athlete mastering the control of a backhand return, a curve ball, a series of turns or leaps on the gymnastics floor. To master any sport, athletes their coaches and trainers break the event into smaller manageable drills to master individually before putting them all together. Drills imply repetition of singular concepts or motions until they become second nature. When we see an athlete or musician and speak of how natural they are, we are seeing the result of hours of practice and drill in order for it to appear natural.

Many of the techniques necessary for an improvising jazz musician are universal for any musician. They must learn to be fluid and in control of their instrument's range of sounds and dynamics, and be in command of the musical heritage and language. At the most basic level all melodies either move in steps or leaps, so they must practice steps and leaps: scales and arpeggios.

While many of the musical techniques necessary are universal, there are some techniques that are unique to the jazz improviser. When the jazz improviser creates music, not only does he need the skills to play notes of the scale or arpeggiate a chord, but he also needs the skills to develop musical ideas in logical ways. Experienced improvisers seem to develop these musical ideas spontaneously and effortlessly. The techniques of developing musical ideas need to be practiced and cultivated along with the muscle skills and techniques.

How does a student develop both sides of this technique dilemma? What actions will develop the muscle skills and the mental control skills to improvise meaningful music?

First, there is no magic solution or shortcut. I had a student who had great difficulty playing a simple scale passage from the week before. I asked him how often he practiced the scale that week. Once. I asked how many tennis serves he practiced. His face lit up when he told me about eight hundred. Guess which area showed the most improvement. Some techniques and skills require hundreds and thousands of repetitions. Routine. Repetition. Major league ball players (even with average salaries over a million dollars) still drill the basics in Spring training. The trick to cultivating the muscle control and mental control is very simple: you have to think while you are practicing. Invent or play exercises that train the muscles and the brain. While you repeat the drills actively think about the musical applications. If the idea works in one musical setting, will it work in another? What if the modality changed? Would it sound good played backwards, upside-down, or fragmented?

BOOK FORMAT

This is not another scale or jazz patterns book. These exercises begin at the source: the improvisations of great jazz artists. Musical ideas are extracted from these excerpts and developed into exercises designed to prepare the improviser to play passages using the extracted idea. The ideas are developed using common compositional devices. The application of compositional devices in the invention of the exercises trains the improviser in the art of composition and the art developing an idea. These skills, exercises and compositional techniques are then applied to etudes and put into useful musical settings. This book will help accomplish the following objectives:

- Playing the exercises will develop physical technique, muscle memory, and mental skills.
- Having the exercises juxtaposed with musical examples expedites the connections and reinforces the practical function of the exercises.
- Thinking through the development of the exercises, seeing from where the exercises were extracted and applying common compositional devices to the extracted ideas, will help the improvising musician acquire the technique of composing "spontaneously."

IMPROVISATION

The dictionary defines the words extemporaneous, impromptu, and improvisation as creation "without advance preparation." Is this what happens? What jazz musician improvises without advance preparation? No one. It reminds me of the story of the man who prayed nightly to God to let him win the lottery. God, after hearing his prayers for weeks, finally spoke to the man and said, "Meet me half-way, at least buy a lottery ticket." Any jazz musician who believes they will go out and create jazz "without advance preparation" is planning to win the lottery without buying a ticket. The exercises in this book at least buy you a ticket (no guarantee of winning).

On what is jazz improvisation based? Can it be defined? Many jazz improvisations fall into the two categories below.

I. Paraphrase the Melody
    A. Adding to the melody
    B. Changing the Rhythmic content
    C. Ornamenting or embellishing the general contour
II. Improvise on the Harmony
    A. Harmonic Generalization
    B. Harmonic Specificity

No single improvisation necessarily adheres strictly to any single structural or theoretical designation. An improvisation may incorporate concepts from either category and maybe both within a single phrase. Why separate them? An improviser may begin a phrase improvising on the harmony, being specific by outlining arpeggios, then suggest the melody, and end the phrase with a harmonically general blues cliché. By separating the approaches, practicing each approach individually, the student improviser has a much better chance of creating lines that incorporate each of these concepts.

There are several devices that all composers and improvisers use. These same devices that can be used to develop ideas in a composition or improvisation can be used to develop individual exercises. Applying motivic devices in the practice room, where time can be stopped, improves the understanding of the devices and prepares the student for using the devices in a real time situation. In order to play a tune at 240 bpm, you need more than just the ability to play scales and arpeggios at 240 bpm. You need to have practiced and cultivated some understanding of fashioning those scales and arpeggios into real musical ideas. Below is a list of devices used in developing motives. Apply these concepts when developing exercises and you will also be exercising compositional techniques. There is an extended discussion of these devices with examples on pp.153-156.

III. Motivic Development Devices

Motives may be derived from the melody or newly invented.

A. Repetition (unless an idea is repeated, it is not a theme.)
B. Transpose
C. Mode Change
D. Fragment
E. Add to (before, in the middle, after)
F. Sequence
G. Embellish or ornament (keeping the general contour, using neighbor-tones and other devices, still keeping the motive recognizable)
H. Augmentation (making the rhythmic unit or the pitch interval larger)
I. Diminution (making the rhythmic unit or the pitch interval smaller)
J. Invert (upside down: what goes up comes down)
K. Retrograde (play backwards)
L. Retrograde inversion (upside down and backwards)
M. Displacement (pitch and & octave displacement; rhythmic displacement)

WHAT'S NEW in THIS EDITION

The format of the book is unaltered. More musical examples have been added from Louis Armstrong, Bach, Beethoven, Stan Getz, John Scofield, Handel, Lizst, Gary Versace, Niels Pedersen, Wes Montgomery, Thad Jones, Sonny Rollins, Kenny Garrett, Sarah Vaughan, and others. Many more exercises have been added to the chapters on triads, diminished scales, motivic and pentatonic patterns, extensions and connections, and dominant cycles. Some exercises were consolidated and duplication was eliminated in order to make room for the additional examples and exercises. Feedback from readers and students prompted the inclusion of more examples of how to apply the exercises. Application examples have been added to most chapters. Chapter 16, already focused on applications, has been enhanced with more applications to standard progressions and several more etudes exploring the use of materials from the book.

> *"We are what we repeatedly do.*
> *Excellence, then, is not an act, but a habit."*
> *—Aristotle*

BERT LIGON is director of Jazz Studies at the University of South Carolina where he directs the big band, teaches jazz theory, improvisation, and arranging. He publishes music for jazz big bands, jazz string ensembles, steel drum ensembles, and orchestra and written award winning music for television and radio. Ligon is the author of *Jazz Theory Resources Volume I & II*, and *Connecting Chords with Linear Harmony*, available from Hal Leonard, Inc. Ligon plays piano, guitar and third base.

> *"I will teach children music, physics, and philosophy; but most importantly music, for in the patterns of music and all the arts are the keys to learning."*
> *—Plato*

I. BASIC EXERCISES

ROUTINE

The first set of exercises is routine. Not routine in the sense of meaningless perfunctory activity, but routine in the sense of habitually repeating important fundamentals. A seasoned athlete or musician will tell you that much of what to practice is still the basics. Catching, throwing, batting for the ball player. Good time, tone, and intonation for the musician.

Since any melody is composed of leaps and steps, it follows that in order to prepare to play melodies, steps and leaps should be practiced. Scales are made of steps and arpeggios are made of leaps. The practice of basics must begin with scales and arpeggios. Scales, arpeggios, and broken chords are the building blocks or the bolt of cloth out of which melodies are created. Practicing scales and arpeggios will help you to learn to move around on the instrument, to make some order and patterns out of the chaos, and will make it easier to learn and play good melodies. It would be difficult to elaborate or chromatically embellish melodies based on scales and arpeggios without first knowing the scales and arpeggios.

Begin the day with scales, arpeggios and broken chords.

TIPS FOR PRACTICE:

1. Practice around the circle of fifths. This reinforces the common root movement prevalent in functional harmony. (C - F - B♭ - E♭ - A♭ - D♭ - G♭ [F♯] - B - E - A - D - G)
2. Don't always start with C. The keys of C, F and B♭ become easier to play, and everything down in the shady area with all the flats and sharps seem to remain in the dark. Note: hard keys become easy keys if you practice them.
3. Use the ***metronome***! For jazz swing playing, put the clicks on 2 & 4 like the hi-hat.
4. Practice it slow enough to get it, then try it faster. Step by step.
5. Practice what you don't do well. If you sound great on something, move on to something you don't do as well.
6. Practice using different phrasing on tunes. Phrases can begin as pick-ups **before** the barline, **on** the barline, or **after** the barline. Try putting the three words in front of you instead of the changes:

BEFORE - ON - AFTER

Try mixing up how you phrase. Too much of one thing becomes predictable, therefore boring.

7. Strive for rhythmic variety. Since jazz is usually based on the eighth-note subdivision, introduce other values for variety. Try placing something like this in front of you when you practice a tune you know:

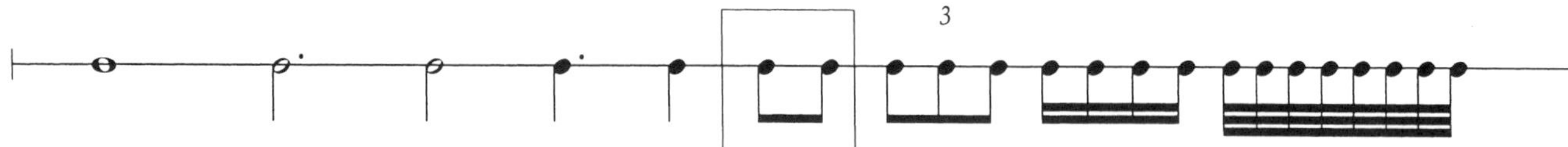

Moving around on either side of the eighth-notes in the middle will help the rhythmic interest of your lines. After introducing rhythmic ideas such as dotted quarters, use the similar accents with your eighth-note feel as a development.

PRACTICE BY LIMITING

1. Fragment tunes; limit to two, four, and eight-bar phrases. Get familiar with these short segments before putting them all together.
2. Drill only specific things. Play a tune using:
   1. only broken chords and arpeggios,
   2. only scale step motion, no leaps and no chromatic alterations,
   3. using a certain motive and make it fit throughout the tune using alterations of the theme and transposition, etc.
3. Practice Contrasts (Angular/smooth; lyrical/agitated; harmonic generalization/harmonic specificity; space/busy; high/low; loud/soft; etc.)
4. Practice some creative doodling. "Go for it" as part of your practice routine. Get the rust off the creative gears. Remember that improvisation is PLAY. Out of your doodling recognize material that is useful. Jot down good ideas for later practice or tunes to compose.
5. Practice what is unique to your instrument besides what is universal. Example: Horns practice extreme registers, trumpets half-valve sounds, bending of tones, tonguing, etc. Rhythm section practice comping; it is what you do at least 80% of the time. Guitar and Piano incorporate chords and double stops into your improvisation, etc.
6. At some time practice playing tunes as a performance. Practice the tune with a beginning, an end and a definite emotional contour.

Always try to sound as musical as possible.

After practice ideas around the circle of fifths, try practicing other orders of the twelve keys such as:

1. Up or down minor thirds:
   C - E♭ - F♯ - A / B♭ - C♯ - E - G / A♭ - B - D - F
2. Up or down major thirds
   C - E - A♭ / G - B - E♭ / D - F♯ - B♭ / A - D♭ - F
3. Up or down whole steps
   C - D - E - F♯ - A♭ - B♭ / D♭ - E♭ - F - G - A - B
4. Up or down half steps
   C - C♯- D - D♯ - E - F - F♯ - G - G♯ - A - A♯ - B

You don't always have to start with C!

If you only practice four keys a day, don't start every time with the key of C. Keep a record of where you leave off and start the next day with a short review, then move on to the next keys.

The typical way to practice scales is beginning with the lowest note, playing to the highest and then back down. Some days play backwards. Begin with the highest note, play down to the lowest and then return to the top. You will be surprised how difficult it may be on keys you thought you knew.

PRACTICE IN ALL TWELVE KEYS?

Why should you practice in all twelve keys?

- Music occurs in all twelve keys. Bach thought it important and wrote preludes and fugues in all twelve major and all twelve minor keys for his students.
- It is a great way to learn your instrument
- You will solve technical problems that will benefit you later
- Solving the technical problems (fingerings, etc.) in one key will help you in another key
- It will prepare you for the inevitable encounter of all keys in reading and improvising music
- Here's a possible four tune jazz set of standard, not obscure tunes, with the keys needed to know listed to the side: all twelve keys are represented.

All the Things You Are	A♭, C, E♭, G , E
Cherokee	B♭, E♭, B, A, G, F
Body & Soul	D♭, D, C
Joy Spring	F, G♭, G, E♭

- Will you always adjust your mouthpiece or empty your spit valve on the bridge to *Cherokee* or *Have you Met Miss Jones?*
- What keys would you omit?
- "hard" keys aren't so hard if you practice them.

TYPICAL DAY

1. Routine to warm-up: maybe not all twelve keys, but at least 2-4
2. Isolate a few technical exercises
3. Isolate a few special scale technical exercises (melodic minor/Diminished, etc.)
4. Apply the above exercises to tunes
5. Practice outlines on tunes
6. Learn new tunes

PRACTICE SLOWLY

If you wish to play Cherokee at 300 bpm, do not practice at 296 and work your way up. Begin at 60-96 bpm. Make it swing at that tempo and every tempo as you work your way up to the faster tempos.

SCALES FOR IMPROVISATION

Some of the basic scales to use with jazz improvisation:

Major Scales Harmonic minor scales

Melodic minor scales Whole-half diminished scales

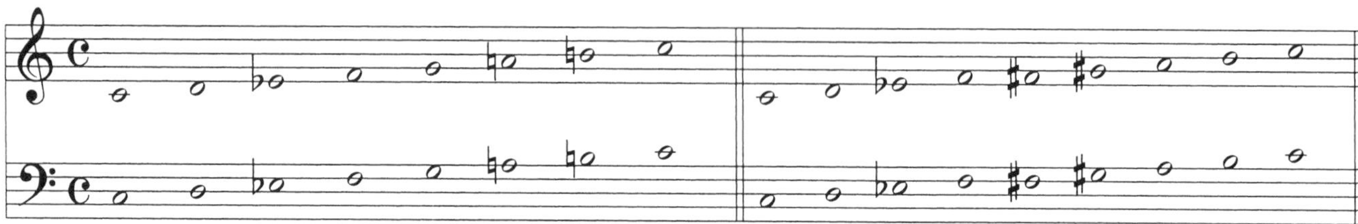

Major pentatonic and blues scales Minor pentatonic and blues scales

Major scales with ♭6 Whole tone scales Augmented Scales

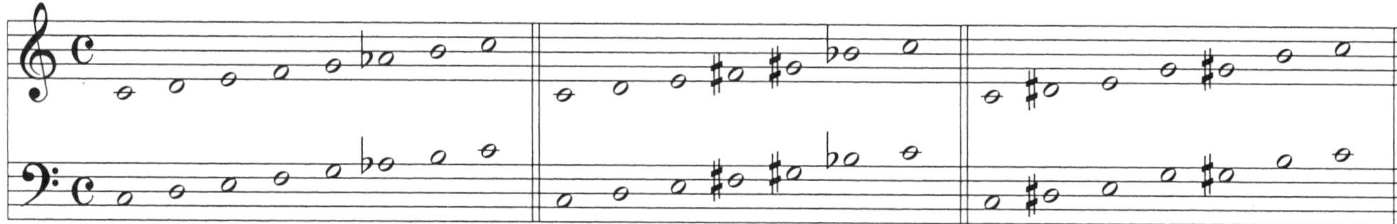

TRANSPOSITION NOTES

- Major, minor, and pentatonic scales can be transposed to all twelve keys.
- A diminished scale can be transposed only three times before repeating. (C diminished is the same as E♭, F♯, and A diminished scales.)
- A whole tone scale can only be transposed once.
- An augmented scale can be transposed four times before repeating. (C augmented is the same as E and A♭ augmented.)

BASIC SCALE PRACTICE

Practice over the full range of the instrument. Pianist should play over four octave range. Think from lowest note on the instrument: i.e. saxophones: start G major on lowest note possible, which is B natural. Always practice with a metronome at a reasonable pulse. First play quarter notes, then move on to triplets, then eight and sixteenth notes. If it is difficult to play sixteenth notes, you may try starting with an eight-sixteenth-sixteenth pattern. Initially, practice with no accents. You may wish to play scales as shown below with accents every three notes. This helps you learn to control accents. If you play these accents as sixteenth notes, this will also help develop a sense of polyrhythm with the accents suggesting a dotted eighth pulse over the metronome pulse of quarter notes.

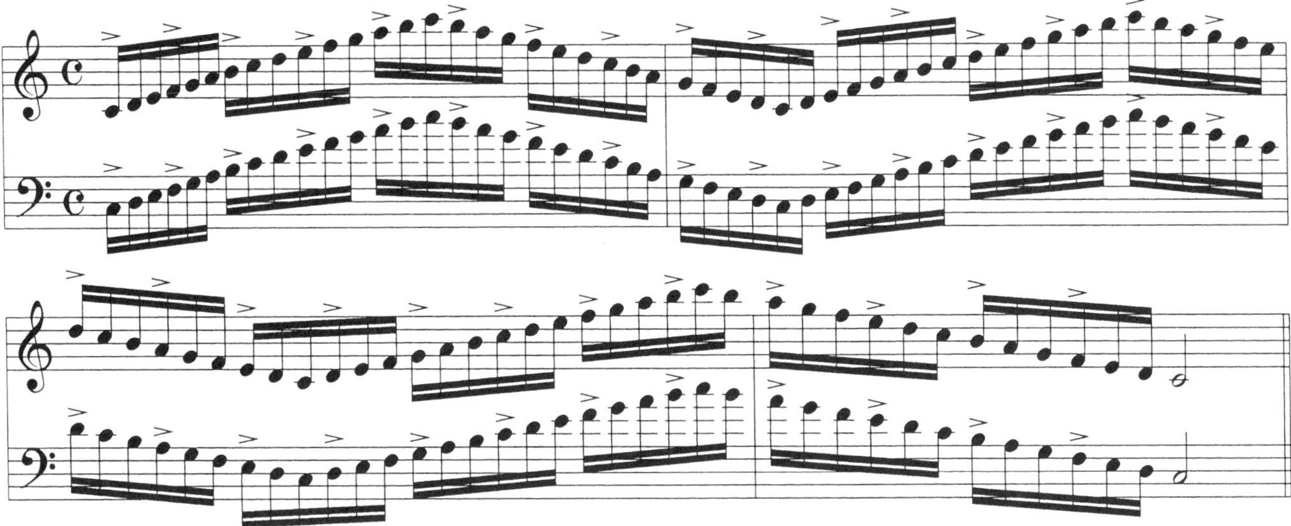

Remember to concentrate on clean execution, good tone, and good time. Play with no errors or hesitation before moving the metronome up a notch. Practice even eighths and then practice swing eighths with alternate tonguing or bowing as applicable.

Concentrate on clean execution, good tone, and good time.

Practice major and harmonic minor scales the full range of the instrument. When these have been mastered, add melodic minor, major with a flat sixth, diminished, and whole tone scales.

SCALE PRACTICE

1.1 Major Scale

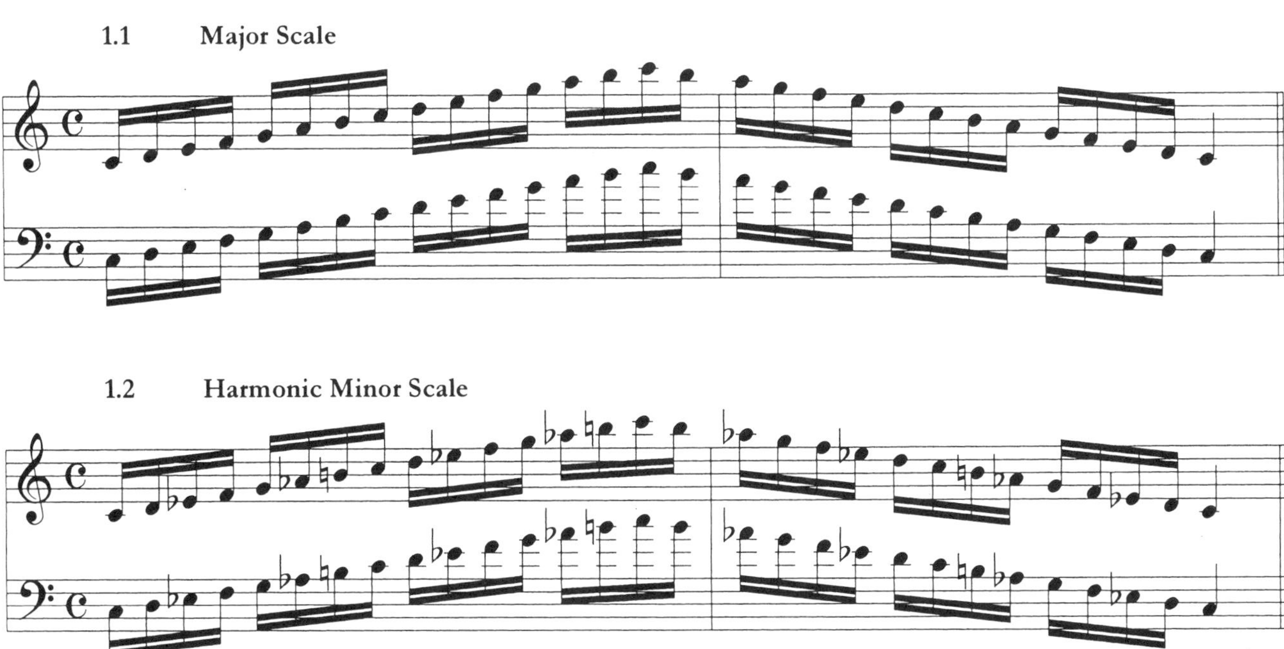

1.2 Harmonic Minor Scale

ARPEGGIO & BROKEN CHORD PRACTICE

1.3 **Major Arpeggio** 1.4 **Minor Arpeggio**

1.5 **Major 7th Arpeggio**

1.6 **Minor 7th Arpeggio**

1.7 **Dominant 7th Arpeggio**

1.8 **Half-Diminished Arpeggio**

1.9 Diminished Arpeggio

1.10 Broken Chord Pattern No.1

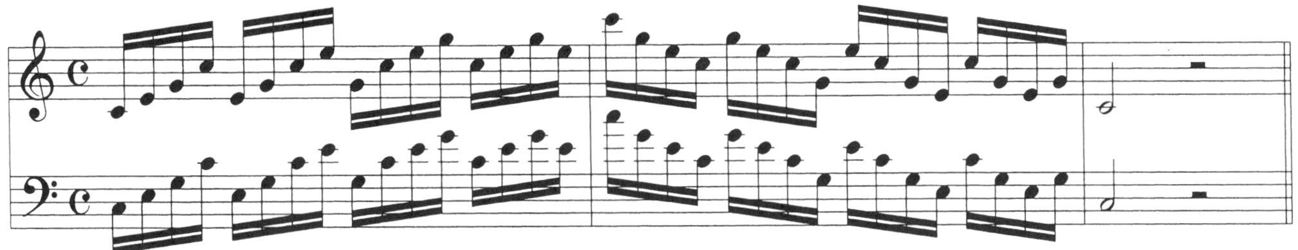

1.11 Broken Chord Pattern No.2

1.12 Broken Chord Pattern No.3

1.13 Broken Chord Pattern No.4

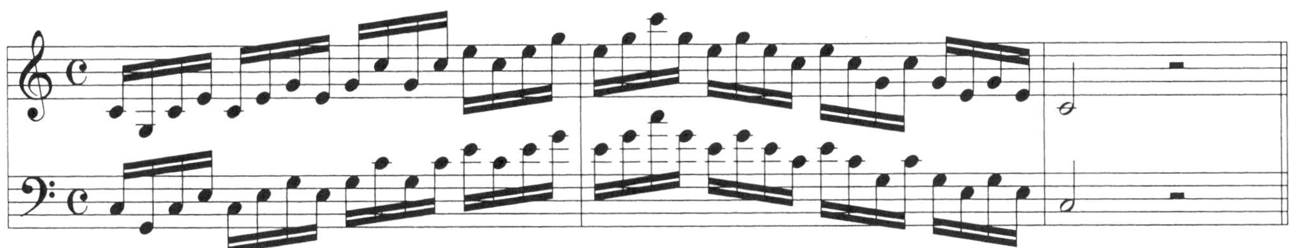

OTHER MELODIC SCALE & ARPEGGIO PATTERNS

Practicing can become dull if all you do is scales and arpeggios, just as improvisation would be dull without some other motion besides scales and arpeggios. Here are some patterns from great improvisers that can be added to the practice routine.

PATTERNS with THIRDS

Clifford Brown and Cannonball Adderley combine scale passages with patterns in thirds in the following examples.

This example from a Charlie Parker solo looks quite complex until you break it down. The top line is the original line from his solo. The second line eliminates the triplet upper-neighbor tone turn to reveal a simple scale pattern in thirds. The third line, when reduced to eighth note values, reveals a simple diatonic line. The fourth line simplifies the line even further to reveal a simple 5-3-1 triad.

The following exercises add the patterns in thirds to the scale routine.

1.14 Ascending Thirds

1.15 Descending Thirds

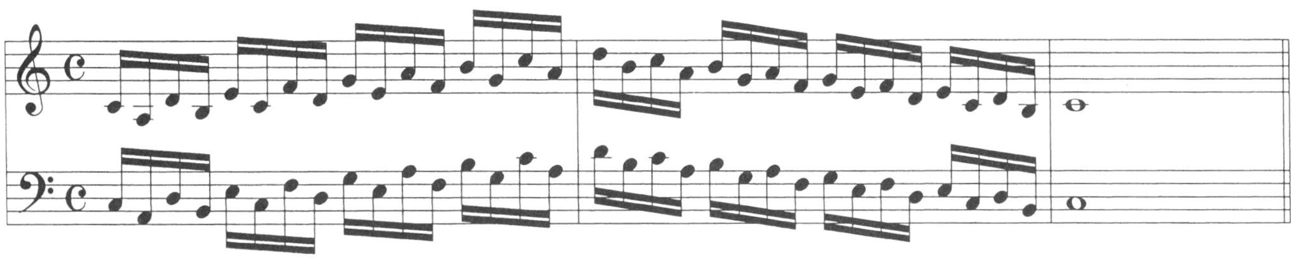

1.16 Alternating Thirds

PATTERNS WITH NEIGHBOR TONES

Apply to all scale practice.

1.17 With Lower Neighbor Tone (LNT) Embellishment ascending, UNT descending

CYCLICAL QUADRUPLETS

One way to embellish a single note is to play the note, move away and back to that same note. A very common pattern that follows this concept involves the primary note and two other notes that return to the primary note. This pattern has four varieties and is has been called a Cyclical Quadruplet (CQ). Cyclical because it cycles back to the first pitch; quadruplet because it is a four note pattern. The four patterns below all have C as the primary pitch. CQ pattern no.2 is the retrograde, no.3 is the inversion, and no.4 is the retrograde inversion of CQ pattern no.1.

Here are some examples of CQ patterns from jazz improvisations by Charlie Parker, Art Farmer, Cannonball Adderley, Sonny Stitt, and Herbie Hancock. Charlie Parker used all four CQ patterns in these two examples. The first includes CQ patterns no.2 & 3; the second, patterns 1 & 4.

CQ pattern no.1

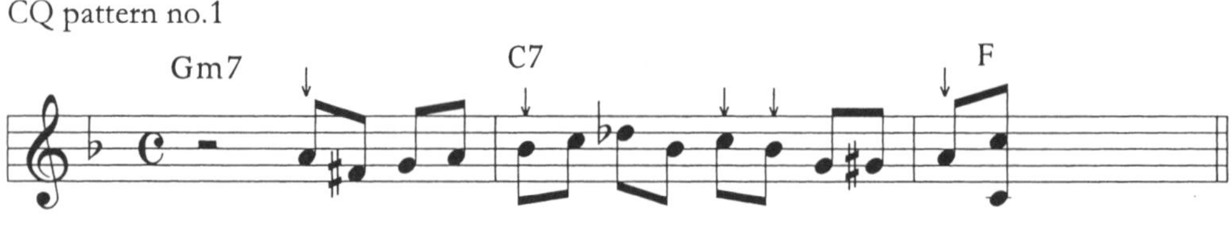

Here are some basic CQ exercises to add to scale routines.

1.22 Cyclical Quadruplet Version No.1 (CQ)

1.23 CQ Version No.2

1.24 CQ Version No.3

1.25 CQ Version No.4

CQ patterns can be applied to arpeggios as they were applied to scales as shown in this excerpt from a Cannonball Adderley improvisation. Adderley used CQ pattern no.1 in the first measure and CQ pattern no.4 in the last two measures outlining a chord.

CQ patterns no.1 and no.4

Here are some basic CQ exercises to add to arpeggio routines. These four exercises are shown applied to a major 9 chord. Practice these patterns applied to minor 9, dominant 9, and other arpeggios.

1.26 CQ Version No.1 applied to C major 9 arpeggio

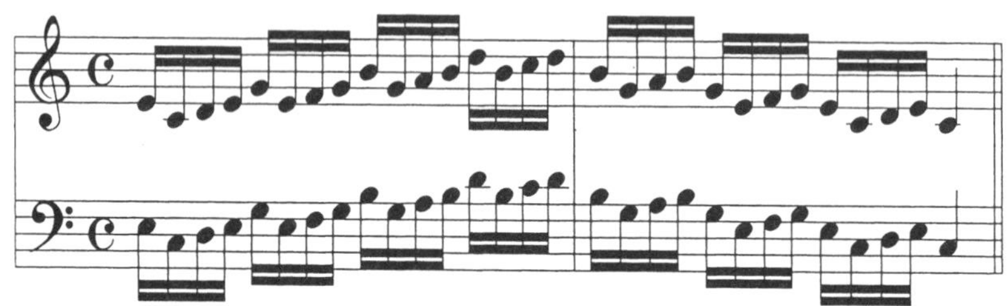

1.27 CQ Version No.2 applied to C major 9 arpeggio

1.28 CQ Version No.3 applied to C major 9 arpeggio

1.29 CQ Version No.4 applied to C major 9 arpeggio

DIATONIC CHORDS

In addition to practicing arpeggios individually, practice arpeggios related to each key center. Triads, seventh and ninth chords can be built on every scale degree of any scale, and often appear in compositions and improvisations. Here are two short examples from Tom Harrell and Dexter Gordon.

Diatonic triads

Diatonic triads

Add these to your scale practice for all major and minor keys.

1.30 Diatonic Triads In Root Position Ascending

1.31 Diatonic Triads In Root Position Descending

Parker and Sonny Stitt used this common pattern that outlines a major triad. The first part of the measure includes passing tones (PT) between the chord tones; the second half uses CQ pattern no.1.

Charlie Parker: Sonny Stitt:

This pattern can be applied to all diatonic triads. This exercise incorporates many of the previous exercises: scales, diatonic triads, CQs.

1.32 Diatonic Triads With PTs And CQs

DIATONIC SEVENTH CHORDS

Triads built in thirds (tertian) occur universally in music. While a triad may be constructed using 1-3-5 of a scale, extended tertian chords can be constructed using 1-3-5-7, 1-3-5-7-9, and even 1-3-5-7-9-11-13. These extended tertian chords occur frequently in jazz. A chord spelled out to the 13th may use all the notes of the scale, and in this way illustrates the equality of the chord and the scale. The scale is a spelling of the seven diatonic notes in steps; the extended tertian chord is a spelling of the seven diatonic notes in thirds. An understanding of basic tertian triads is necessary in order to understand seventh chords. A seventh chord is created by adding the interval of a third to the top of a tertian triad and a ninth chord is created by adding another interval of a third to the top of the seventh chord. The seventh chord exercises will provide a background to understanding extended tertian chords and connections covered later in chapter 10.

Hank Mobley ended his improvisation using diatonic seventh chords.

McCoy Tyner used them in conjunction with other elements in the following excerpt. (Diatonic triads and 1235 pattern)

The following are exercises designed to aid the mastering of diatonic seventh chords in root position and in all inversions. Begin practicing in all major scales first. They can be quite useful built on each scale degree of all scale types.

1.33 Diatonic Seventh Chords In Root Position

1.34 Diatonic Seventh Chords In First Inversion

1.35 Diatonic Seventh Chords In Second Inversion

1.36 Diatonic Seventh Chords In Third Inversion

1.37 Diatonic Seventh Chords Alternating Ascending And Descending

HROMATIC EMBELLISHMENT

DIATONIC SEVENTH CHORDS

Any diatonic note of the scale can be embellished with chromatic leading tones. This is not unique to jazz or Western Art Music. Chromaticism can make the music more interesting; the chromatic notes adding a tension not available with the diatonic notes alone. The diatonic scale, diatonic triads, and diatonic seventh chords must be first mastered individually before attempting chromatic embellishment. If you have a command over the diatonic vocabulary, then this next section will help add chromaticism to your vocabulary.

Clifford Brown used ascending diatonic seventh chord arpeggios in the following example, but added an element of chromaticism. Several of the seventh chords are preceded with chromatic leading tones.

McCoy Tyner used descending seventh chord arpeggios in the following passage.

DIATONIC TRIADS WITH LT EMBELLISHMENT

Here are some consummate examples of diatonic triads embellished by leading tones (LT). All of these great lines use the same basic diatonic triads with the added LT to the root of each chord. Some use the pattern of LT-1-3-5. The example from Mozart may be the most interesting because of the angularity created by the 5-3-LT-1 pattern.

This improvisation ends in a similar method to the earlier Hank Mobley diatonic seventh example from p.14.

Mozart: Clarinet Quintet, K.581

Any of the previous exercises can be practiced using chromatic leading tones. Here are some suggested exercises to get started adding chromaticism to the routine vocabulary.

1.38 Ascending Diatonic Chords With Chromatic Leading Tone (LT)

1.39 Descending Diatonic Chords With LT

NEIGHBOR TONES APPLIED TO ARPEGGIOS & BROKEN CHORDS

Previous examples have shown leading tones (which are always, by definition chromatic), and passing tones. Any diatonic note may have an upper neighbor tone (which is usually diatonic), and may have a lower neighbor tone (which, like the leading tone, is usually chromatic). The following examples illustrate common embellishment of diatonic material using diatonic upper neighbor tones (UNT).

UPPER NEIGHBOR TONES (UNT)

This first example is a line that most jazz musicians learned from Louis Armstrong. Each chord tone was preceded with a diatonic upper neighbor tone. The second example was from a scat solo by Sarah Vaughan, who paid respect to the Armstrong line. In the third line, Stan Getz made an ascending triad interesting by preceding each chord tone with an accented upper neighbor. The basic structure of each line is shown below the example.

It may look like the UNTs in this Chopin example are chromatic which contradicts the previous paragraph. At this point, the piece is in the key of F minor. The C triad (shown with circled notes) is elaborated using the diatonic notes from the key of F minor. The UNT of C is D♭, the UNT of E is F, and the UNT of G is A♭. The UNTs are chromatic, but in this case, also diatonic to the key of F minor.

Chopin: Op.9 No. 2

The F triad is stated as a broken chord in the first measure and in the second is elaborated with passing tones and diatonic UNTs in this example from Bach.

Bach: Two-Part Invention No. 8

Cannonball Adderley appears to have borrowed this UNT idea from the previous Bach example.

Here are several basic arpeggio and broken chord exercises from earlier in the chapter with UNTs added.

1.40 Arpeggio with chord tones preceded by UNT

1.41 Broken chord pattern (from exercise 1.13) with chord tones preceded by UNT

1.42 Arpeggio with UNTs

1.43 **Broken chord pattern (from exercise 1.11) with UNTs**

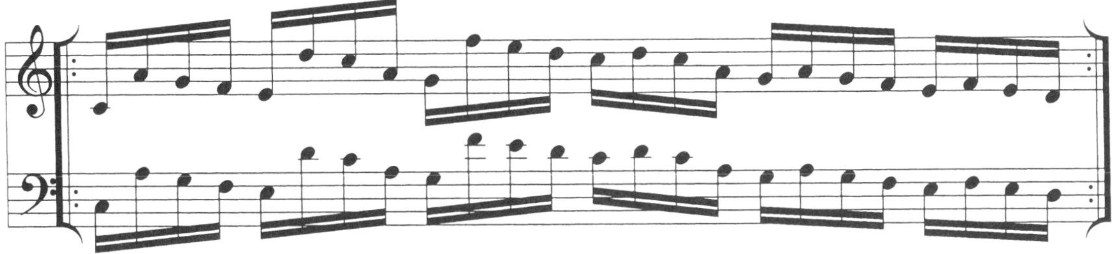

1.44 **Broken chord pattern (from exercise 1.11) with UNTs**

LOWER NEIGHBOR TONES (LNT) & LEADING TONES (LT)

The following examples illustrate common embellishment of diatonic material using chromatic lower neighbor tones (LNT). *Joshua Fought the Battle of Jerico* begins with the root of the minor triad, moves to the LNT, returns to the root, and continues using the second degree as a passing tone before repeating the pattern on the third of the chord. Cannonball seems to have quoted *Joshua Fought the Battle of Jerico* in the second example.

Joshua Fought the Battle of Jerico

Quote?

Sonny Stitt took the LNT idea and applied it to the diminished chord. The sum of all the LNTs and PTs added to the diminished chord creates the half-whole diminished scale, also called the octatonic scale. (Many of the notes in this passage do not appear to relate to the indicated chords). The diminished scale will be looked at more closely in chapter 5.

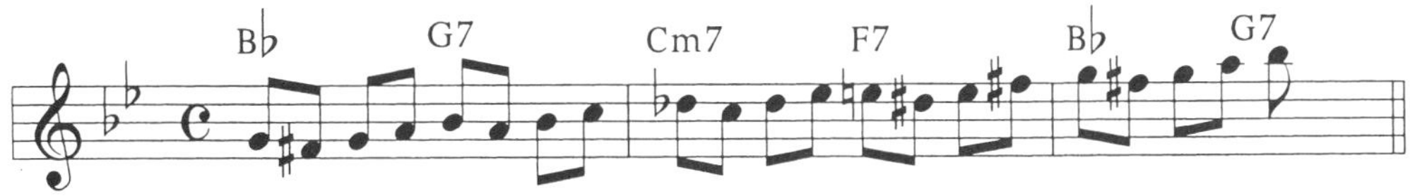

Brown and Parker approached simple triads with LTs. In both the following excerpts the tonic triad is used for generalization. More on triadic generalization can be found in chapter 3.

Triad with LNTs

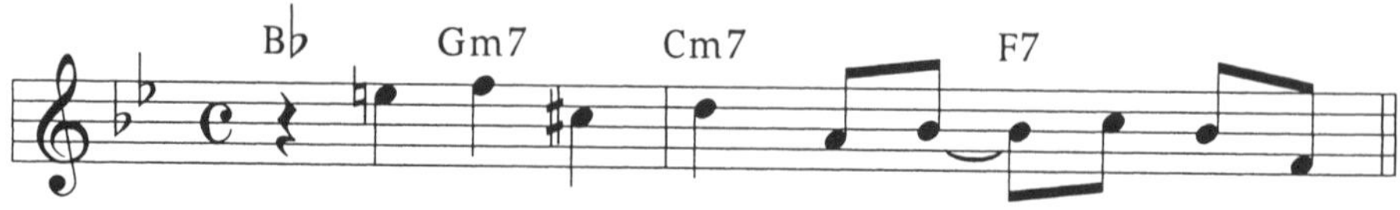

The triad embellished by LTs can be found in this Beethoven sonata and a Wes Montgomery improvisation.

Beethoven: Piano Sonata Op.14, No. 2 (G triad embellished with LTs)

(C triad embellished with LTs)

Parker embellished a diminished chord with LTs and the sum of the notes, like the previous Sonny Stitt example, creates the half-whole diminished scale.

After ascending arpeggios on upper structures (3-5-7-9-11) of the E♭ minor chord, Bill Evans used LNTs preceding the notes of the basic triad in the last measure of this example.

E♭m9 8va

Lou Donaldson played this excerpt in an improvisation:

Can you see the triad as the basic musical idea in the above Lou Donaldson excerpt? PTs are added to the triadic idea, and then eighth note chromatic leading tones are added.

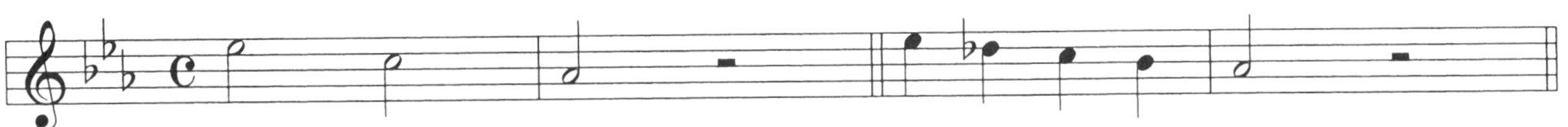

Here are several basic arpeggio and broken chord exercises from earlier in the chapter with LNTs and LTs added.

1.45 Arpeggio with chord tones preceded by LNT

1.46 Broken chord pattern (from exercise 1.13) with LNTs

1.47 Arpeggio with LNTs

1.48 Broken chord pattern (from exercise 1.11) with LNTs

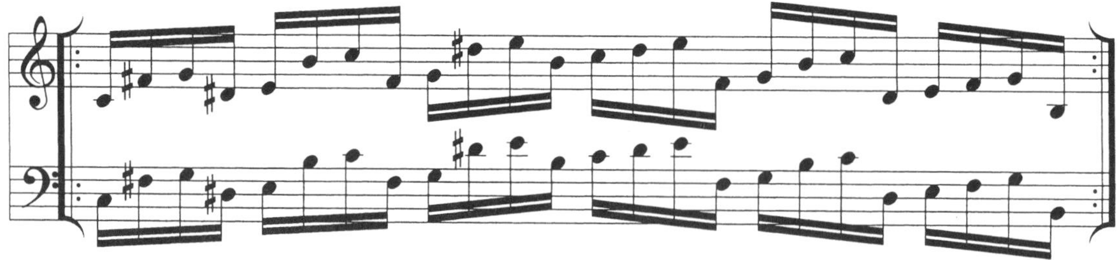

COMBINING UNT & LNT ON ARPEGGIO/BROKEN CHORD EXERCISES

Master the arpeggios and scales first, then master LNTs and UNTs individually to prepare for practicing combinations of UNTs and LNTs added to arpeggio and broken chord exercises.

1.49 Combination. Broken chord pattern (from exercise 1.13) with LNT ascending & UNT descending

1.50 Arpeggio with UNTs and LNTs

Charlie Parker played a broken chord idea in the first two measures below with a mixture of UNTs and LNTs. It would be a mistake to analyze the melodic pitches in the first two measures related to the indicated chords. Parker seemed to focus on the B♭ tonic chord for two measures, and then addressed specific chords. This line is very similar to the Armstrong excerpt shown on page 19.

This exercise is based on the previous example. The first measure illustrates the simple broken chord on which this exercise is based. The first measure must be mastered before attempting to surround these chord tones with chromatic embellishment. This can be applied to major triads (as shown) and minor triads.

1.51 Broken chord pattern (related to exercise 1.11) with mixture of UNTs and LNTs.

ENCIRCLING CHORD TONES WITH UNT & LNT

Thousands of melodic figuration examples involve the triadic chord tones encircled by their UNTs and LNTs. As stated before and shown below, the UNTs are almost always diatonic, the LNTs chromatic. Sonny Rollins surrounded each chord tone of a simple F arpeggio with the upper neighbor tone (UNT) – chord tone (CT) – lower neighbor tone (LNT) and chord tone in the first measure below. The second measure recalls the pattern from Armstrong's West End Blues solo – a broken arpeggio with upper neighbor tones.

UNT-CT-LNT-CT pattern & UNT patterns

Charlie Parker and Oscar Peterson ignored the individual harmonic details and generalized the tonic triad in the following examples. The four note pattern follows the arpeggio. The first note of the pattern is the UNT followed by the chord tone (CT), the LNT and the CT again, then a jump is made to the next chord tone's UNT.

Tonic triad encircled with UNT-CT-LNT-CT pattern

Tonic triad encircled with UNT-CT-LNT-CT pattern

As you can see from the following Beethoven example, this encircling idea is not new or unique to jazz. The pattern is the same one used by Parker and Peterson: UNT-CT-LNT-CT.

Beethoven from the 3rd movement of the 9th Symphony

Chopin's Etude No.2, Op.25 is an excellent study in the use of neighbor tones over simple triads. It seems to swing because of the use of the triplets and the polyrhythms over the left hand (not shown here). Danilo Perez has used excerpts of this etude in his improvisations. Shown below are two short excerpts illustrating the simple F minor and A♭ major triads embellished identically in parallel phrases. The circled notes indicate the triad. The chord tones, even though surrounded by chromatic and diatonic neighbors are stressed in part due to their location on the strong beats, and because all surrounding notes point back directly to the chord tones. It is interesting that if all the neighbor tones were removed, what remains is a quarter note triplet melody of the chord tones: 5-5-5-3-3-3-1.

Chopin: Etude No.2, Op.25 (F minor)

Chopin: Etude No.2, Op.25 (A♭ relative major)

Mozart used the pattern found in Beethoven, Parker and Peterson, buts added a leap away to another chord tone and back to the original chord tone before continuing the sequence in the following two examples. Leaping away to another chord tone is called an arpeggiated tone.

Mozart: Piano Sonata in F major, K.332, Allegro Assai

Mozart: Sonata in F major, K.547a, Allegro

Lee Morgan made this line interesting with the use of chromatic encircling of an F minor triad. Like the Chopin example, the chord tones 5-3-1 occur on the downbeats so that not only do the chromatic notes resolve to the chord tones, but do so at significant rhythmic locations.

F minor triad with NTs

Tete Montoliu displaced the rhythmic accent in this syncopated example. He used a three note pattern of UNT-LNT-CT.

Triad with NTs on the Blues

Tom Harrell makes a case for practicing in all twelve keys in the next two examples. These are from different tunes, different tempos and a half-step apart. The material is identical with the exception of rhythmic displacement. These examples should inspire you to try rhythmic displacement as a developmental tool in your improvisation and practice. The encircling pattern is LNT-UNT-CT. He encircled the third and root of the chord in two octaves, but played the fifth of the chord without any embellishment.

E minor triad with NT elaboration

E♭ minor triad with NT elaboration

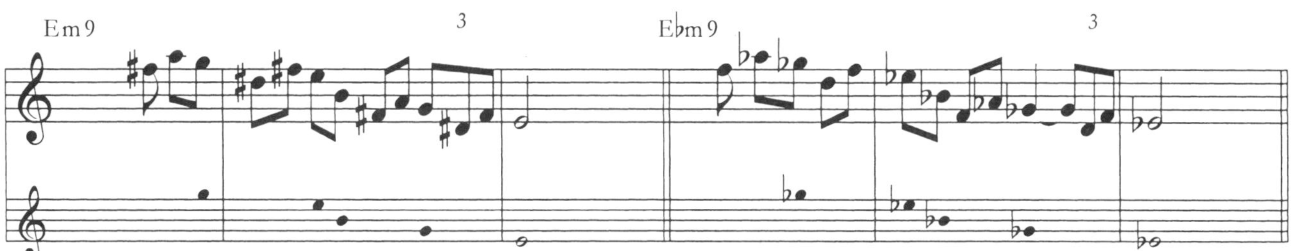

Joe Pass used encircling patterns often. In the following excerpt, Pass began a scale passage that became outline no.2 in the first measure, but relied on the encircling pattern CT-LNT-UNT-CT for the rest of the passage.

Encircling patterns

In order to be fluent with encircling patterns, you must first be fluent with the basic triads. Begin by identifying the triad and the appropriate UNTs & LNTs remembering that UNTs are usually diatonic and LNTs usually chromatic. In the example below, the C minor triad is assumed to be from the key of C minor, and therefore the UNT to G is A♭. If the C minor triad was from dorian mode or as a ii chord in the key of B♭ major, the UNT to G would be A natural.

Encircling a C Major Triad

Encircling a C Minor Triad

The following exercises will help you incorporate neighbor tone encircling ideas in your improvisations and compositions. There are six basic neighbor tone patterns; two containing three notes; four containing four notes. The four note patterns are: CT-UNT-LNT-CT and its inversion CT-LNT-UNT-CT, and UNT-CT-LNT-CT and its inversion LNT-CT-UNT-CT. The three note patterns are: UNT-LNT-CT, and the inversion, LNT-UNT-CT.

The first set of exercises deal with four note patterns and are shown for major triads and minor triads. Two rhythmic settings are shown for each. There are endless rhythmic variations considering the variety of subdivisions and displacements available, so be creative in your practice as you take these through the different keys.

1.52 CT-UNT-LNT-CT pattern for major triad

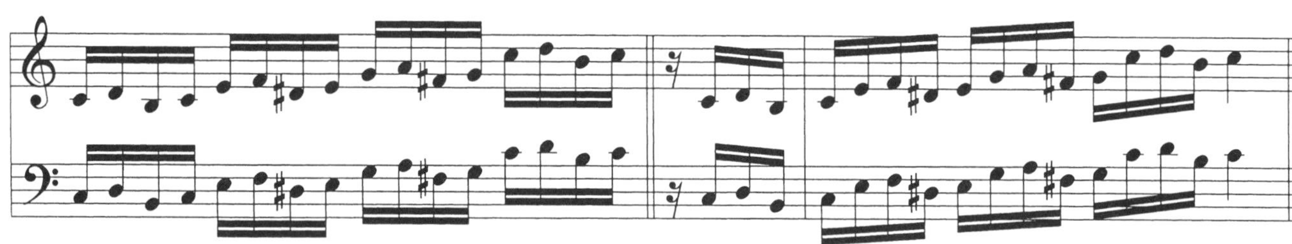

1.53 CT-UNT-LNT-CT pattern for minor triad

1.54 CT-LNT-UNT-CT pattern for major triad

1.55 CT-LNT-UNT-CT pattern for minor triad

1.56 UNT-CT-LNT-CT pattern for major triad

1.57 UNT-CT-LNT-CT pattern for minor triad

1.58 LNT-CT-UNT-CT pattern for major triad

1.59 LNT-CT-UNT-CT pattern for minor triad

The next sets of exercises are created using three note encircling patterns. Three note patterns can be rhythmically interesting. The accents created by groupings of three eighth notes may imply a dotted quarter note pulse over the underlying quarter note pulse. Experiment with different variations of rhythmic placement of these three note patterns.

1.60 UNT-LNT-CT pattern for major UNT-LNT-CT pattern for minor

1.61 LNT-UNT-CT pattern for major LNT-UNT-CT pattern for minor

SCALES PRECEDED WITH UNT & LNT ENCIRCLING

The exercises up to this point have concentrated on using neighbor tones to encircle triad shapes. Exercises 1.62 and 1.63 are based on the next three examples that show how neighbor tones are also useful for starting scale passages.

UNT and LNT precede scale passage

UNT and LNT precede scale passage

UNT and LNT precede scale passage

1.62 UNT and LNT precede the 1-2-3-4-5 scale pattern for all twelve major triads. Note that the scale passage still accentuates the basic triad since chord tones land on the downbeats, so that the scale notes 2 and 4 are really just passing tones between the circled chord tones shown in m.1.

1.63 UNT and LNT precede the 1-2-3-4-5 scale pattern for all twelve minor triads.

The previous exercises began with neighbor tones and ascend the scale. Would the same idea work if the scale descends? Transpose these to all keys.

1.64 UNT and LNT precede the 5-4-3-2-1 scale pattern in major and minor

Exercise 1.65 is a one octave scale, but every time the scale reaches a tonic chord tone (1-3-5) the CT-UNT-LNT-CT encircling pattern is inserted before continuing up or down the scale. This exercise opens up new challenges for playing simple scales. This idea could be applied to any scale and infinite combinations of encircling patterns.

1.65 Scale with tonic triad encircled with CT-UNT-LNT-CT pattern

COMMON CHROMATIC APPROACH

There is an ubiquitous pattern for approaching the third of the tonic triad that is illustrated in the following example from Sonny Stitt. The cyclical quadruplets, discussed earlier, begin this example creating a step progression as shown by the arrows below. The D natural, the third of the tonic B♭ chord, is approached using a common pattern beginning on the F, down the scale to the E♭, skips over the D to another chord tone of the F chord, the C, then the chromatic passing tone C♯.

Chromatic approach to 3rd of tonic shown in box

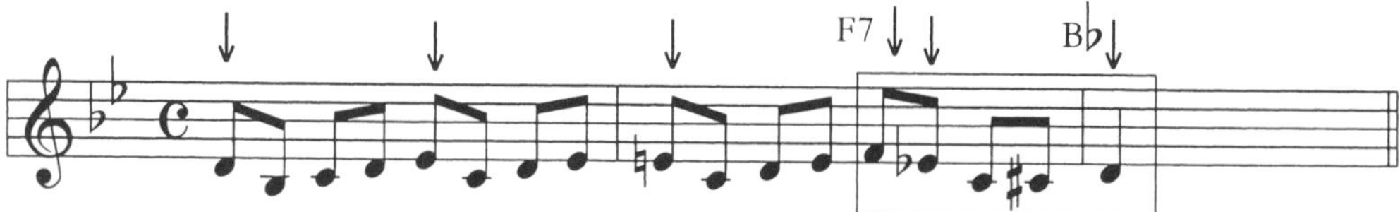

Herbie Hancock used cyclical quadruplets to create a step progression indicated by the arrows, and ended with a chromatic approach to the third of the F chord.

Here are two different examples from Clifford Brown. In the first, the chromatic approach leads to the fifth, and then is sequenced to finally arrive at the third of the tonic chord. In the second example, the chromatic approach leads to the third of the tonic chord F, but by the time it gets there, the chord has changed to D. Brown again sequenced the line to eventually arrive at the third of the D7 chord.

Chromatic approaches

The illustration below may help the understanding of how this chromatic approach works. In the following example consider the melodic motion from the fifth to the third of an F triad (a.). The same passage with a B♭ passing tone added (b.). The same motion with chromatic approach from below (c.) Look at the passage again as if the melodic motion was from the ♯9 of an A7 chord resolving to the fifth of a D minor chord (a.). In this context, the B♭ passing tone can also be heard as the ♭9 of the A7 chord and still leads to the fifth of D minor (b.). The addition of the chromatic approach takes nothing of the clarity away from the passage and mirrors the kind of approach used by Clifford Brown above.

Practice the following chromatic approach exercises for all keys.

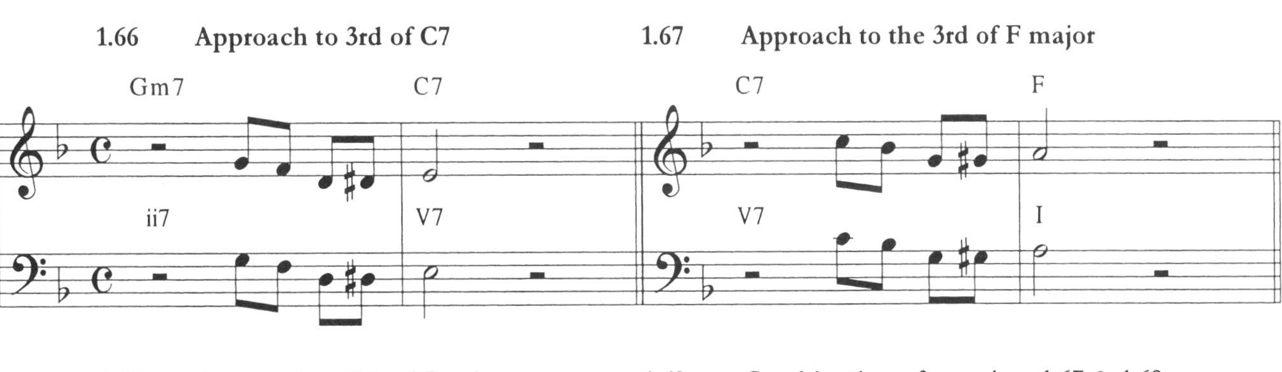

In the following exercise, chromatic approaches (marked with brackets) are used to approach the following notes:

m.2	A (3rd of F)
m.2	F♯ (3rd of D7)
m.3	E (3rd of C7)
m.5	D (3rd of B♭)
m.6	A (root of Am)
m.6	F♯ (3rd of D7)
m.8	C (5th of F)
m.1	on repeat, D (5th of Gm).

Transpose this exercise to all twelve keys.

1.70 Chromatic approach exercise in the progression in the key of F.

> *"Genius begins great works;*
> *labor alone finishes them."*
> *—John Joubert*

II. 7th & 9th CHORD ARPEGGIOS

In addition to the routine scales, arpeggios and broken chords, time should be spent honing specific melodic fragments and concepts. Each chapter will focus on a specific area of melodic material. It would be impossible to practice everything in the book in any one day or week, so the ultimate decision of how much and what areas to explore should be up to the individual.

SEVENTH CHORDS

Familiarize yourself with the following charts that identify where these chords came from and how they may function.

CHORD TYPE (symbol suffix)	FUNCTION IN MAJOR KEY	FUNCTION IN MINOR KEY*
Major 7 (maj7)	I, IV	VI
Minor 7 (m7)	ii, iii, vi	iv
Dominant 7 (7)	V7	V7
Half-diminished 7 (ø7)	viiø7	iiø7
Diminished 7 (°7)	n/a	vii°7

*When discussing functional harmony of minor keys, this book will be referring to harmonic minor only.

These exercises begin with basic seventh chord arpeggios:

a.	Major 7	(M-m-M)
b.	Dominant 7	(M-m-m)
c.	Minor 7	(m-M-m)
d.	Half-diminished 7	(m-m-M)
e.	Fully diminished 7	(m-m-m)

Practice the seventh chords as shown in the following exercises.

2.1 All Major 7th chords beginning with I(maj)7 in the key of C major

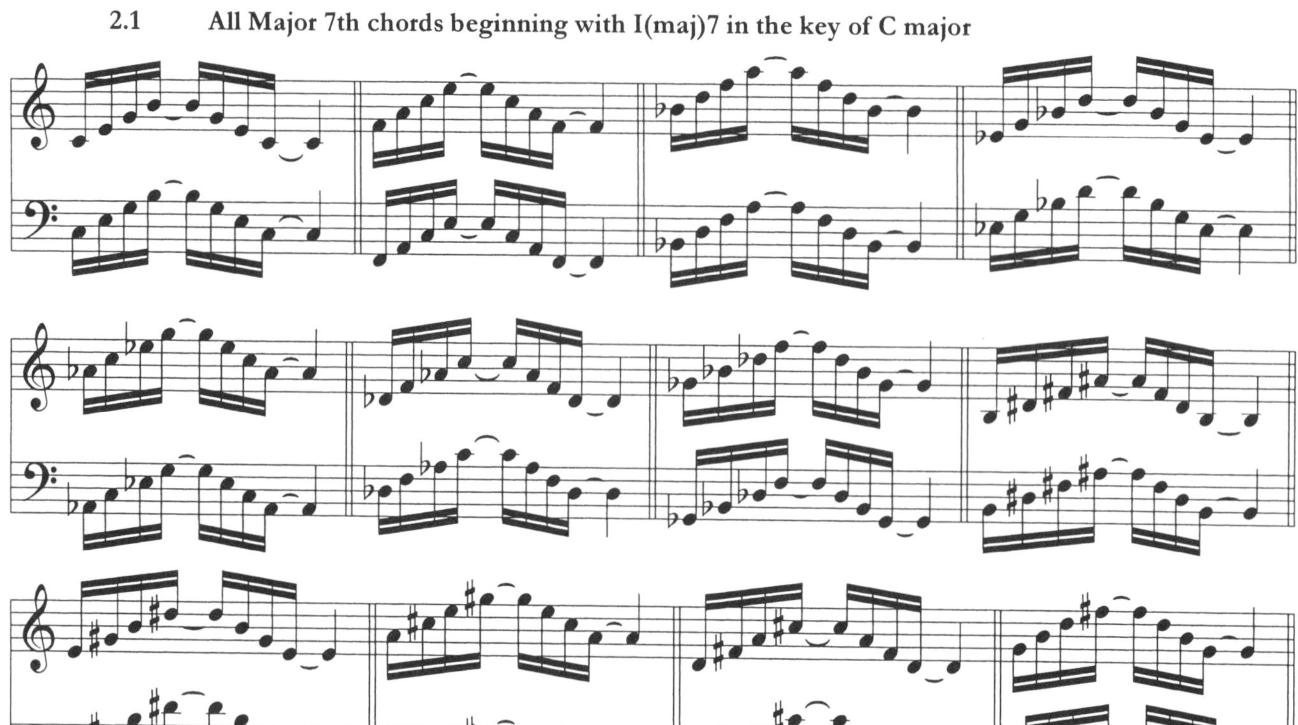

2.2-5 Repeat for all dominants 7th chords beginning with the V7 of C major; all minor 7th chords beginning with the ii7 chord of C major; all half-diminished chords beginning with the viiø7 of C Major or the iiø7 chord of A minor; all diminished chords beginning with the vii°7 of A minor.

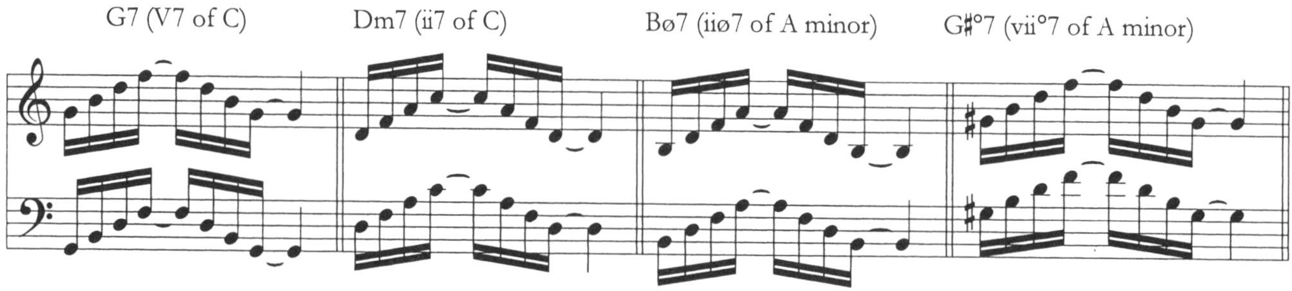

2.6 **Cycle through all the chords in a key center. Roman numerals indicate key function.**

2.7 **Another cycle through all the chords in a key center ending on vi. This progression occurs many times in jazz, pop, and European art music.**

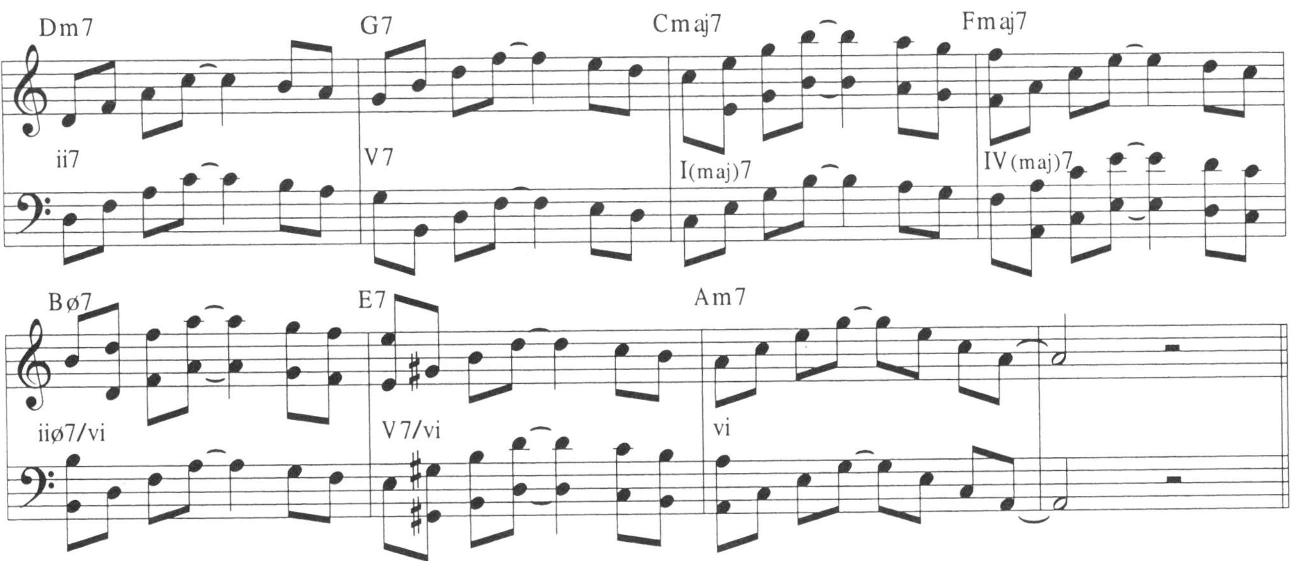

2.8 **Cycle through the key center alternating between inverted arpeggios and traditional ascending arpeggios.**

2.9 Cycle through the key center playing the first inversion of the seventh chord. By beginning with the thirds of the chord, this exercise assures a good counterpoint to the roots in the bass. Notice the voice leading over the measure line: the 7th of each chord resolves by step to the 3rd of the next.

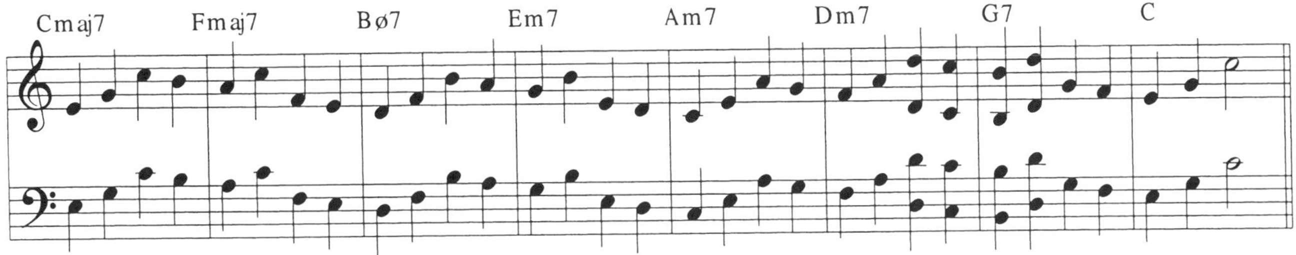

2.10 Cycle through the key center with first inversion of the seventh chord. By beginning with the thirds of the chord, this exercise assures a good counterpoint to the roots in the bass. Notice the voice leading over the measure line: the 7th of each chord resolves by step to the 3rd of the next.

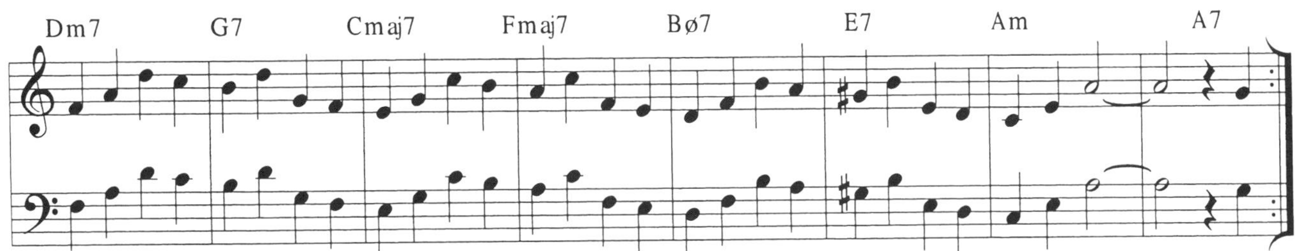

2.11 This exercise is the same as exercise 2.9, but with octave displacement of the first or last two notes in each measure. The 7th of each chord resolves by step to the 3rd of the next.

2.12 This exercise is the same as exercise 2.10, but with octave displacement of the first or last two notes in each measure. The 7th of each chord resolves by step to the 3rd of the next.

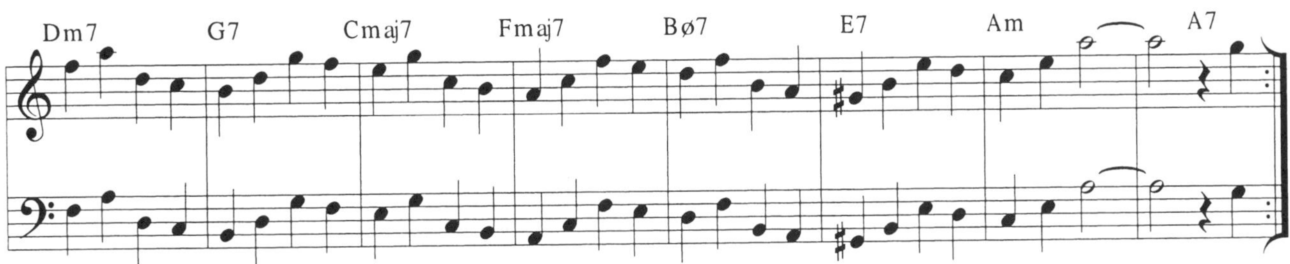

NINTH CHORDS

2.13 Practice these ninth chords in all twelve keys. Major ninth chords can be found as I or IV in major, dominant ninths as V9 in major, minor ninths as ii or vi in major, iv in minor.

2.14 Broken chord variation for ninth chord practice

2.15 Broken chord variation for ninth chord practice

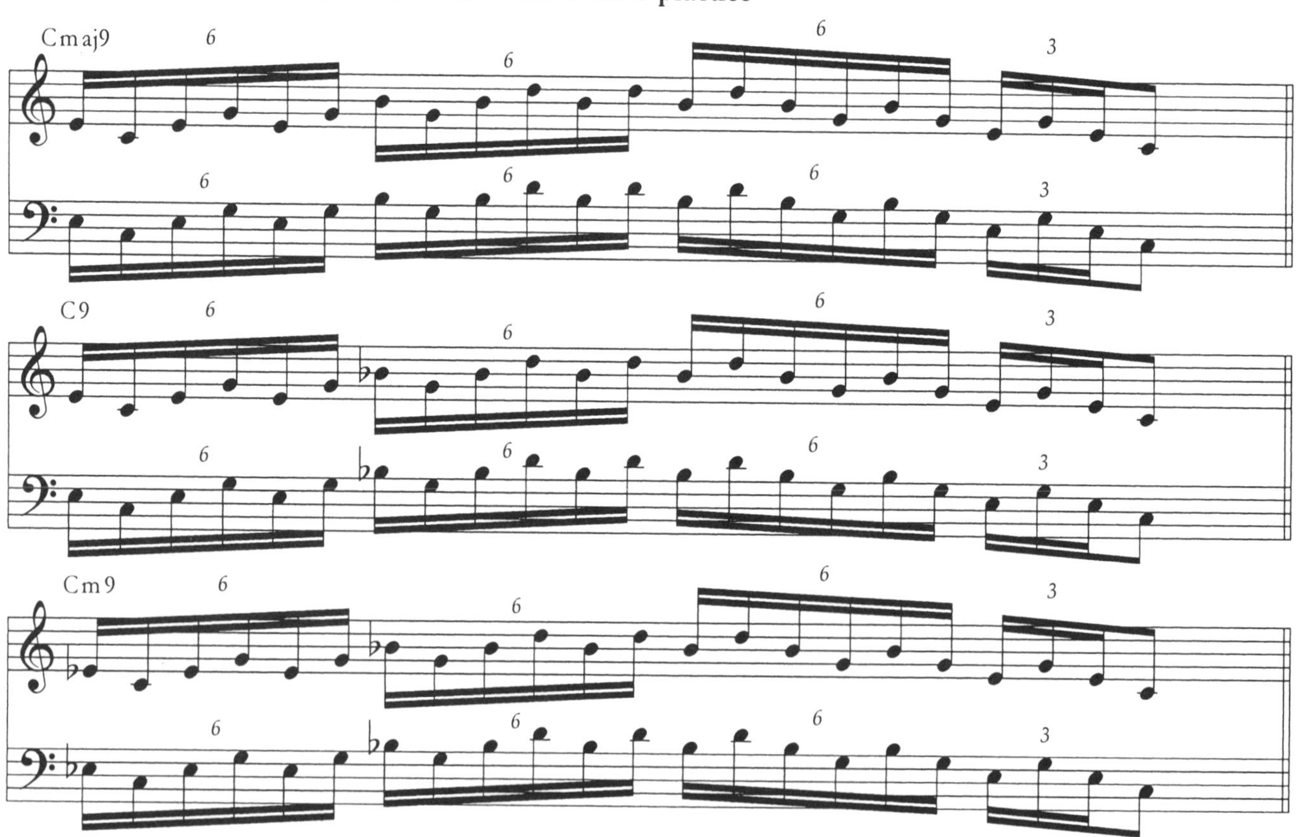

2.16 **Ninth chord arpeggios broken into two segments: 3-5-7-9 and 1-3-5-7. When inverted, as in the second half, they create at once an angular line due to the leaps, and a simple step line created by the top circled notes.**

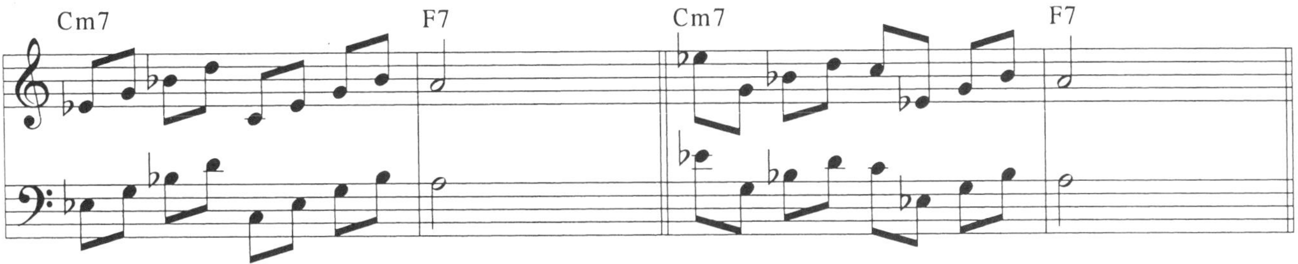

2.17 **The arpeggios as shown in exercise 2.16 can be connected in cycles as shown below, since each begins on the third and resolves to the third of the next chord. Here it is applied to a turn around progression (ii7 – V7 – I – V7/ii).**

ARPEGGIOS PRECEDED WITH UNT & LNT ENCIRCLING

Tom Harrell played around the third of each of the chords in the following examples using upper and lower neighbor tones before arpeggiating 3-5-7-9. These are ninth chord arpeggios with the root supplied by the bass.

Encircled third and 3-5-7-9 arpeggio

Encircled third and 3-5-7-9 arpeggio sequence

In order to incorporate these ideas into your vocabulary, you must first practice all the ninth chord arpeggios without playing the root. Practice all the major ninth, dominant ninth and minor ninth chords as shown in exercise 2.18 starting with the third. You will be playing arpeggios you have already practiced, but will be thinking of them in new ways. For instance, a 1-3-5-7 Em7 arpeggio (E-G-B-D) is the same as a 3-5-7-9 rootless C major 9 arpeggio (E-G-B-D).

2.18 3-5-7-9 arpeggios for Major 9, Dominant 9 and Minor 9 chords

2.19 3-5-7-9 arpeggio exercise preceded by UNT and LNT

Playing a seventh chord arpeggio starting on the 3rd of a chord is actually arpeggiating the 3-5-7-9 of that chord. So a B♭ major 7 arpeggio over a G minor chord sounds like the 3-5-7-9 of the G minor chord. Exercise 2.20 is an excellent cycle to practice because it reinforces aiming for the third of the chord instead of the root. In a jazz setting, the bass player will usually have the root as his goal, so having the third as a goal assures good counterpoint. Exercise 2.20 is based on 3-5-7-9 arpeggios. It begins with a 3-5-7-9 arpeggio over the Gm7 chord, but the 3-5-7-9 arpeggio is inverted over the C7. The arpeggios alternate throughout the exercise. For the second half of the exercise the alternations are reversed as it starts with an inverted 3-5-7-9 on the Gm7 and ascends 3-5-7-9 on the C and alternates to the end of the exercise. It is important to notice the resolution of the seventh of each chord. The seventh resolves by step into the third of the next chord.

2.20 3-5-7-9 Arpeggio exercise with diatonic resolution

Each 3-5-7-9 arpeggio in exercise 2.20 was followed by step motion down to the third of the next chord. The following melodic ideas can be added to the 3-5-7-9 arpeggios shown in 2.20.

2.21 3-5-7-9 arpeggio exercise with the addition of a chromatic approach to the third

2.22 3-5-7-9 arpeggio exercise with the addition of another chromatic approach (from exercises 1.66-1.70)

2.23 3-5-7-9 arpeggio exercise with the addition of an escape tone and then various chromatic

III. TRIADS & GENERALIZATION

ITCH HIERARCHY

There are twelve pitches in the chromatic scales, but in the major/minor system they are not of equal importance. The twelve pitches can be divided into a hierarchy of four categories of importance. The most important pitch is, by definition, the tonic (1), the home pitch or the musical center. The second most important pitches are the dominant (5) a perfect fifth above the tonic, which helps establish the tonic as the principal tone, and the mediant (3), which establishes the modality as minor or major. The third class of pitches are the remaining diatonic pitches (2, 4, 6, & 7), which provide some contrast to the main three pitches and usually function to lead back to the tonic, dominant and mediant. Thousands of simple melodies illustrate these principles. The fourth pitch class would be any chromatic alterations of any of the scale tones. An excerpt from *Joy to the World* and a theme from a Beethoven trio provide a brief confirmation of the principles. The Tonic begins and ends the phrase. The dominant and the mediant are the other points of rest on the way to the final note of the phrase. The importance of the tonic, dominant and mediant is reinforced by the rhythmic value and rhythmic location on strong beats. The other scale degrees are on weaker beats and provide a path to the important pitches.

George Frederick Handel

Beethoven: Piano Trio in B♭ Major, op. 97

PITCH HIERARCHY

I. Tonic (1)
II. Dominant (5)
Mediant (3)
III. Supertonic (2), Subtonic (4), Submediant (6), & Subtonic or Leading Tone (7)
IV. The remaining five chromatic pitches

Many melodies can be constructed almost solely of triadic material. A triadic melody may have other pitches other than the 1-3-5, but those other pitches occur in a subordinate role. This basically describes most of the tonal music in existence. Some of the gravity associated with the triad pitches can be attributed to their occurrence as the first three separate pitches in the overtone series.

The triad establishes the stability, the other pitches provide a departure and a degree of instability, and stability is restored on the return to triad pitches. Since most of the settings for jazz improvisation are still based on the major minor system, an improviser should have a large vocabulary of ideas for elaborating major and minor triads

BASIC ELABORATION OF TRIADS:

The next few pages are a catalog of possibilities for elaborating the three basic pitches of an F major triad. Isolating the individual choices will aid the understanding of how to combine each of these to make longer lines and yet keep the focus on the primary triadic pitches. Under each note of the triad is a chart of possible notes to surround, embellish or elaborate the note at the top of the chart.

F MAJOR TRIAD, cont.

TONIC MEDIANT DOMINANT

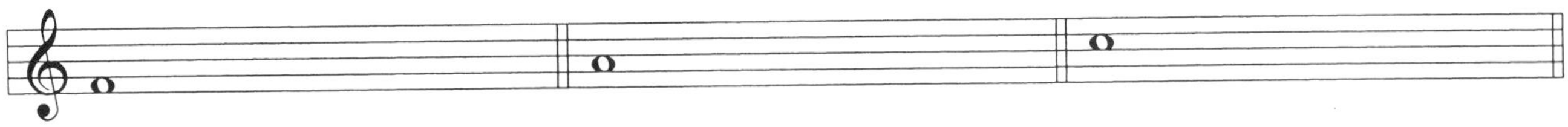

Encircling using CT-LNT-UNT-CT:

Chromatic approach from UNT or LNT through a chromatic passing tone (PT)

Encircling with NTs including chromatic passing tone (PT)

Arpeggiate: approach by leap from other chord tones above:

Arpeggiate: approach by leap from other chord tones below:

Using passing tones (PT) to pass between two chord tones:

F MINOR TRIAD
TONIC
MEDIANT
DOMINANT
Leading tones (LT) or lower neighbor tones (LNT) from half step below:
Upper neighbor tones (UNT) a diatonic step above:
Encircling using UNT-LNT-chord tone (CT):
Encircling using UNT-CT-LNT-CT:
Encircling using LNT-CT-UNT-CT:
Encircling using CT-UNT-LNT-CT:
Encircling using CT-LNT-UNT-CT:
Chromatic approach from UNT or LNT through a chromatic passing tone (PT)

F MINOR TRIAD, cont.

TONIC MEDIANT DOMINANT

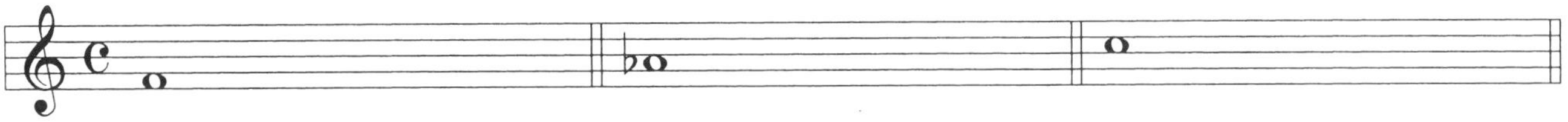

Encircling with NTs including chromatic passing tone (PT)

Arpeggiate: approach by leap from other chord tones above:

Arpeggiate: approach by leap from other chord tones below:

Using passing tones (PT) to pass between two chord tones:

Using passing tones (PT) to pass between two chord tones:

There are four different versions shown (above) of the passing tones between the dominant and tonic that illustrate aeolian or natural minor, dorian mode, harmonic minor, and melodic minor, respectively.

TRIAD MOTIVE DEVELOPED

The triad arpeggio excerpt below is hardly interesting enough by itself to be considered a theme. Bach used this basic structure to create a memorable and workable theme for the Two-part Invention No. 8. In the first measure, the ascending arpeggio is transformed into a broken chord, which is more interesting because of its angularity. In the second measure, the descending arpeggio is transformed into a smoother line with the use of passing and upper neighbor tones. The two parts of the theme, one angular and one smooth, provide a contrast of musical ideas for development.

Simple arpeggio idea Transformed to a theme by J. S. Bach

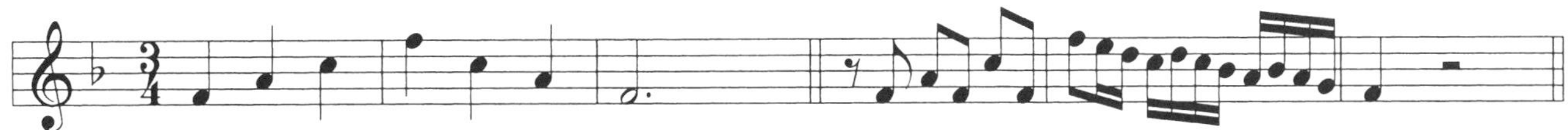

The last nine pitches of the Bach theme can be changed to eighth note values:

Changing the direction of the line produces the following lines:
Opposite motion with LNTs

In minor

Arpeggio tones could be inserted where the UNT tones were, and the motive remains musical. This idea is found in a John Coltrane improvisation.

Bach theme with arpeggio tones:

line:

If the idea works in major will it work in minor? Below are three more variations of the idea: the Coltrane line in minor, inverted in minor and in major. Listen to the Coltrane/Bach idea inverted and in a major key; it is the same as the Shaker tune *Simple Gifts*.

in minor

inverted in minor

inverted in major

Parker used chromatic passing tones to outline the F major triad in this excerpt from a blues improvisation. The F major triad pitches still occur on the strong beats. Lou Donaldson used almost the exact Parker line, adding only arpeggio tones. With the arpeggiated tones added to the Donaldson idea, the result is a jazzy version of *Simple Gifts*.

Parker:

Donaldson:

Shapes related to the Bach theme can be found in these selected improvisation excerpts:

Descending using UNTs and PTs

Ascending idea using LNTs

Ascending idea using LNTs

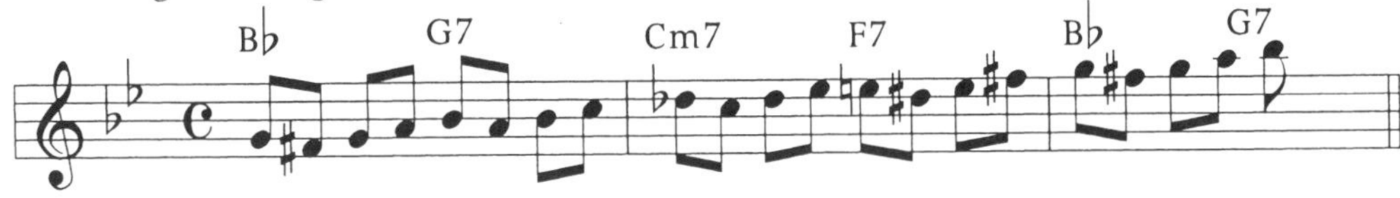

These lines echo this familiar melody:

Joshua Fought the Battle of Jerico

TRIADIC ELABORATION

Here are two triads are shown as a descending arpeggios. Beneath each is a series of possible elaborations utilizing the number of chromatic and diatonic neighbors available. Practice for all twelve major and minor triads.

F major **F minor**

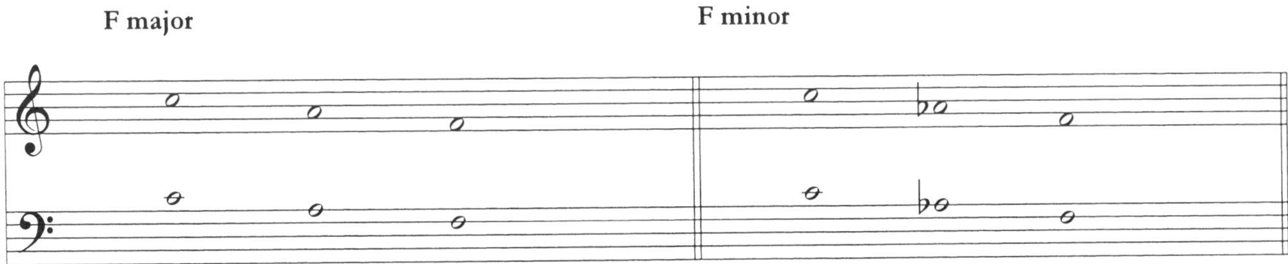

3.1 UNT & PTs

3.2 LNT & PTs

3.3 Encircling with LNT-UNT-CT pattern

3.4 LTs, encircling, chromatic approaches

3.5 Encircling with NTs

3.6 Encircling with NTs

3.7 Encircling with CT-LNT-UNT-CT pattern

3.8 UNTs

This excerpt is an example of Clifford Brown ignoring the harmonic implications in favor of the tonic triad generalization. Brown preceded each chord tone with a leading tone.

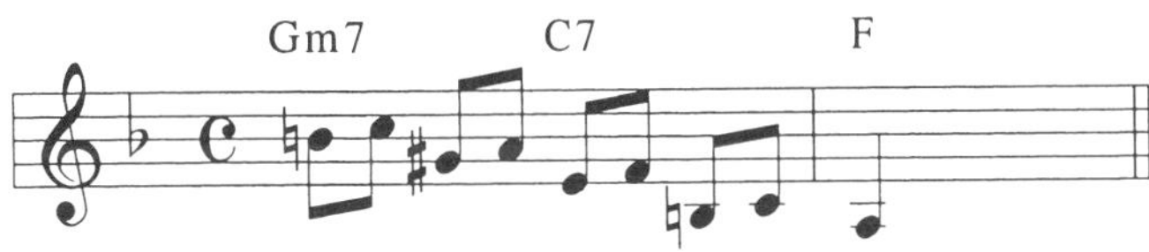

3.9 Using LTs

Lee Morgan embellished the F minor triad with UNT and LNTs. One of the LNTs, G, is preceded by a LT. This type of chromatic encircling is common in the improvisations of Bill Evans, Tom Harrell and many other contemporary players.

3.10 Encircling with UNT & LNTs

3.11 Encircling with UNT, LNTs & chromatic approaches

3.12 Encircling with a mixture of NT patterns

Here are some examples of triad pitches with a mixture of chromatic approaches from Sonny Stitt, Ray Nance, and Clifford Brown.

F triad with a mixture of chromatic approaches

A♭ triad with a mixture of chromatic approaches

F triad with a mixture of chromatic approaches

Triadic Generalization B♭ triad with chromatic approaches

3.13 Chromatic approaches

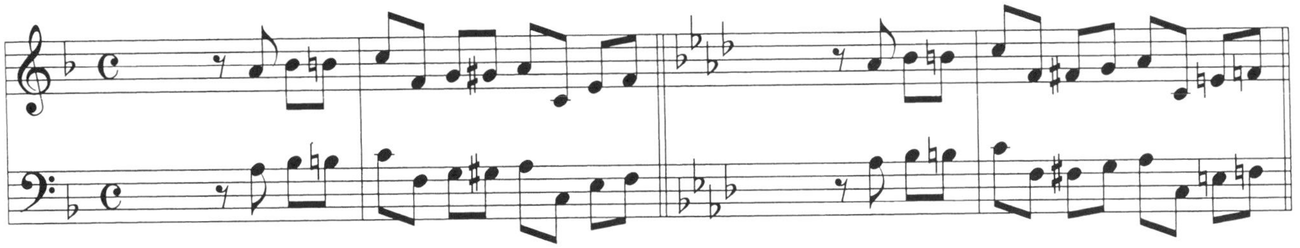

3.14 Arpeggio note and leading tones

3.15 Chromatic approaches

3.16 Encircling using notes from the V9 and V7♭9 chords

There is a familiar logo that is nothing more than a triad shape in inversion. It is a good vehicle for developing more interesting and involved melodic ideas.

The logo shape is at the heart of this John Coltrane excerpt. Coltrane leaped to the UNT of the G and then encircled the E♭ using UNT and LNTs.

LOGO VARIATIONS

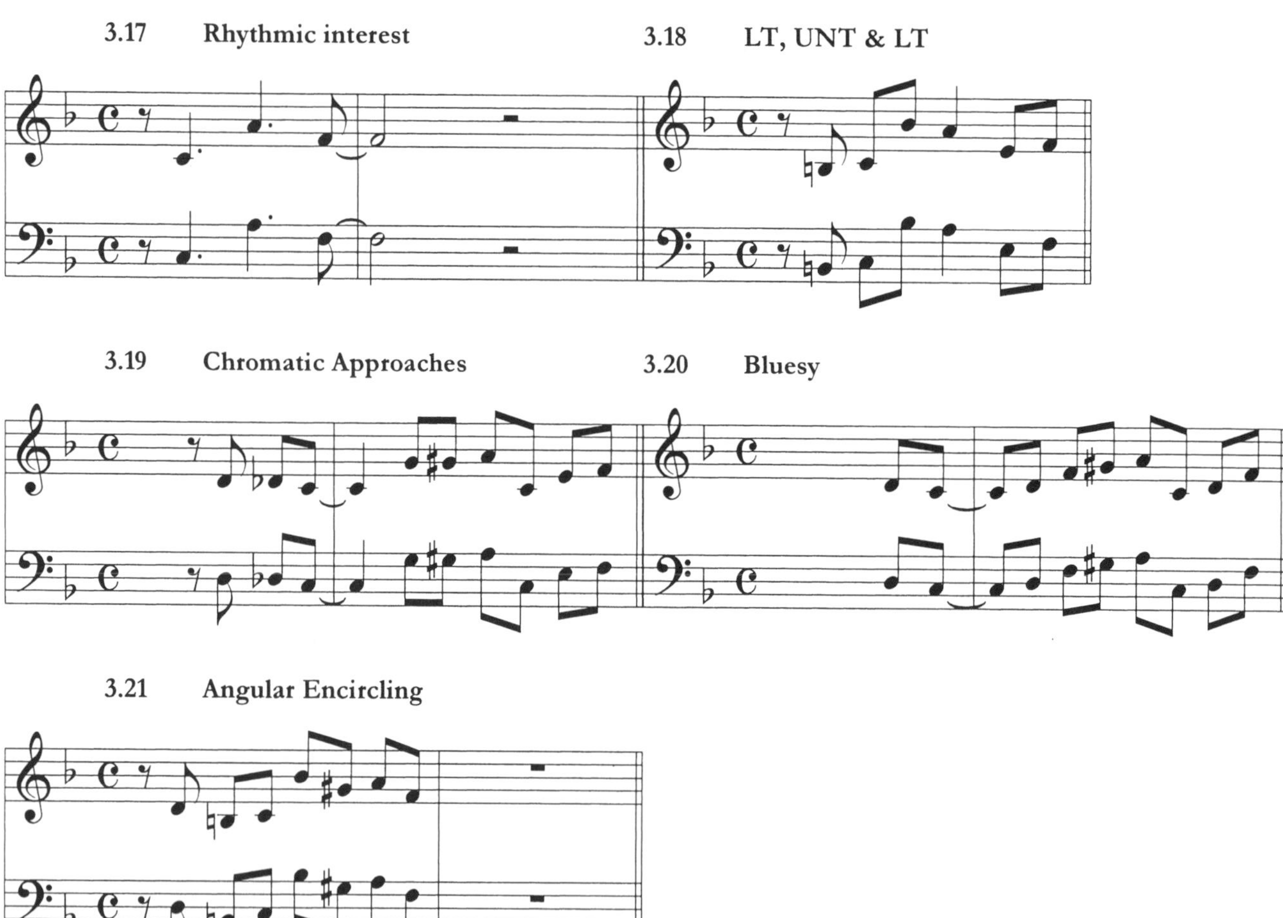

RIADIC GENERALIZATION

An improviser has a choice when dealing with the harmony. The harmony implications can be adhered to specifically, generally, or ignored.

When being specific the improviser pays careful attention to all harmonic implications: the proper thirds, sevenths and ninths resolving appropriately, adherence to the implicit or explicit alterations. When being general the improviser, rather than deal with the specifics, may generalize large areas of the music by key area, tonic triad generalization, and blues generalization. Experienced, mature improvisers will be both specific and general within the same improvisation and even within the same phrase. An example of generalization by key area would be thinking in the tonic key regardless of modulations or secondary dominants. This may work well on some tunes like *All of Me*, Blues or Rhythm Changes. In a more complex tune, like *All the Things You Are*, it can be done, but in smaller chunks. For instance, the first eight measures may be harmonically generalized as follows:

vi	ii	V	I	IV	iiø/iii –V/iii	I/III	
Fm7	B♭m7	E♭7	A♭maj7	D♭maj7	Dø7 G7	Cmaj7	

A♭ major scale or A♭ triad. . . . . C minor . . . . . C major . . . .

If the melody is pointing to A♭ triad and all the chords are functioning to point to the A♭ triad, then the two elements are functioning the same in the linear dimension. This is why it works and sounds good, even if there are some vertical discrepancies along the way.

Any of the exercises dedicated to embellishing the triad will be useful to the improviser when generalizing the harmony or when being specific.

TRIADIC MUSICAL EXAMPLES

Here are a few phrases that might inspire you to create some lines or exercises to prepare you to create triadic lines.

Listen to how interesting this Tete Montoliu line is on the first three measures of a blues in F, using only triad notes as goals and encircling several notes and using interesting rhythms.

Triad & NTs

Brown ignored the Cm7 and F7 chords and just aimed for B♭ triad sounds in this excerpt.

Triadic Generalization

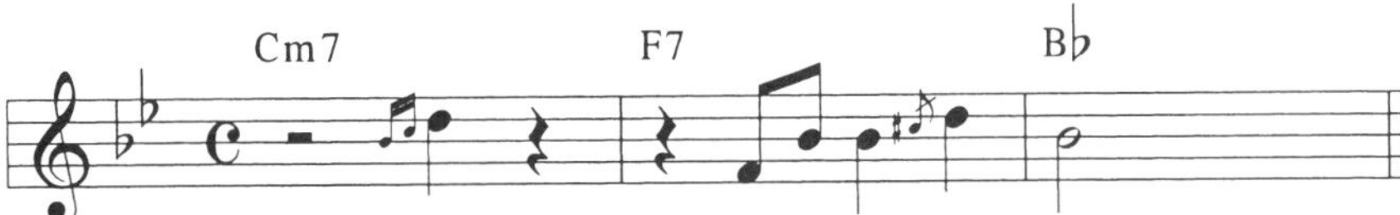

Parker used triadic notes with a variety of NTs in this phrase from the first four measures of a blues in F. Parker sometimes skipped from one chord tone to the neighbor tone of a distant chord tone as in m.2, but the neighbor tones behave and resolve where expected. After all the triadic generalization in the first three measures, Parker was very specific about the F7 leading to the E♭ chromatically and had it resolve down to the third of B♭ in m.5.

Triad Generalization

Tete Montoliu used primarily the F major triad with some interesting chromatic encircling and approaches on blues in F in the next three examples.

Notice the simple rising chromatic line A - B♭ - B, made more angular with the use of an arpeggiated tone (F) used as a pivot. You can hear him rhythmically and melodically leading to a C natural on the downbeat of m.2, but instead, he leaped to the UNT of C and displaced it rhythmically. He played the C in two octaves before encircling the A. The F triadic idea continues until the introduction of the E♭, the seventh, which leads to the third of the B♭ chord. The last five notes of the line are outline no.1 (see chapter 15).

Triadic Generalization

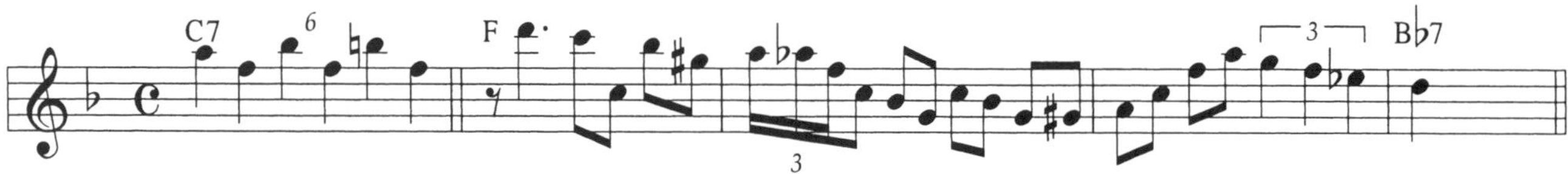

Montoliu arpeggiated down the F chord, uses B♭ as an UNT and a PT in m.1 below. The second measure has a chromatic approach to C from above and below before using outline no.3 to arrive at the B♭. In both examples, after using chiefly triadic material, he aimed for the seventh (E♭) that propels the line into the B♭ chord. The E♭ has more of an impact because of its absence from the measures preceding its use. The last five notes are outline no.3 (see chapter 15).

Triadic Generalization

If you analyze the example below in a strictly vertical framework, you get some odd results. Over the C7: a ♮11, ♯5, 13, 9, ♭9, major 7th? But, if you analyze vertically, you see F triad with neighbor tones and chromatic approaches. Why does it work over C7? Because both the C7 chord and all the melodic neighbor tone embellishments point to the F triad.

Triadic Generalization

The two phrases that follow are from the same improvisation based on Rhythm Changes. In the first example, Kenny Dorham ignored the harmonic implications of the secondary chords. He used no arpeggios of any chord except the B♭ chord. There is no B♭ on either G7 chord and he did not aim for clear chord tones for Cm7, F7 or Dm7. If you play the line outside the context of the harmony you would hear only the implied B♭ triad, and yet, it also sounds musical in the harmonic context. In fact, playing just the circled triad notes without any embellishment makes musical sense.

Triadic Generalization

Dorham's approach was different in this next phrase extracted from the same improvisation. It began the same as the previous phrase but gradually becomes more harmonically specific to each chord. An E♭ occurred under the F7 leading it to D. The G7 chord was arpeggiated (3-5-7-♭9), the seventh of G led to the third of Cm. He landed on consecutive thirds in m.4, the seventh of each chord resolving appropriately to the third of the next chord. The B♭7 was arpeggiated (3-5-♭7-9), led to more arpeggios in m.6 and finally a 3-5-7-9 arpeggio of the B♭ in m.7. The different approaches between these two phrases strengthened the entire improvisation by providing contrast and balance.

Harmonic Specificity and Generalization

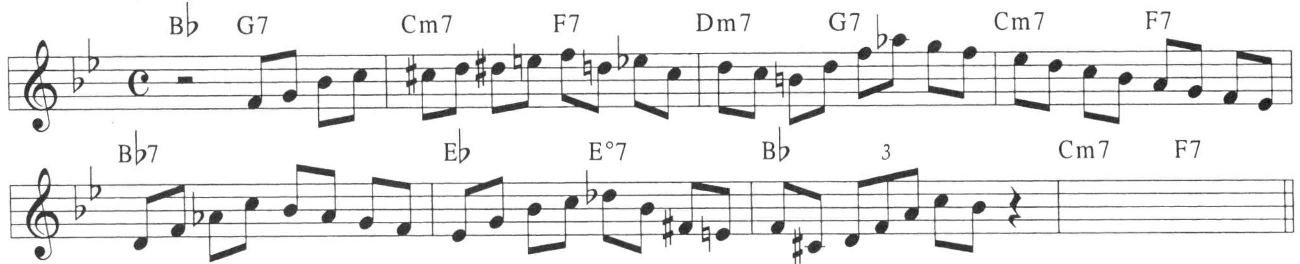

A triad can be used structurally to create longer lines. Below is a simple version of *Amazing Grace* in the key of F major.

Amazing Grace:

Notice that only F triad notes occur on the downbeats. This version, even though extremely simple, still works musically and has a sense of musical form.

Amazing Grace: Basic melodic substructure

If the simple structure works after removing any secondary notes, would it still work with a different, more complex set of auxiliary notes? The following "improvisation" aims for the basic triad notes shown previously as the structural form of *Amazing Grace*. The auxiliary notes and rhythms are drawn from the jazz tradition. Sing and play through this version with a swing or straight eighth note feel. Structurally it is identical to *Amazing Grace*: it begins and ends the same, arrives at the same pitches in corresponding measures, and has its high point at the same place.

"Improvisation" on the basic melodic structure of *Amazing Grace*:

Compare the *Amazing Grace* structure to this famous theme from Beethoven:

APPLICATION OF TRIADIC GENERALIZATION

Compose some very simple melodies using longer note values limited only to the notes of the triad. Superimpose these simple triadic melodies over jazz standard tunes whose progressions primarily stay in one key. Two good progressions to begin with are the blues and rhythm changes. Try improvising using the basic structure and applying a variety of embellishing figuration devices you have learned. Away from your instrument write out a few simple framework melodies. Make sure that the melodies make sense in their simplicity and have a clear sense of phrasing with a beginning and an end. Sing the melodies and then try improvising following the written notes. If the fundamental structure works, then any improvisation over the structure has a chance. If the elaborate melody does not work, it is often a flaw in the underlying structure and not the actual figurations.

A simple triadic framework for improvisation:

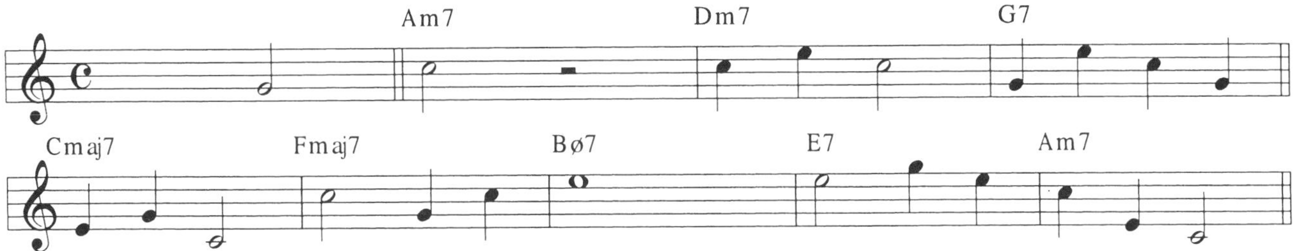

"Improvisation" based on the preceding triadic framework.

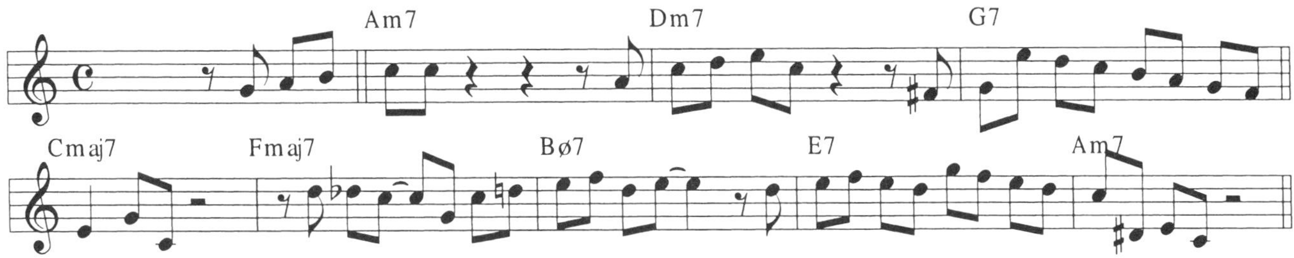

Notice that the improvisation is not "wall to wall" with notes. It begins with five eighth notes and answers with five rhythmically displaced eighth notes before creating some longer lines. Many improvised melodies begin quite simply with a few notes. Intensity is increased by creating longer, busier lines with more chromaticism. Sometimes the lines must return to some very simple ideas to allow the listener to digest complex lines.

BROKEN CHORD EXERCISES

The exercise below may be very difficult to play at first, but it would be easier to play if broken down into components and then pieced back together. This exercise will add some angular broken chord elaborations to your vocabulary and illustrate how to break an exercise down into manageable segments and piece them together.

3.22 Broken chord NT exercise

Exercise 3.22 will be easier to play if you see this substructure of a simple broken chord pattern.

3.22a

The eight pitch broken chord pattern can be broken down into seven pairs of pitches.

3.22b

Practice each pair of pitches individually adding a UNT to the higher note and a LNT to the lower note.

3.22c

After mastering each pair individually, try combining them in groups of three pitches and their neighbor tones, as shown below.

3.22d

Combine in groups of four pitches with their neighbor tones.

3.22e

It should now be easier to practice the original exercise for all major and minor triads after breaking it down into smaller components.

3.22f

BLUES LINES

Are there really blues scales? They, like many aspects of music theory may be the result of academic labeling and codification. There is a certain grain of truth to the existence of blues scales. A blues improvisation by Parker, Clifford Brown and Wynton Kelly may have elements of what we label a blues scale, but they also draw on many other elements in the course of the improvisations. Also, many phrases that we would without a doubt call a blues lick may not be constructed strictly out of a blues scale. These blues licks will probably have elements found in blues scales and triadic generalization.

What is commonly called the blues scale is the Minor Blues Scale (3.23). Every high school jazz band member knows it, as often that is all the band director is able to teach them about jazz improvisation. The minor blues scale is really nothing more than a Minor Pentatonic scale with a chromatic note added. I have watched students play this over a major blues and have fun to a point. Their frustration comes at the point where they intuitively begin to realize there is more to jazz than that minor blues scale. They also begin to sense the missing major third, and after playing the ♭3rd and 4th over and over are ready to hear it resolve to the major third, but alas, it is not in the scale they have been taught. Actual jazz artists will use the minor blues scale as a color but will mix it in with other concepts and sounds. One of these other sounds is what can be called the Major Blues Scale (3.23).

The major blues scale is nothing more than a major pentatonic with a chromatic tone added. The chromatic tone will sound like a chromatic approach tone to the major thirds, or in another context, will sound like a minor third. The two blues scales are related in the same way major and minor are related. A C major blues scale has the same notes as an A minor blues scale. A C minor blues scale is related to an E♭ major blues scale. In a major context both blues scales are often called upon. In a C major tune, you could use C major or C minor blues scale.

Aside from the obvious application (minor blues for minor tunes, major blues for major tunes) a minor blues scale can often be used in a major key, but it would be hard to find an example of major blues played in a minor key setting. The imposition of the minor blues flatted third, flatted fifth and flatted seventh, notes often labeled "blue notes," creates a nice tension over the major harmony, which is often resolved to the major triad notes. One can tell quite a good story just going back and forth between the gritty minor blues scale and the major blues scale with the "pretty notes."

Blues scales are another form of triadic generalization. The following chart makes it clear how the extra tones of the pentatonic and blues scales, shown in black, are auxiliary tones to the triad.

3.23 BLUES & PENTATONIC SCALES

Major Pentatonic Scale Major Blues Scale Minor Pentatonic Minor Blues Scale

BLUES SCALE MUSICAL EXAMPLES

Here is a brief collection of major and minor blues scale ideas and a few examples with combinations of the two. Search for your own examples and create some lines based on what you find here and in your search.

MAJOR BLUES SCALE

Below are several straight forward and familiar examples of the major blues scale used in compositions and improvisations. The third note of the major blues scale can sound like a raised second or a lowered third depending on the context. In the first example, it sounds like a flatted third. In the second and third examples, the note is a raised second leading into the major third. The fourth example uses the same pitch twice in two different ways: the first as a leading tone (G♯) to the third, the second time as the minor third (A♭).

Major Blues Scale

Major Blues Scale

Major Blues Scale

Major Blues Scale

MINOR BLUES SCALE

Wynton Kelly used the minor blues scale emphatically in the climax to this B♭ blues improvisation.

Minor Blues Scale

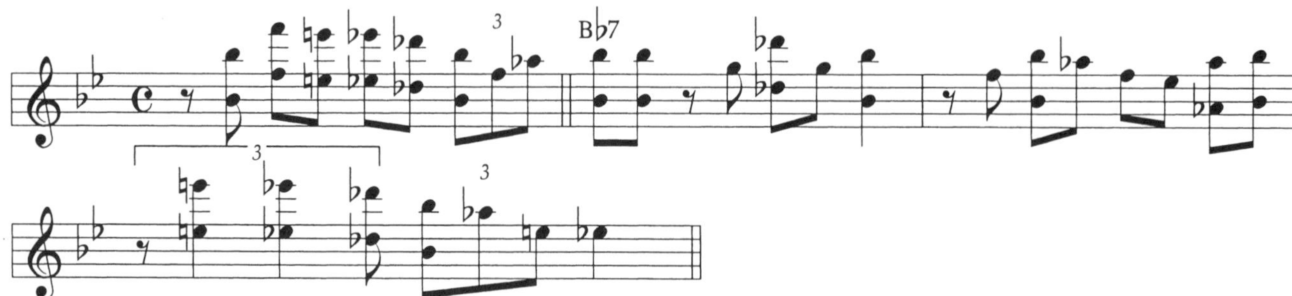

Adderley also made the minor blues scale work over the B♭ major blues progression.

Minor Blues Scale

Carl Fontana ignored the harmonic implications and drove this minor blues scale through to an exciting conclusion in this improvisation. Notice that at the end, the minor third is resolved to a major third. It would be foolish to analyze each note in relationship to the chords above them. It would be better to recognize the strength of the line through the use of the minor blues scale as a generalization, and the use of a repeated sequential idea that leads to a logical conclusion.

Minor Blues Scale

COMBINATIONS of MAJOR & MINOR BLUES SCALES

These Charlie Parker and Wynton Kelly examples show how the two scales, although different in character, can be used side by side for an effective blues line. Both are from a blues in C, both begin with a major and end with a minor blues scale idea.

Major & Minor Blues Scales

Major & Minor Blues Scales

GENERAL BLUES EXERCISES

Here is a set of blues lines that incorporate major and minor blues scales, triadic generalization ideas, and combinations. These are meant to be a point of departure. All of the following lines are shown for C or C minor. Make up your own, change them to suit your needs, invent new ones, borrow ideas from the examples above. Find places where these kinds of lines will work. Certainly they will work in blues and rhythm changes, but they will also work in many places as harmonic generalization. Pick the ones you like, learn them in the keys you need. You could, for instance, practice 3.24 transposed to B♭ for the A section, then D7, G7, C7, and F7 for the B section to Rhythm Changes.

3.24 Major Blues Scale **3.25 Minor Blues Scale**

3.26 Blue 3rds & 7ths **3.27 Combination of 3.24 & 3.26**

3.28 Minor with Major answer **3.29 Minor with Major answer**

3.30 Longer line created out of previous exercises

3.31 Major Blues Line

3.32 Playing Chromatically to the 5th & 7th

3.34 Chromatic Approach

3.35 1 to 5 and back

3.36 Encircling idea

3.37 Chromatic PT to ♭7

3.38 Emphasizes the major 6 and ♭3

3.39 Ends with ambiguous 9th

3.40 Longer lines created from combinations of previous ideas

3.41 One good closing or ending line

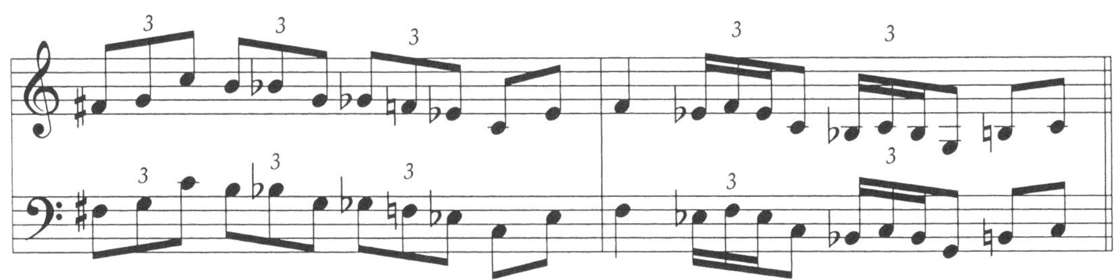

3.42 Sequencing an idea at different pitch levels

3.43 Testifyin'

3.44 Eight measure phrase constructed from previous exercise ideas

3.45 Four measures based on rhythmic idea displaced and compressed

3.46 Blues line based on displaced quarter note triplet

LUES LINES & ENDING RIFFS

These triadic and blues lines can be used effectively as endings to solos, phrases and for the ends of tunes.

3.47 Common "Ellington" ending **3.48 Common Variation**

3.49 Major triad ending **3.50 Major triad ending**

3.51 Common ending **3.52 From Count Basie**

3.53 Longer ending lines using triadic and blue lines

3.54 Longer ending lines using triadic and blue lines

3.55 Longer ending lines using triadic and blue lines

IV. MELODIC MINOR SCALE EXERCISES

MELODIC MINOR SCALE & MODES

Melodic minor is used quite differently in jazz than in traditional Western art music. Melodic minor and its modes are used as a way of coloring the existing major/minor framework and as a palette for creating new music not based on the major/minor system. Each of the modes of melodic minor has a unique sound and each is linked to a particular chord sound. Chords can be built in thirds off each of the scale notes.

The common names of the seven modes of melodic minor are:

1. Melodic Minor
2. Dorian ♭2
3. Lydian Augmented
4. Lydian Dominant, Lydian ♭7
5. Mixolydian ♭6
6. Locrian ♮2
7. Superlocrian, Altered, Diminished whole-tone

There are two ways to define any mode: by its relationship to a single scale; and by its relationship related to a single pitch or root. Both ways are shown in the following examples.

The seven melodic minor modes shown in relation to C melodic minor scale:

The seven melodic minor modes shown in relation to C melodic minor scale. Each is paired with its related chord symbol and voicing:

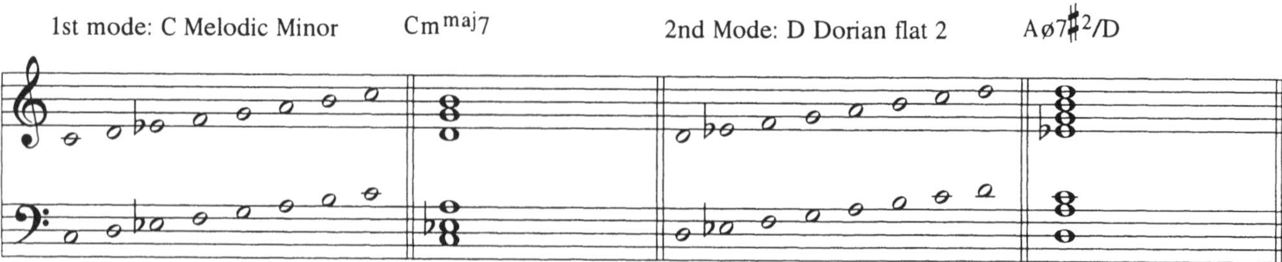

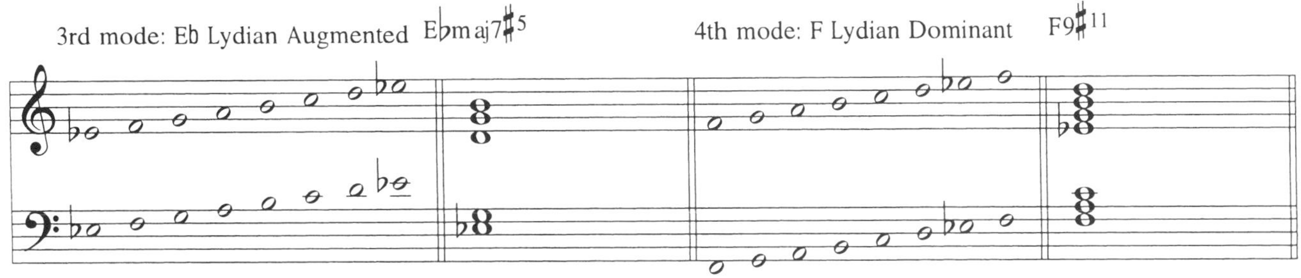

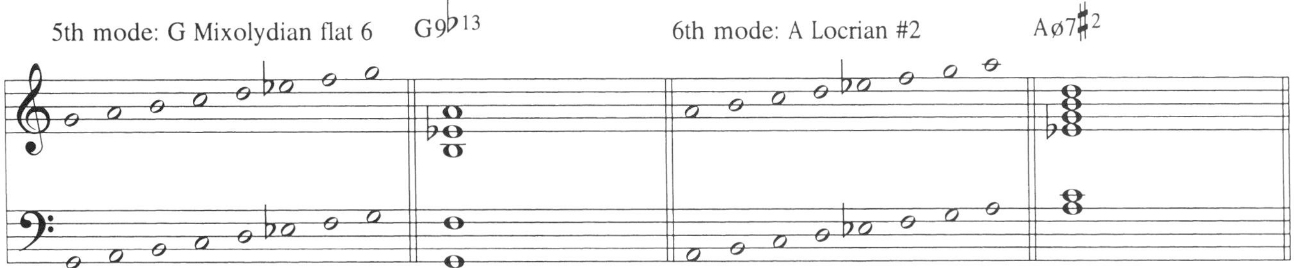

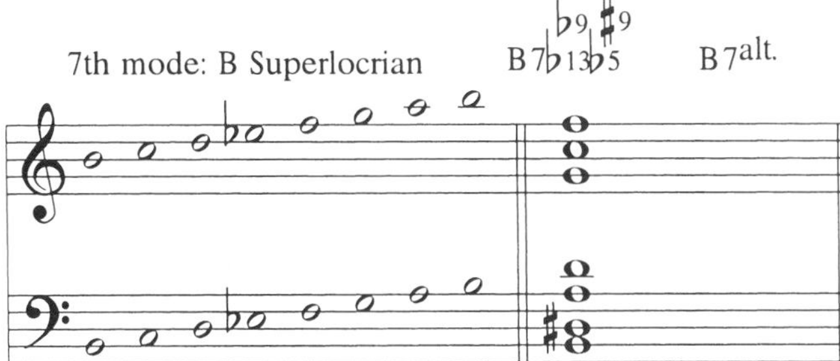

The seven modes related to the pitch C. Each is paired with its related chord symbol and voicing:

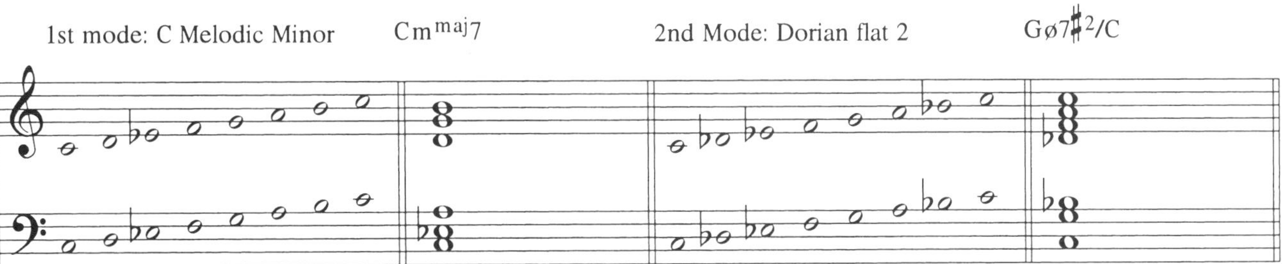

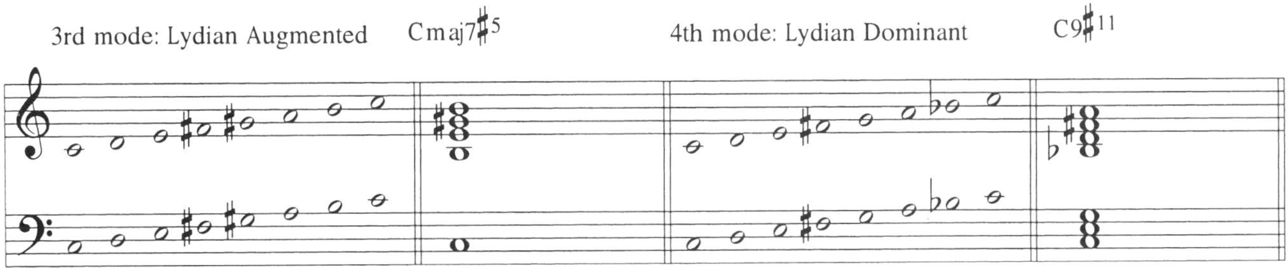

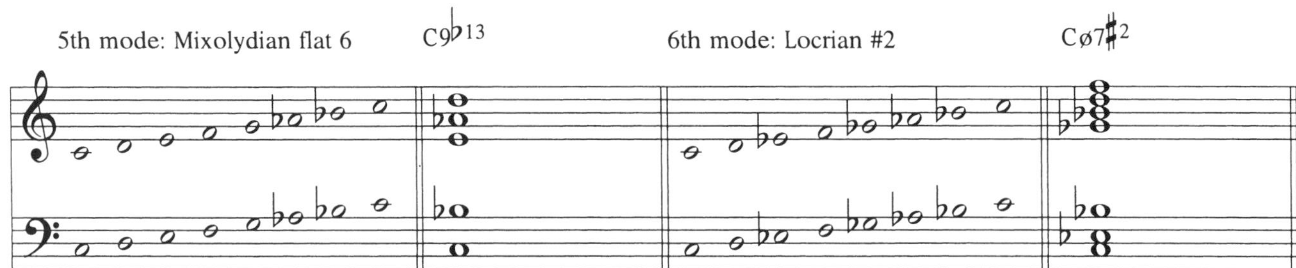

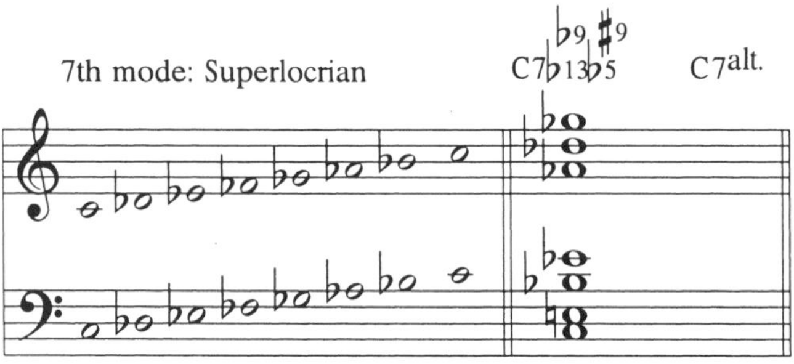

The following examples are excerpts from improvisations that include melodic material derived from melodic minor modes. Remember that when an artist plays melodic patterns, they may not be thinking of any scales or modes. I do not presume to tell you what these artists were thinking when they played. One can draw useful conclusions about the content after the fact. Sometimes a melodic pattern will not include all the notes of the scale, but the remaining pitches can often be deduced. The same is true for any mode or scale. We would assume that *Amazing Grace* is derived from the major scale, even though two significant tones are missing: the fourth and the seventh. How can we deduce that? Sing the melody and afterwards sing the complete scale. Do you hear an augmented fourth indicating Lydian or a minor seventh indicating mixolydian? Probably not.

7th MODE: SUPERLOCRIAN/ALTERED/DIMINISHED WHOLE TONE

The seventh mode may be one of the most used modes. It is often superimposed over dominant chords leading to major or minor tonic chords. A common motive that can be derived from the seventh mode is a ♯9-♭9-R-7 pattern. The 7th usually resolves to the third of the following major or minor chord. The next three examples are from Tom Harrell followed by one from Randy Brecker and McCoy Tyner.

♯9-♭9-R-7 PATTERN

♯9-♭9-R-7 pattern to major

♯9-♭9-R-7 pattern to minor

♯9-♭9-R-7 pattern to major, includes all the notes of the scale

Entire scale ending with the ♯9-♭9-R-7 pattern

Entire scale ending with the ♯9-♭9-R-7 pattern

McCoy Tyner used the G superlocrian sound in m.1, then the F superlocrian sound in mm.2-5 before ending with the ♯9-♭9-R-7 pattern.

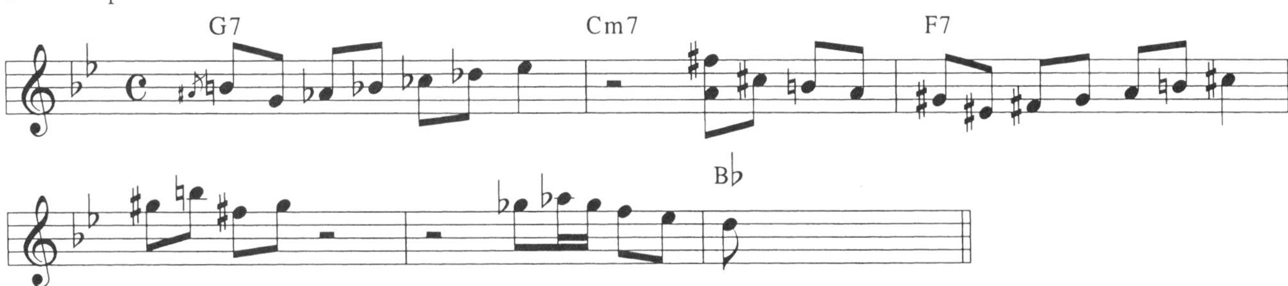

Lee Morgan called attention to relationship between A♭ melodic minor and G superlocrian in these passages. These lines end with the ♯9-♭9 resolving to the fifth of the Cm chord.

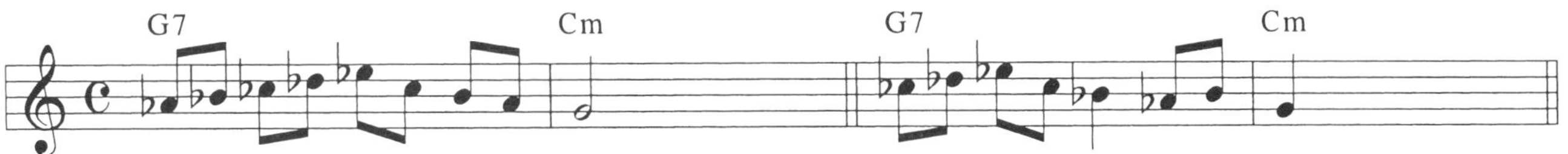

MINOR 1-2-3-5 PATTERN

Lee Morgan called attention to the minor scale above by playing the first few notes of the minor scale over the dominant chord. Here is another ubiquitous pattern containing the 1-2-3-5 of the melodic minor scale a half-step above the root of the dominant chord. Any 1-2-3-5 melodic pattern is so common in traditional music, folk, & pop, that it retains its musical strength when imposed over other chords. The minor pattern over the dominant chord half-step below contains the colorful notes: ♭13, 3, ♯9 and ♭9. In the following examples, Tom Harrell and McCoy Tyner used the pattern to resolve to F major; Harrell used it again pointing to A minor; Lee Morgan used it to point to D♭ and A♭ chords; Woody Shaw used it pointing to E♭; and Harrell used it again pointing to the Dm and Cm chords.

C♯m 1-2-3-5 pattern over C7

C♯m 1-2-3-5 pattern over C7

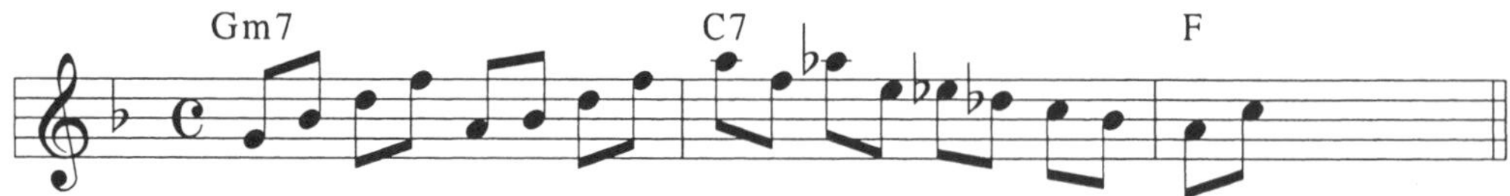

Fm 1-2-3-5 pattern over E7

Am 1-2-3-5 pattern over A♭7 Em 1-2-3-5 pattern over E♭7

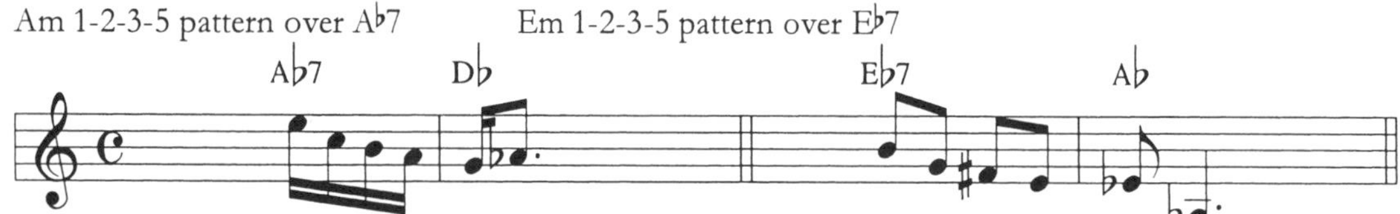

Bm 1-2-3-5 pattern over B♭7

B♭m 1-2-3-5 pattern over A7 A♭m 1-2-3-5 pattern over G7

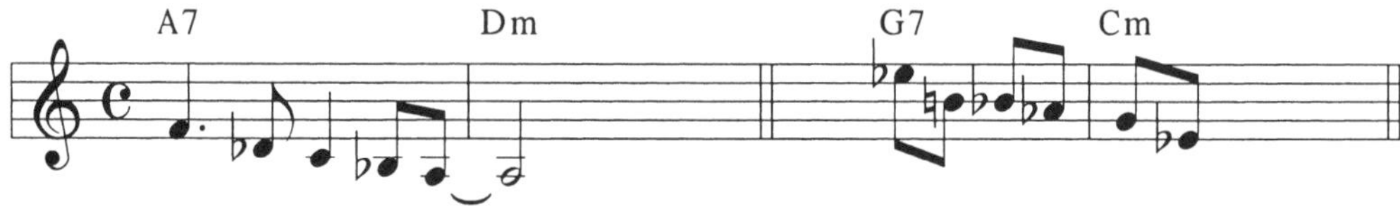

MAJOR 1-2-3-5 PATTERN

Any 1-2-3-5 melodic pattern is so common in traditional music, folk, & pop, that it retains its musical strength when imposed over other chords. There are two major 1-2-3-5 patterns found in a melodic minor scale. Over the dominant chord, the major 1-2-3-5 patterns are found on the ♭5 and ♭13. Woody Shaw used the major 1-2-3-5 pattern found on the ♭5 (♯4, E) of B♭ and Lee Morgan used the 1-2-3-5 pattern from the ♭13 (E♭) of the G7.

E Major 1-2-3-5 over the B♭7 (acting as tritone substitution?)

E♭ Major 1-2-3-5 over the G7

COMBINATION OF 1-2-3-5 PATTERNS

One of the most common minor 1-2-3-5 patterns is sometimes called the *Cry Me a River* (CMAR) lick because of its similarity to the opening line of the tune. Here are examples of it from improvisations by Tete Montoliu, Tom Harrell, and Joe Pass.

G minor CMAR pattern over F♯7 — C minor CMAR over B7

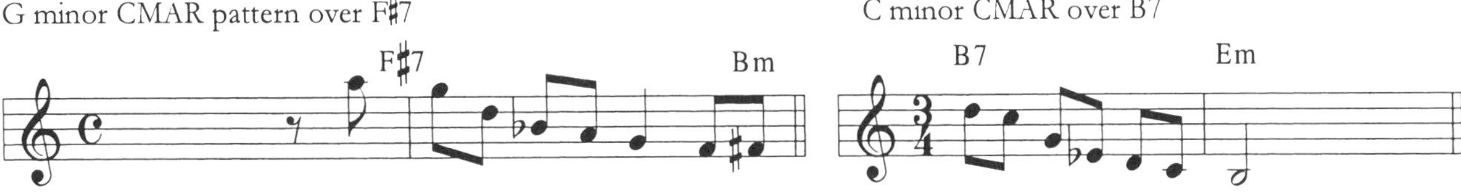

E♭ minor CMAR pattern over D7

B♭ minor CMAR pattern over A7

ø7 ARPEGGIO OVER ALTERED DOMINANT 7TH

A half diminished seventh chord can be found on the sixth degree of a melodic minor scale, which is the seventh degree of superlocrian. An Fø7 chord can be found in an A♭ melodic minor scale and can be used over the G7. The notes of the Fø7 sound the important pitches, 7th, ♭9, 3 and ♭13, which identify the chord quality. Below shows the Fø7/G7 and how it might resolve to the Cm. For the D7, use the half diminished chord on its seventh degree — Cø7. The D7 is shown with its resolution to major. The voice leading is smooth and is the same for each. In the examples that follow, Cannonball Adderley, Charlie Parker and Tom Harrell illustrate how the smooth voice leading translates into smooth linear motion.

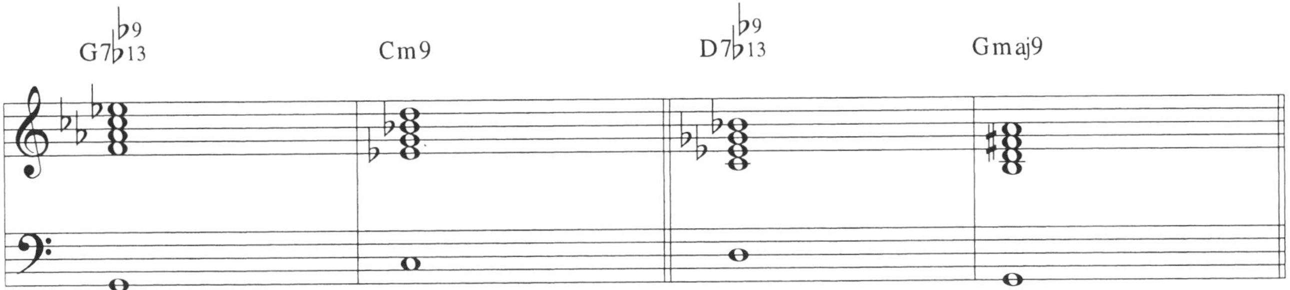

If you begin an arpeggio on the seventh of an altered dominant, you get the following notes: 7-♭9-3-♭13-R-♯9. If you use the same arpeggio, but change the bass note to a tritone substitute the notes become 3-5-7-9-♯11-13 of the new chord. The new chord has a lydian dominant sound.

Tete Montoliu used this extended tertian arpeggio in the following example. We can only guess whether he was thinking C7 or G♭7, but either way the results are the same.

LYDIAN DOMINANT

So much of the music we hear and study is based on the uniquely European model for major and minor that we forget sometimes that in other parts of the world, music is created out of many different modes and scales. The are many folk melodies from places as different as Hungary and Brazil which are composed using the fourth mode of melodic minor, lydian dominant. This scale is sometimes called the overtone scale. It is not unique to jazz as evidenced by the following example.

Béla Bartók: A♭ Lydian Dominant

Here are a few examples using the lydian dominant sound. Charlie Parker used it as a colorful dominant on the bridge to rhythm changes. The connection to A melodic minor is clear as he arpeggiated an A minor 1-3-5-7-9 over the D7.

Wynton Kelly suggested the upper structures 7-9-♯11-13 of the A♭7 and E♭7 chords and Tete Montoliu chose to play the entire descending scale over the B7.

D Lydian dominant outlines upper structure: 5-7-9-♯11-13

Lydian dominant upper structure 7-9-♯11-13 for these two arpeggios

Lydian dominant scale passage

LYDIAN AUGMENTED

The lydian augmented scale is used less than other modes of melodic minor primarily because of the rarity of major seventh chords with augmented fifths. Contemporary jazz composers have been using more of these sounds as substitutions for tonic chords and as independent color chords in non-traditional progressions. Harrell suggested the lydian augmented sound in these two examples that ultimately resolved to C major.

Lydian Augmented

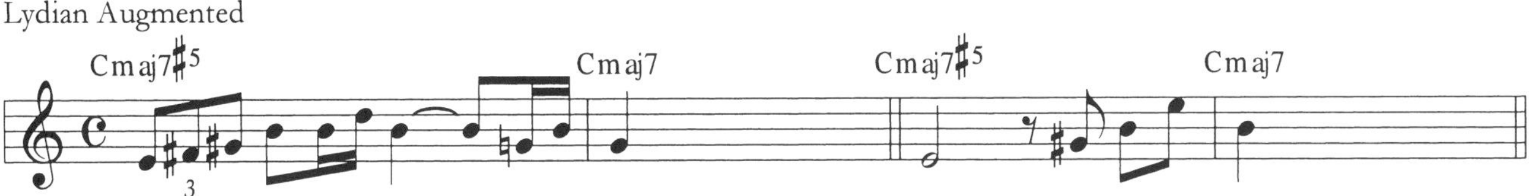

LOCRIAN ♮2

Is a half diminished with a raised second degree a bright chord or a dark chord? The two chords are exactly the same in the example that follows. Played by themselves they will sound exactly the same. However, chords are never played by themselves except in music theory classes. If these two chords occur in the context of the key signatures in which they are shown, the perception of bright and dark will change. In the key of B♭ major we expect to hear a Cm7 or Cm9 as the ii chord. If the G is flatted, the chord becomes Cø7♮2, and will sound darker in that context because of the lowered note. In the key of B♭ minor we expect a G♭ and would expect a Cø7 as the iiø chord. Raising the D♭ to a D♮ will certainly make the Cø7♮2 sound brighter in the context of B♭ minor.

Cø7♯2: Dark Cø7♯2: Bright

The squares below illustrate how context changes our perceptions. The inner squares are the same shade of gray, however the inner square on the left appears lighter surrounded by the dark edge, and the inner square on the left appears darker.

Cannonball Adderley used the Cø7♯2 in the place of the Cm9 chord in the key of B♭ major. The contrast between the darker G♭ (from the parallel minor key) and the brighter D♮ (suggesting B♭ major) is carried over to the F7 chord.

Cø7♯2 arpeggio

COMBINATIONS OF MODES

Sounds and chords created from melodic minor modes can often occur in succession. In the next example Harrell used a A♭ø7 (locrian ♯2, enharmonic 6th mode of B melodic minor) in m.1, D♭7 (superlocrian, enharmonic 7th mode of D melodic minor) sound in m.2, and G♭maj7♯5 (Lydian Augmented, 3rd mode of E♭ melodic minor) in m.3.

Mixture of Melodic Minor Modes

Bill Evans used an Fø7 (locrian ♯2, 6th mode of A♭ melodic minor) followed by a B♭7 (superlocrian, 7th mode of B melodic minor). The line ascends the arpeggio over the Fø7 and descends over the B♭7. The CMAR lick is followed by the ♯9-♭9-R-7 pattern on the B♭7 chord.

This line is very similar to the line above, but is in C minor. The lines for the dominant chords are identical. Dø7 (locrian ♯2, 6th mode of F melodic minor) G7 (superlocrian, 7th mode of A♭ melodic minor).

The raised second degree and altered ninths are not just modern jazz inventions. Clifford Brown played Gø7 (locrian ♯2, 6th mode of B♭ melodic minor) and C7 (superlocrian, 7th mode of C♯ melodic minor) in the following example.

MELODIC MINOR EXERCISES

This collection of exercises is designed to make melodic minor patterns more familiar. Begin by practicing the scale as any other scale, taking it through normal scale patterns shown in previous chapters, and practicing them in all keys. Then look at arpeggios that are unique to the melodic minor scale. Below there are three arpeggios shown that can be found in the C melodic minor scale: Cm maj7, E♭ maj7♯5 and Aø7. All of these by themselves can be found elsewhere. The Cm maj7 on the first degree of C harmonic minor; the E♭ maj7♯5 on the third degree of C harmonic minor; the Aø7 on the seventh degree of B♭ major or G harmonic minor. Stacked on top of each other as shown in m.5 below, they can only be found in the C melodic minor scale.

ARPEGGIO MELODIC PATTERNS FROM MELODIC MINOR

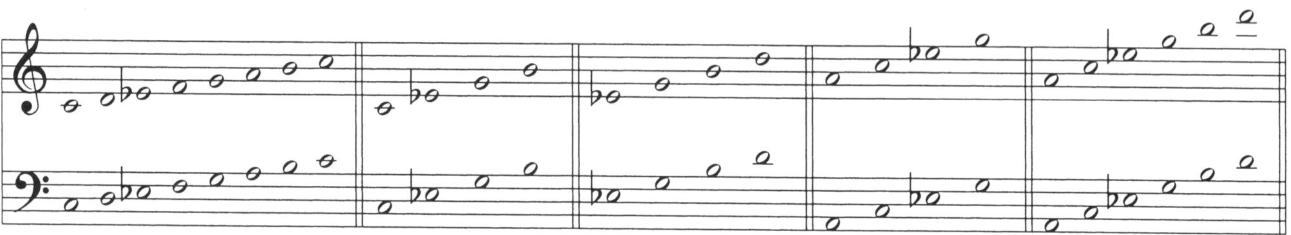

Remember that each of those melodic patterns can be used in a number of different situations. All of the patterns above work for Cm maj7, E♭ ma7♯5, F9♯11, Aø7♮2, or B7 (♯9 ♭13). All melodic minor exercises should be transposed to all keys and applied to standard harmonic progressions.

4.1 Diatonic triads

4.2 Cyclical Quadruplet (CQ) patterns emphasizing the arpeggiated notes A - C - E♭ - G - B - D

4.3 CQ patterns applied to a progression. (Dø7 = F melodic minor, G7 = A♭ melodic minor, Cm & F9 = C melodic minor)

4.4 Extended arpeggios applied to a progression. (Dø7 = F melodic minor, G7 = A♭ melodic minor, Cm & F9 = C melodic minor).

Each of the following pairs of extended arpeggios begins on the same pitch. Several pitches stay the same from the ø7 to the Dominant 7 chord. The notes that change follow voice leading principles. The seventh of Eø7 (D) resolves to the third of A (shown as enharmonic D♭); the F♯ resolves down to the F (9 resolving to the ♭13).

4.5 Extended arpeggios applied to an excerpt of a familiar standard jazz progression

4.6 Extension on standard progression

If a line works for any of the following chords, then they will work on all of the other chords in the following progression. The trick is to play the pattern from the appropriate melodic minor scale. In the following exercises the scales are: Aø7 = C melodic minor; D7 = E♭ melodic minor; Gm and C7 = G melodic minor.

4.7 Extension sequences on a typical progression

4.8 Extension sequences on a typical progression

4.9 CMAR quote over a iiø7 - V7 - i progression

4.9b CMAR quote in C minor works for all of these chords.

Simple triad shapes can be found in melodic minor scales that sound musical when superimposed over other chords as in the following exercise. G and Cm triad shapes are played over the Aø7; B♭ and E♭m triad shapes over the D7; and D and Gm triad shapes over the Gm followed by the CMAR quote.

4.10 Triads over standard progression

1-2-3-5 & 1-2-3-4-5 PATTERNS from MELODIC MINOR

If triads (1-3-5) can be superimposed over other chords, then the 1-2-3-5- and 1-2-3-4-5 melodic patterns will work. For the C melodic minor scale, two choices would be the Cm and the G major triads and corresponding patterns.

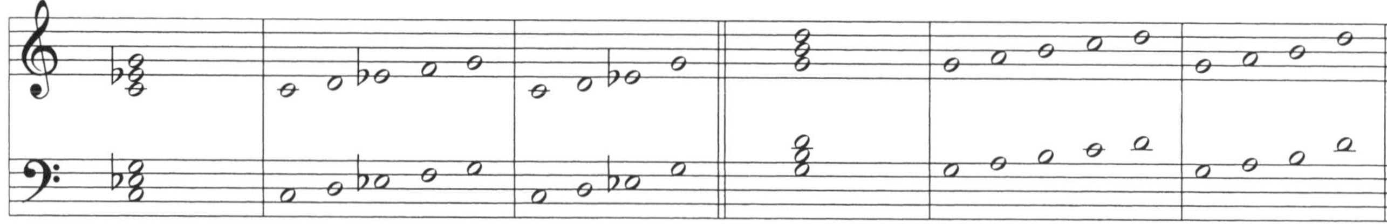

Although it is physically easy to play a five finger exercise pattern such as 1-2-3-4-5 in major; implementing the idea when the beginning note is the ♭13 of a dominant chord or the ninth of a 9♯11 chord is mentally challenging. Practice these simple patterns as shown below, exercising the thought process so that when you need it and want to use these concepts and melodic patterns, it will not be necessary to perform some mathematical calculations first. Chord symbols show various progressions with which these melodic figures work.

4.11 **Simple 1-2-3-4-5 and 1-2-3-5- pattern applications**

4.12 **1-2-3-5 pattern variation = 3-5-2-1:**

4.13 **5-4-3-2-1 pattern over an altered dominant becomes ♯9-♭9-R-7 pattern shown with possible resolutions:**

4.14 **Shown with a deceptive resolution.**

4.15 A♭ melodic pattern resolving to C major.

4.16 1-2-3-5 pattern variations. 3-5-2-1 with and without octave displacement.

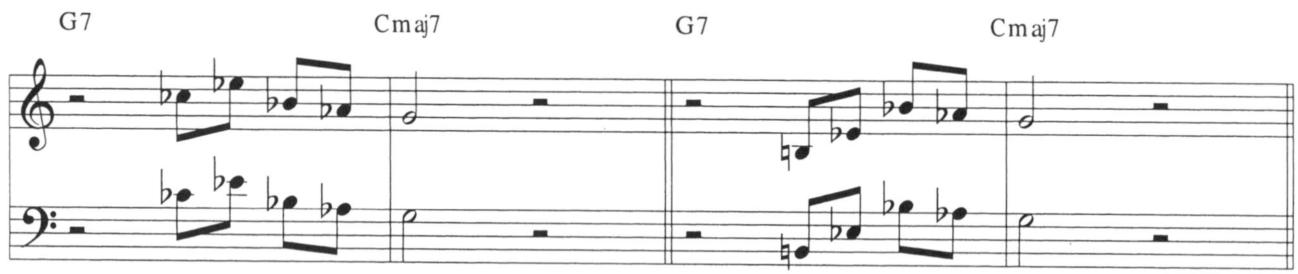

4.17 Practice resolving to major and minor.

4.18 1-2-3-5 patterns in sequence over progression.

4.19 **1-2-3-5 patterns in sequence over progression.**

4.20 **1-2-3-5 patterns in sequence over progression.**

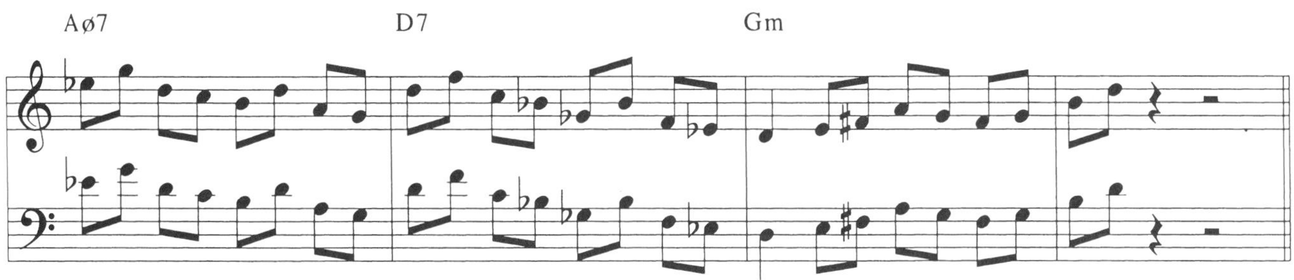

4.21 **1-2-3-5 patterns in sequence over progression.**

4.22 **1-2-3-5 patterns in sequence over progression.**

4.23 1-2-3-5 patterns in sequence over progression.

1-2-3-5 PATTERN VARIATIONS

Consider that a major or minor 1-2-3-5 pattern may be inverted to be 3-5-2-1 or 3-5-2-1 with octave displacement. Then consider that a major 1-2-3-5 and two variations and a minor 1-2-3-5 and variations could be imposed over half-diminished chords, and the same for a dominant seventh chords. There are six possible patterns to be plugged in over each chord in a iiø7 – V7 progression, which means that thirty six distinct patterns can be created. All thirty six patterns are shown in Chapter 7.

4.24 Six possible 1-2-3-5 patterns for Bø7

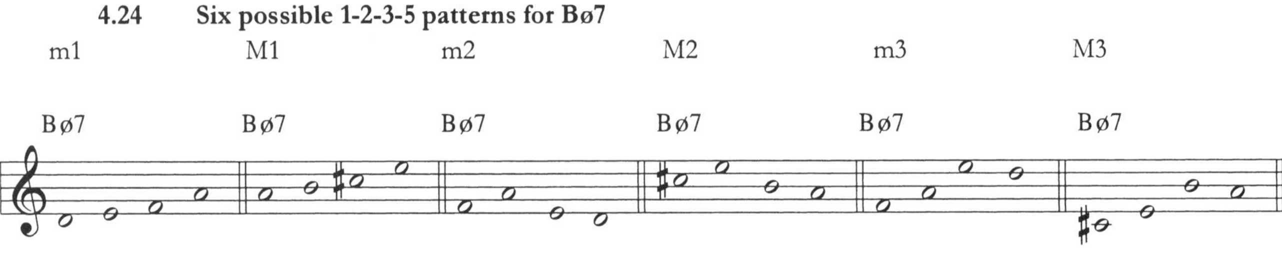

4.25 Six possible 1-2-3-5 patterns for E7

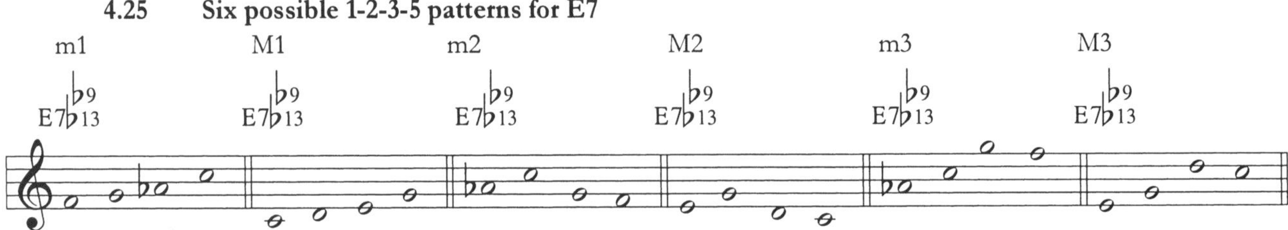

TRIADS

Two of the diatonic triads found in the melodic minor scale are major triads. Superimposing these simple triads over other chords related to the melodic minor modes can create some interesting harmonic colors. Superimposing the D♭ and E♭ major triads found in the A♭ melodic minor scale creates the two chords shown below over a G7. Developing lines based on these triads are harmonically colorful since the triads yield the ♭5, ♭9, ♭13, and ♯9—all of the altered tones, yet since the lines could be based on simple triads, may be simple in melodic conception at the same time. Polytonal lines can be suggested by superimposing triadic shapes over other chords.

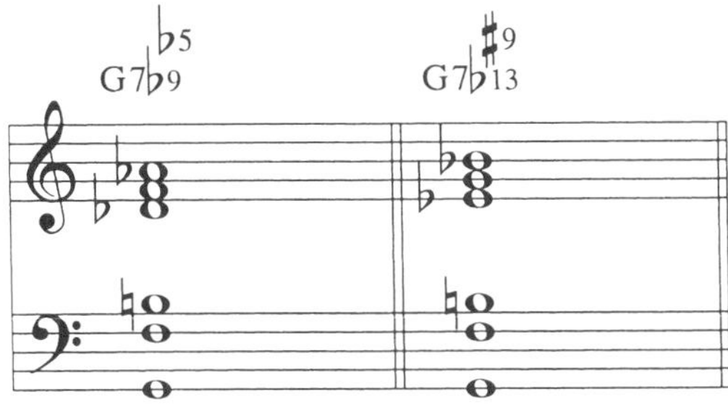

4.26 **D♭ and E♭ major triads over G7 altered. This same exercise works for a D♭9♯11**

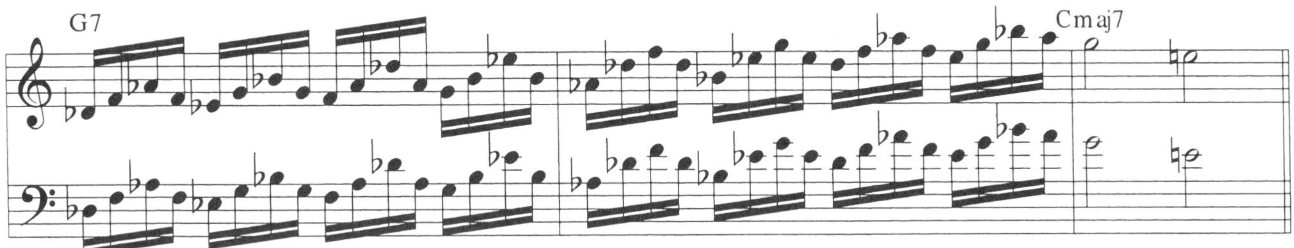

TRITONE SUBSTITUTION & MELODIC MINOR CHORDS

Two dominant chords a tritone apart, such as D♭7 and G7 share the same tritone. The unstable tritone is what necessitates the motion from V7 to I. Since the two dominants share the unstable tritone pitches, although enharmonically spelled below, they can function in the same way. The D♭7 chord is spelled like an augmented sixth chord (D♭ – B = augmented sixth) but sounds like a D♭7 chord. The unstable tritone notes can resolve to the stable C major tones as shown below. The D♭7 can substitute for G7 in the ii - V7 - I progression as shown below.

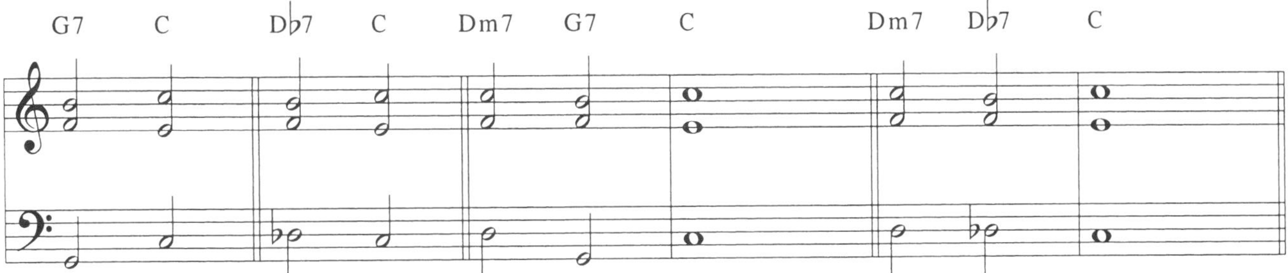

In a tritone substitute relationship, the third and seventh of one chord becomes the seventh and third of the other. A G7 altered dominant and a D♭9♯11 are both sounds that can be created using the A♭ melodic minor scale. The example below shows the relationship of each note of the A♭ melodic minor scale to the respective chords.

G7♯9♭13
R ♭9 ♯9 (3) ♭5 ♭13 7 R

D♭9♯11
♯11 5 13 7 R 9 3 ♯11

Spelling a tertian chord from the third of the D♭9♯11 yields these pitches shown with their relationship to the two chords.

G7♯9♭13
7 ♭9 (3) ♭13 R ♯9 ♭5

D♭9♯11
3 5 7 9 ♯11 13 R

RELATIONSHIP of ALTERED DOMINANTS, LYDIAN DOMINANTS & MELODIC MINOR SCALES

ALTERED DOMINANT	LYDIAN DOMINANT	MELODIC MINOR SCALE
G7 ♯9/♭13	D♭9 ♯11	A♭ Melodic Minor
C7 ♯9/♭13	G♭9 ♯11	D♭ Melodic Minor
F7 ♯9/♭13	B9 ♯11	F♯ Melodic Minor
B♭7 ♯9/♭13	E9 ♯11	B Melodic Minor
E♭7 ♯9/♭13	A9 ♯11	E Melodic Minor
A♭7 ♯9/♭13	D9 ♯11	A Melodic Minor
D♭7 ♯9/♭13	G9 ♯11	D Melodic Minor
F♯7 ♯9/♭13	C9 ♯11	G Melodic Minor
B7 ♯9/♭13	F9 ♯11	C Melodic Minor
E7 ♯9/♭13	B♭9 ♯11	F Melodic Minor
A7 ♯9/♭13	E♭9 ♯11	B♭ Melodic Minor
D7 ♯9/♭13	A♭9 ♯11	E♭ Melodic Minor

Lydian dominant chords often function as substitute dominants, but may also be used as what has been called "Backdoor Dominants." These dominants are usually preceded by a IV and resolve from the flatted seventh to the tonic. They are related to the traditional plagal, IV- I or iv - I, cadence as illustrated below. The backdoor dominant could be heard as pointing to the vi chord as a tritone substitution, so when acting as a backdoor dominant it is really a deceptive resolution.

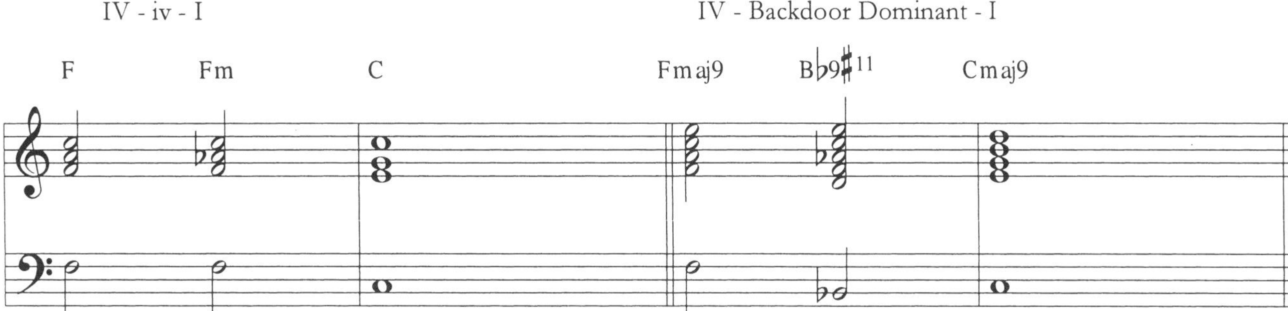

SECONDARY DOMINANTS & TRITONE SUBSTITUTIONS

In C major, a piece may modulate to any of the diatonic key centers one accidental either way:

ii	key of D minor	1♭
ii	key of E minor	1♯
IV	key of F major	1♭
V	key of G major	1♯
vi	key of A minor	no ♯s or ♭s

The tonic chord is often preceded by its dominant (the primary dominant) or the tritone substitution dominant. These new secondary key areas or tonicizations are preceded by their dominants (secondary dominants) and often in jazz with their tritone substitution dominant:

NEW KEY AREA	SECONDARY DOMINANT	TRITONE SUBSTITUTION DOMINANT
D minor	A7	E♭7
E minor	B7	F7
F major	C7	G♭7
G major	D7	A♭7
A minor	E7	B♭7

It would be helpful to make a chart like the one shown above for all keys.

The following arpeggio exercise looks at secondary dominant tritone substitution chords in the key of F major. It begins with extended arpeggios on the tonic chord and modulates around in fifths following the pattern: I - IV - iii - vi - ii - V - I. The exercise uses tritone substitute dominants instead of traditional dominants.

- The B9♯11 is substituting for F7 pointing to the key of IV, B♭ major
- The B♭9♯11 is substituting for E7 pointing to the key of iii, A minor
- The E♭9♯11 is substituting for A7 pointing to the key of vi, D minor
- The A♭9♯11 is substituting for D7 pointing to the key of ii, G minor
- The D♭9♯11 is substituting for G7 pointing to the key of V, C major
- The G♭9♯11 is substituting for C7 pointing to the tonic key of F major

4.27 Arpeggio Exercise Through Diatonic Modulations Using Tritone Substitute Dominants

4.28 Alternating ascending and descending patterns using cycle of altered dominants

4.29 Alternating ascending and descending patterns using cycle of lydian dominants

This line may be practiced thinking of the progression: D♭9 ♯11 — C7 ♯9♭13 — B9 ♯11, etc.

Try using these lines with one of these turnaround progressions shown in the key of C:

↓
| Dm7 / / / | G7 / / / | B♭9 ♯11 / A7 ♯9♭13 / | A♭ 9♯11 / G7 ♯9♭13 / | C

| Dm7 / / / | G7 / / / | E7 ♯9♭13 / E♭ 9♯11 / | D7 ♯9♭13 / D♭ 9♯11 / | C

4.30 Alternating ascending and descending patterns using cycle of altered dominants
4.31 Alternating ascending and descending patterns using cycle of lydian dominants

This line may be practiced thinking of the progression: A9 ♯11 — G♯7 ♯9♭13 — G9 ♯11, etc.

Try using these lines with one of these turnaround progressions shown in the key of C:

↓
| Dm7 / / / | G7 / / / | B♭9 ♯11 / A7 ♯9♭13 / | A♭ 9♯11 / G7 ♯9♭13 / | C

| Dm7 / / / | G7 / / / | E7 ♯9♭13 / E♭ 9♯11 / | D7 ♯9♭13 / D♭ 9♯11 / | C

The next two exercises incorporate several extended arpeggios and scale passages derived from the melodic minor scales. Try practicing this as an altered dominant (or its tritone substitute) resolving to major or minor.

4.32 Ascending lines using diatonic arpeggios from melodic minor

G7♯9♭13 or D♭ 9♯11 Cmaj7 or Cm

4.33 Descending lines using diatonic arpeggios from melodic minor

G7♯9♭13 or D♭ 9♯11 Cmaj7 or Cm

V. DIMINISHED SCALE EXERCISES

Major and minor scales can be transposed to all twelve pitch degrees and have unique pitch classes. Diminished scales are scales of limited transposition. There are only three pitch collections with each having only two modes. The diminished scale is also known as the octatonic scale and the symmetrical scale. Part of the charm and attraction to the diminished scale is its ambiguity.

The three diminished modes with the whole-step/half-step pattern are shown below. Each scale, when transposed up by minor thirds contains the same pitch sets. Whole-half diminished scales beginning on C, E♭, F♯, and A♮ share the same pitches.

WHOLE-HALF DIMINISHED SCALES

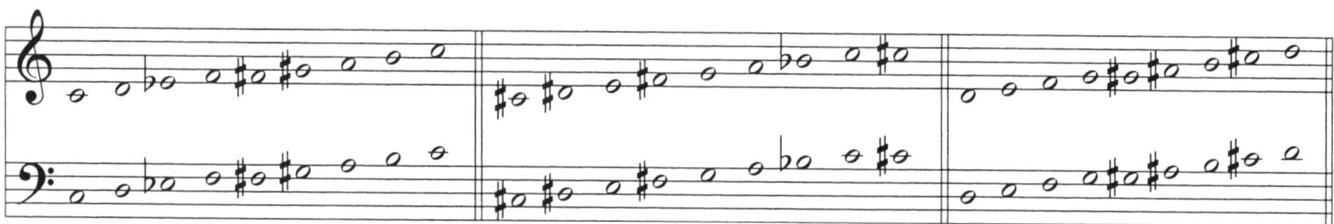

The three diminished scales with the half-step/whole-step pattern are shown below. Each scale, when transposed up by minor thirds contains the same pitch sets. Half-whole diminished scales beginning on C, E♭, F♯, and A♮ share the same pitches.

HALF-WHOLE DIMINISHED SCALES

The following chords and sonorities can be derived from diminished scales starting on C. The first set is from the whole-half scale, the second set from the half-whole scale.

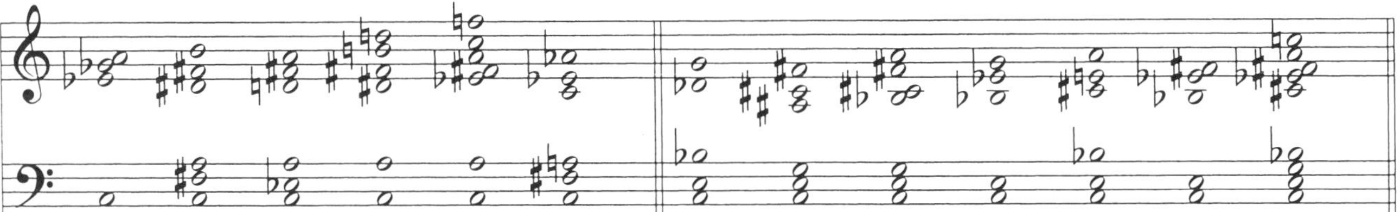

The whole-half scale is used over diminished chords. C°7, E♭°7 (D♯°7), F♯°7, and A°7 all share the same whole-half diminished scale. The half-whole scale is used over dominant seventh chords. C7, E♭7, F♯7, and A7 all share the same half-whole diminished scale.

The ambiguity of the diminished scale is apparent after looking at the usual function of a diminished chord as the vii°7 in minor. The whole-half scale in the first measure above would work with F♯°7. Typically, an F♯°7 points to G minor. The whole-half scale beginning on F♯ does not have a G or a B♭, the important identifying notes of G minor, instead it has the ambiguous G♯ and B♮.

The half-whole scale in the second measure corresponds with C7. Typically, a C7 would points to F major or F minor. The notes of the scale include a ♯9 and ♭9 which would suggest resolution to F minor. It also includes a ♮13, which would suggest resolution to F major. The F♯ does not suggest a C7 pointing to F major or minor, but suggests C7 as a tritone substitution (for F♯7) pointing to B minor or a C7 as a backdoor dominant resolution to D major.

The symmetry of the diminished scale allows any melodic material found in the scale to be transposed up in a series of minor thirds. Any motive is available a minor third, tritone, and a major sixth above the original. As shown below, D, F, A♭ and B major triads can be found in the following whole-half diminished scale.

These major triads are related to functional harmony. The above C whole-half diminished scale would work with C°7 (B♯°7), D♯°7, F♯°7, and A°7. If C°7 (B♯°7) functions to point out D♭ (C♯) minor then so does the A♭ (G♯) triad. The other diminished chords correspond with the triads shown above as well: D and F♯°7 can point to G minor; F and A°7 can point to B♭ minor; B and D♯°7 can point to E minor.

These major triads can be found in the following half-whole diminished scale. This scale works for C7, E♭7, F♯7 (G♭7), and A7 chords with these alterations: ♭9, ♯9, ♯11, & ♮13.

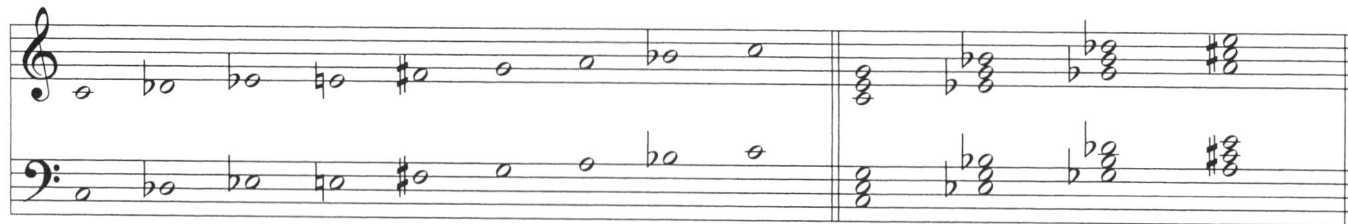

DIMINISHED SCALE MUSICAL EXAMPLES

Bill Evans used the half-whole diminished scales over dominant chords and whole-half diminished over diminished chords in the following examples. Cannonball Adderley used the scale as a generalization over Rhythm changes.

Half-whole diminished over dominant chords. Diatonic diminished chords.

Whole-half diminished over diminished chords. Ascending scale pattern.

Diminished scale pattern from Rhythm changes.

Many melodic patterns derived from the diminished scale emphasize the available symmetrical qualities and patterns. Any interval that can be found in the scale can be found in at least four separate places. These next few patterns emphasize perfect fourths and major seconds. Depending on the analysis, the following Cannonball Adderley line is built on seconds or fourths. The four pairs of seconds are: F–E♭; A♭–G♭, B–A, and D–C. The four pairs of perfect fourths are: E♭–A♭, G♭ (F♯)–B, A–D, and C–F.

Diminished pattern emphasizing symmetrical intervals transposed up in minor thirds from Blues.

Some diminished patterns emphasize symmetrical intervals transposed up in minor thirds. Do these Cannonball and Harrell excerpts below emphasize seconds? fourths? both?

Half-whole over dominant chord emphasizing symmetrical intervals transposed up in minor thirds.

These melodic patterns emphasizing symmetrical intervals transposed up in minor thirds are not unique to jazz as shown by the following two examples. The first is from Paul Hindemith; the second from Béla Bartók.

Tom Harrell used the diminished scale over a traditional ii - V - I progression. The melody seems to slide in and out of the key. The first four notes are common to the key of B, while the next four notes are not. The melody line is not resolved to the key of B until the third beat of the fourth measure.

Descending diminished Scale over ii - V - I.

Art Farmer and Harrell used the ascending scale over these examples. The G7 chords are pointing to a C minor chord, so the diminished scale creates an ambiguity: the ♭9 and ♯9 point to C minor; the ♮13 points to C major; ♯11 could point to F♯ with G7 being a tritone substitute dominant.

Half-whole over dominant chord.

Half-whole over dominant chord.

Half-whole over dominant chord.

After ascending an E♭m arpeggio up to A♭, Randy Brecker used the descending diminished scale to lead back to the D♭ chord.

Half-whole over dominant chord.

The four triads arpeggiated in the following Harrell example are found in the C half-whole diminished scale.

C, A, F♯, and E♭ triads suggested over C7

Gustav Holst used two triads available from the half-whole diminished scale a tritone apart.

While the diminished scales yield many melodic patterns such as triads that are common to traditional scales, they also yield patterns unique and removed from traditional melodic patterns. Here are a number of examples from Béla Bartók. If you listen to many contemporary jazz musicians (Chick Corea, Tom Harrell, Michael Brecker, and others) these examples will sound familiar.

Tete Montoliu played this half-step/perfect fourth motive that could have been influenced by Béla Bartók patterns.

Leaps create dramatic interest as illustrated by this Jeff Andrews sequence from a blues solo.

Diminished scales are employed to add color to this saxophone line by Thad Jones.

DIMINISHED SCALE EXERCISES

Practice this collection of diminished scale exercises as all other exercises. Keep the metronome clicking. The exercises begin by just isolating the scale and specific patterns from the scale. Later exercises introduce applications of the scale patterns in traditional settings. These scales can only be transposed three times before repeating themselves, but it is a good idea to be able to play these exercises from any pitch. Avoid the temptation of only practicing from three pitches.

5.1 Diminished Exercises emphasizing (a) ascending scale and half steps, then (b) whole Steps and descending scales.

5.1.a **5.1.b**

5.2 Diminished scale with traditional scale pattern ascending and descending.

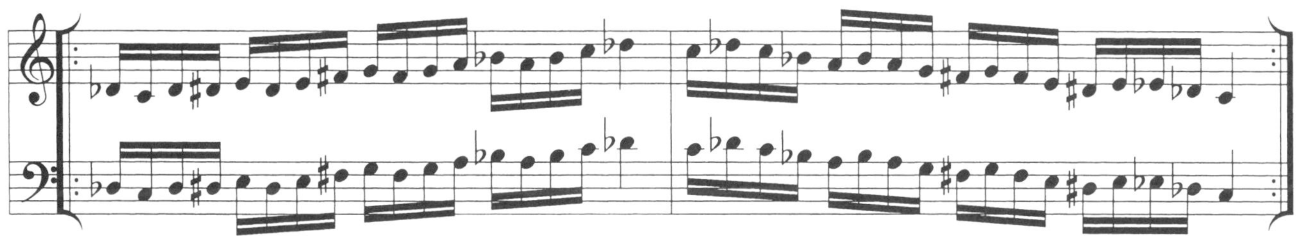

5.3 Encircling the diminished chord tones using the pattern: CT-UNT-LNT-CT.

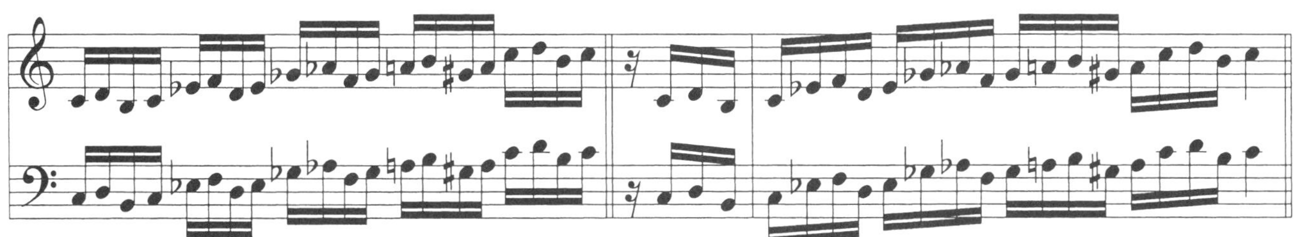

5.4 Encircling the diminished chord tones using the pattern: CT-LNT-UNT-CT.

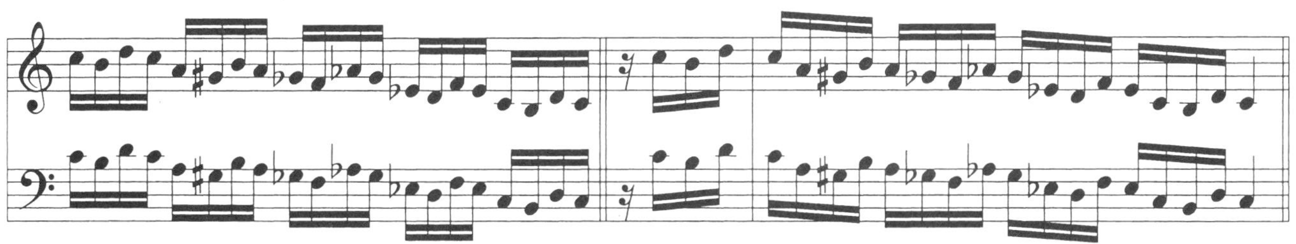

5.5 Encircling the diminished chord tones using the pattern: UNT-CT-LNT-CT.

5.6 Encircling the diminished chord tones using the pattern: LNT-CT-UNT-CT.

5.7 Encircling the diminished chord tones using the pattern: UNT-LNT-CT & the pattern: LNT-UNT-CT

5.8 Arpeggiated ascending diatonic diminished triads.

5.9 **Arpeggiated diatonic diminished triads alternating ascending and descending.**

5.10 **Arpeggiated diatonic seventh chords.**

5.11 Other diatonic seventh chords unique to diminished scales. Note the first two notes are echoed a tritone away: C–E & G♭–B♭, C♯–F♯ & G–C, etc.

5.12 This exercise isolates the first chord from exercise 5.11 and sequences it up and down in minor thirds.

5.13 This exercise isolates the second chord from exercise 5.11 and sequences it up and down in minor thirds.

5.14 **Major triad arpeggios found in diminished scales.**

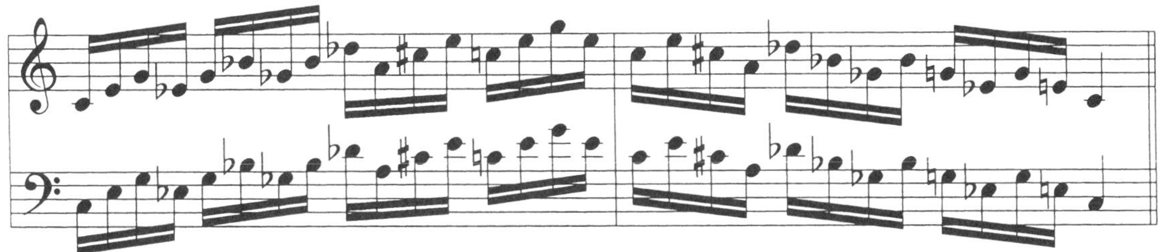

5.15 **Isolating ascending minor third intervals.**

5.16 **Isolating descending minor third intervals.**

5.17 **Alternating ascending & descending minor third intervals.**

5.18 **Alternating descending & ascending minor third intervals.**

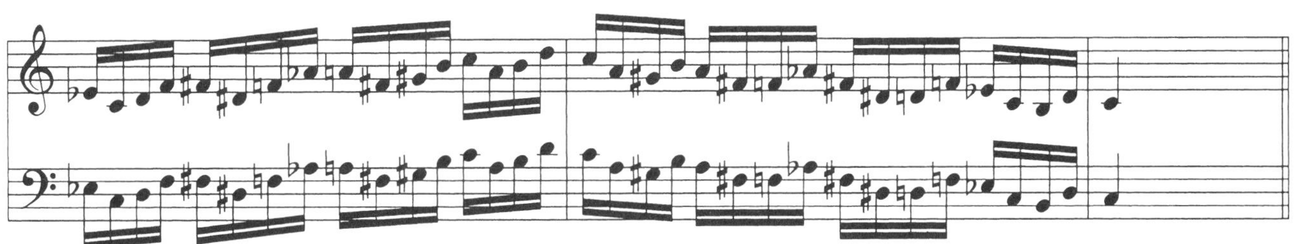

5.19 **Melodic pattern (M2-m3) sequenced at a minor third.**

5.20 **Melodic pattern (m3-M2) sequenced at a minor third. (Retrograde inversion of 5.19)**

5.21 **Melodic pattern (M2-M3) sequenced at a minor third.**

5.22 **Melodic pattern (M3–M2) sequenced at a minor third. (Retrograde inversion of 5.21)**

5.23 **Melodic pattern (m6–M2) sequenced at a minor third.**

5.24 Melodic pattern (m2–m6) sequenced at a minor third.

5.25 Melodic pattern (m2–P4) sequenced at a minor third.

5.26 Retrograde inversion (P4–m2) of 5.25 sequenced at a minor third.

5.27 Melodic pattern (d5–P4) sequenced at a minor third.

5.28 Melodic pattern (m2–m3–M2) sequenced at a minor third.

5.29 **Melodic blues pattern sequenced at a minor third.**

5.30 **Melodic pattern (m2–P4–m2) sequenced at a minor third.**

5.31 **Melodic pattern (M2–M3–M2) sequenced at a minor third.**

5.32 **Melodic pattern (P4–M3–M2) sequenced at a minor third.**

5.33 **Melodic pattern (m3–M2–m3) sequenced at a minor third.**

5.34 **Melodic pattern (m3–M2–m3) sequenced at a minor third and rhythmically displaced.**

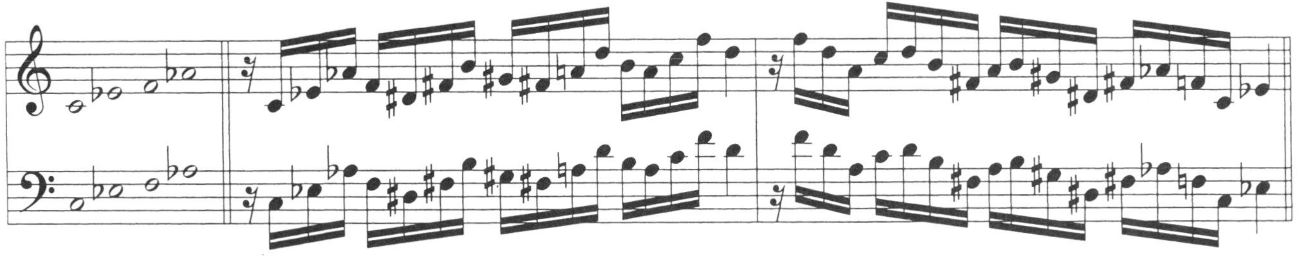

5.35 **Melodic pattern (m3–M2–m3) sequenced at a minor third and rhythmically varied.**

5.36 **Melodic pattern (m3–P4–m3) sequenced at a minor third and rhythmically displaced**

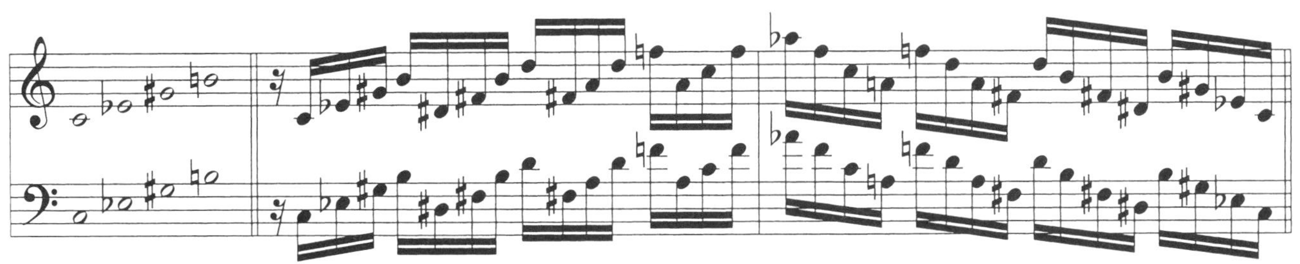

5.37 Minor third and seventh chord patterns.

5.38 **Minor third and seventh chord patterns.**

5.39 **Minor third and seventh chord patterns.**

5.40 **Minor third and seventh chord patterns.**

5.41 **Triad arpeggios a tritone apart.**

5.42 **Triad broken chords a tritone apart.**

5.43 **Triad inversion arpeggios a tritone apart.**

5.44 **Parts of triads a tritone apart: 2 & 3 note groupings**

5.45 **Descending scalar four-note groupings.**

5.46 Major seventh leaps sequenced at the minor third.

5.47 Melodic pattern (m2–M7) sequenced at a minor third.

Most triadic and seventh chord melodic patterns are traditionally contained within an octave. Some contemporary composers and improvisers are experimenting with larger interval chords that go beyond the octave. One way to create these chords is to octave displace one note.

The chords in exercise 5.48 may be found by themselves or superimposed over other chords. By themselves, these chords are either notated as °7 chords or as slash chords (B/C). (The slash chord, B/C, indicates a B major triad over a C bass note.) If superimposed over dominant chords, they create very colorful dominant structures. For instance, the first chord below over a D7 creates a D13♭9.

5.48 Large interval four-note chords.

The chords in exercise 5.49 are also often superimposed over dominant chords. The following can be played over a D7, F7, A♭7, and B7. This chord occurs in many compositions by Mike Stern and other contemporary jazz composers. What alterations would each create?

5.49 **Large interval four-note chords.**

5.50 **Diminished triad with first note encircled creating a five-note pattern.**

DIMINISHED SCALE LINES OVER TRADITIONAL HARMONY

5.51 **Alternating thirds melodic pattern over traditional ii - V7 - I progression.**

5.52 Triad arpeggios over V7 - I progression.

5.53 Triad arpeggios over V7 - I progression.

5.54 Triad arpeggios over V7 - I progression creating a repeating five-note pattern

5.55 Triad arpeggios over V7 - I progression creating a repeating five-note pattern.

5.56 Pattern from exercise 5.25 over typical jazz progression.

5.57 Scale and half-step patterns over typical jazz progression.

5.58 Pattern from exercise 5.22 over typical jazz progression.

5.59 Neighbor tone pattern from exercise 5.5 over typical jazz progression.

When reading through this book, I hope that you imagine exercises that are not included. Follow your instincts and write them down and practice them. Inventing your own exercises is a way to develop your own voice and vocabulary. One of the goals of a teacher is for the student to develop to the point where the teacher is not needed. Teach the teacher some new exercises.

VI. MOTIVIC & PENTATONIC PATTERNS

In the European Western Art Music tradition, one tends to think of the major scale as the primary building block for melody construction. If one studies and listens to music around the world one may find the pentatonic scale to be more universal than the major scale, and that the pentatonic scale did not originate with Debussy. Jazz improvisers and composers have often used pentatonic scales as a basis for melodies superimposed over traditional harmonies and over modal and pedal structures. Closely associated with the use of pentatonic scales in jazz is the use of motivic devices to develop melodies from simple pentatonic scale patterns.

There are many kinds of pentatonic scales. In fact, any five tones could be called a pentatonic scale. The most common pentatonic scale is the one shown below in major and in minor form. The two forms share the same pitches as do a major and natural minor scale. These scales can be formed by removing the active tritone pitches (B & F) from the major and natural minor scales. The major pentatonic includes the 1-2-3-5-6 of a major scale; the minor pentatonic includes the 1-♭3-4-5-♭7 of the natural minor scale. The triad is an important part of these scales. Many tunes based on pentatonic scales come to rest on the triadic tones (1, 3 & 5) and use the remaining tones (2 & 6) as secondary auxiliary tones moving to the primary pitches. Sing through the pentatonic melody *Amazing Grace* and note how all points of rest and all strong beats are the primary triadic tones.

C MAJOR PENTATONIC SHOWN WITH ITS RELATIVE A MINOR

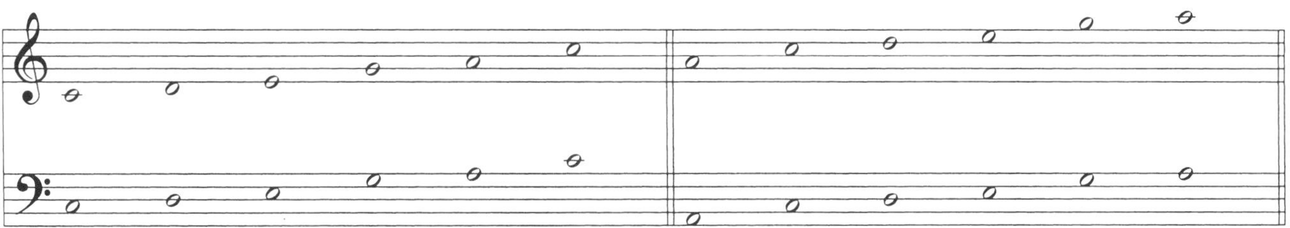

C MAJOR PENTATONIC SHOWN WITH ITS PARALLEL C MINOR

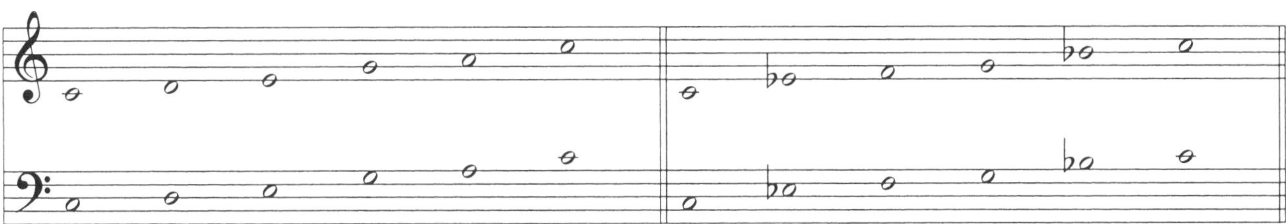

There are other pentatonic scales used throughout the world. Here are a few that have names and melodic potential. These scales can be used by themselves or superimposed over certain harmonies. some possibilities are shown below.

Kumoi	Hirajoshi	Flatted 6th	Pelog	All tones flatted
				(A♭ sounds like tonic)

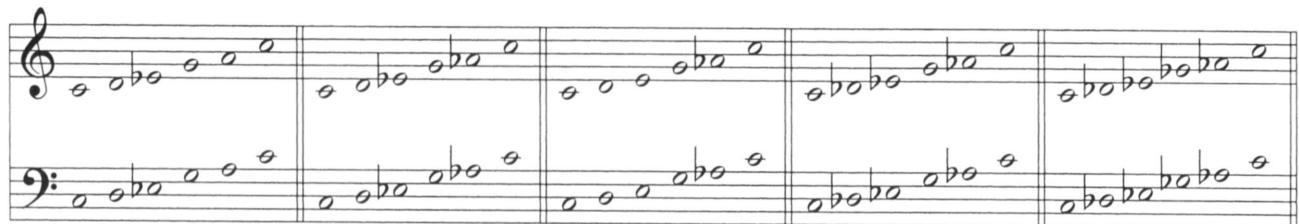

Kumoi scale:	Cm6/9, Aø7, F9, B7(♯9 ♭9 ♭13), E♭maj7 ♯11
Hirajoshi:	Cm, A♭maj7 ♯11
Flatted 6th:	A♭maj7♯5, B♭9#11, Dø7♯2, E7(♯9 ♭13), Fm^maj7
Pelog:	C phrygian, Fm7, A♭maj7, D♭maj7
All tones flatted:	A♭ mixolydian

BASIC PENTATONIC SCALE EXERCISES

The following exercises are designed to introduce the pentatonic scales and should be transposed to all twelve major keys.

6.1 Major pentatonic scale with three note groupings

6.2 **Major pentatonic scale with four note groupings**

6.3 **Major pentatonic scale with four note grouping played with triplet subdivision creates interesting rhythmic material.**

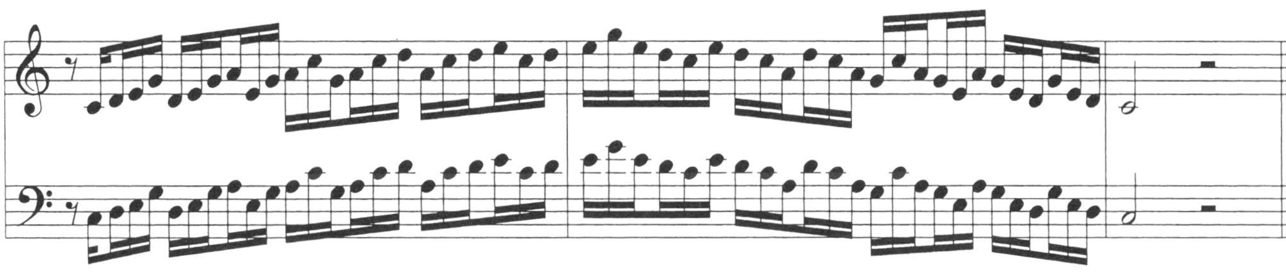

If traditional diatonic tertian triads are found by skipping over notes in the major scale, then the following triads, created by skipping notes in the pentatonic scale, could be considered the diatonic triads (not necessarily tertian) of the pentatonic scale.

DIATONIC TRIADS OF THE MAJOR PENTATONIC SCALE: (QUARTAL & TERTIAN MIXTURE)

6.4 Diatonic triads exercise

The previous exercises use three and four note groupings arranged ascending going up the scale and descending going down the scale. Exercise 6.5 alternates between ascending and descending. The alterations between ascending and descending could also be applied to the previous exercises.

6.5 Diatonic triads exercise alternating ascending and descending.

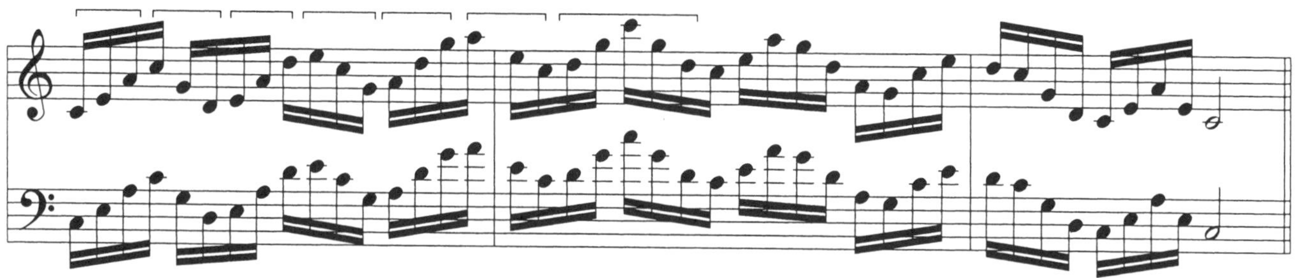

6.6 Broken chord exercise applied to diatonic triads of the major pentatonic scale.

All triads can be played in root position and inverted. Below are the five diatonic triads from a major pentatonic scale shown in root position, first and second inversions. The first chord is a traditional tertian minor chord; the fourth is a major chord; the second third and fifth chords are quartal.

DIATONIC TRIADS OF THE MAJOR PENTATONIC SCALE:
Shown in all inversions.

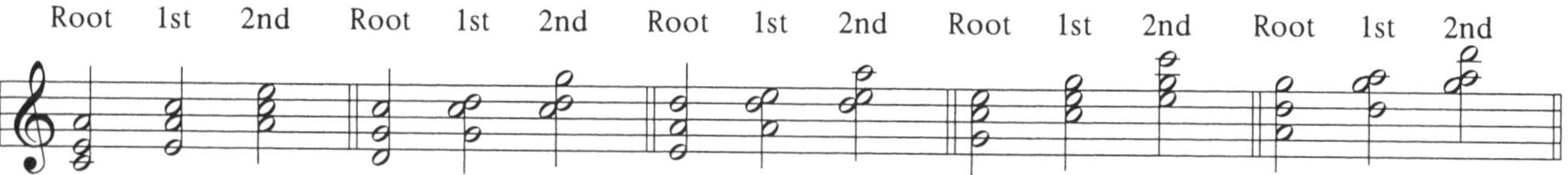

6.7 **Diatonic triads: 1st inversion.**

6.8 **Diatonic triads: 2nd inversion.**

6.9 **Alternating 3rds & 4ths.**

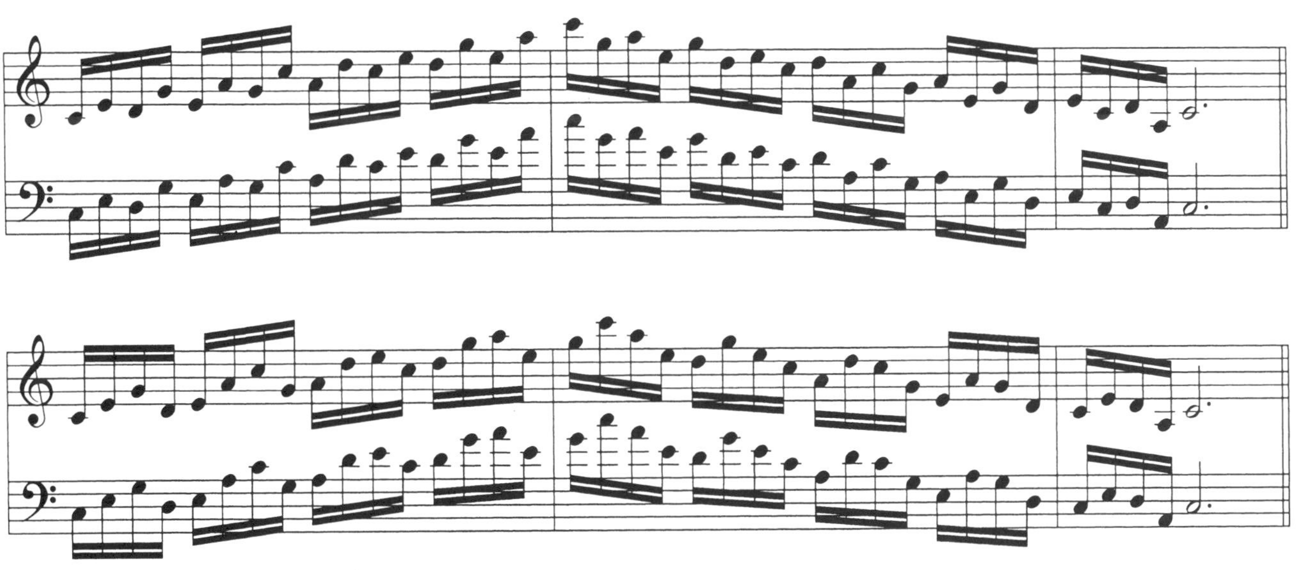

6.10 Four note pentatonic scale pattern.

6.11 Four note pentatonic scale pattern.

6.12 Four note pentatonic scale pattern.

6.13 **Six note pentatonic scale pattern.**

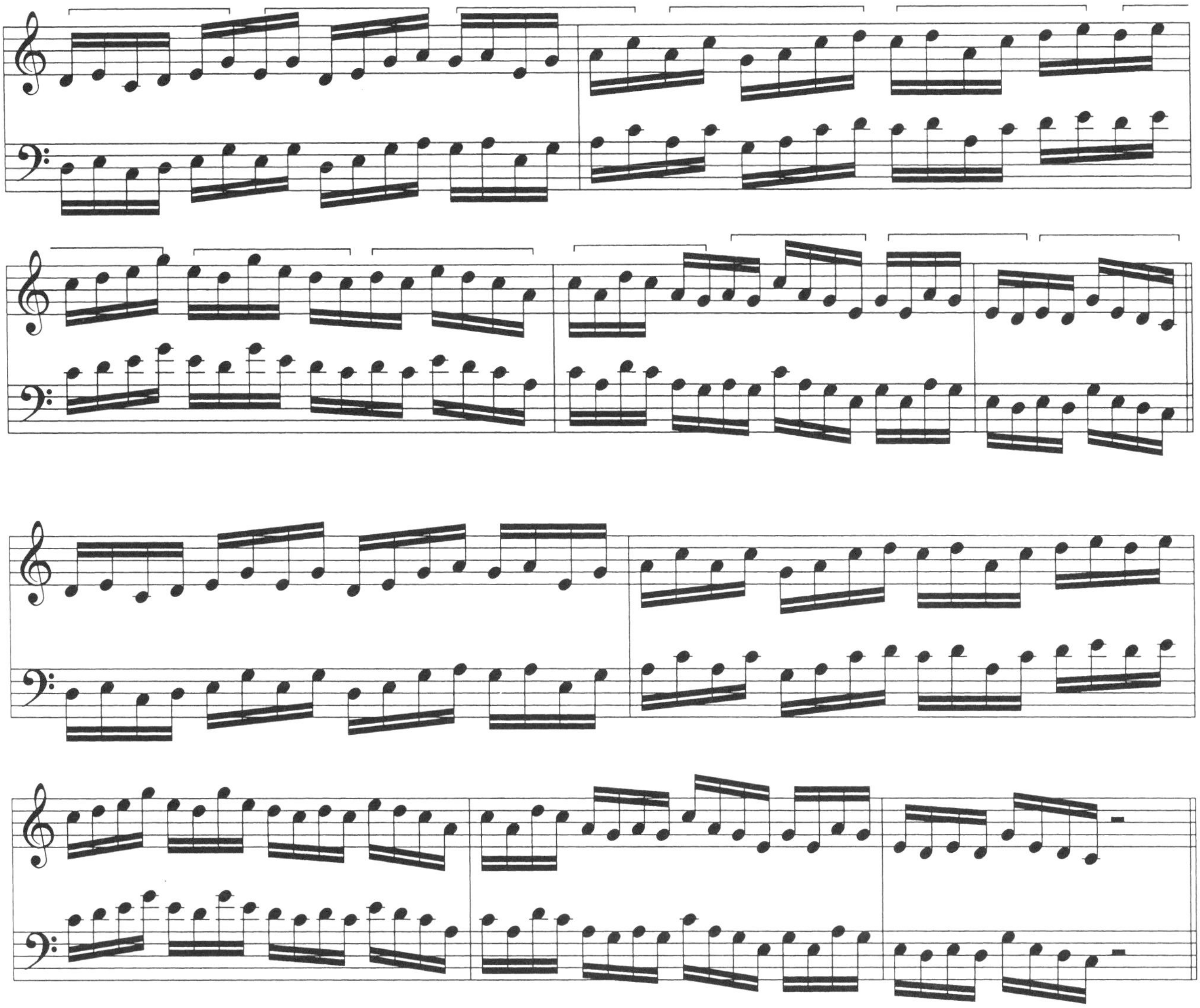

By skipping another note in the scale a fourth note can be added to the diatonic triads creating the following large interval patterns:

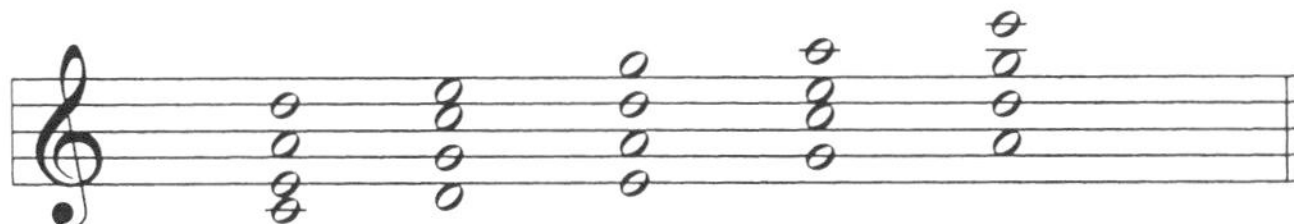

6.14 **Large interval arpeggios**

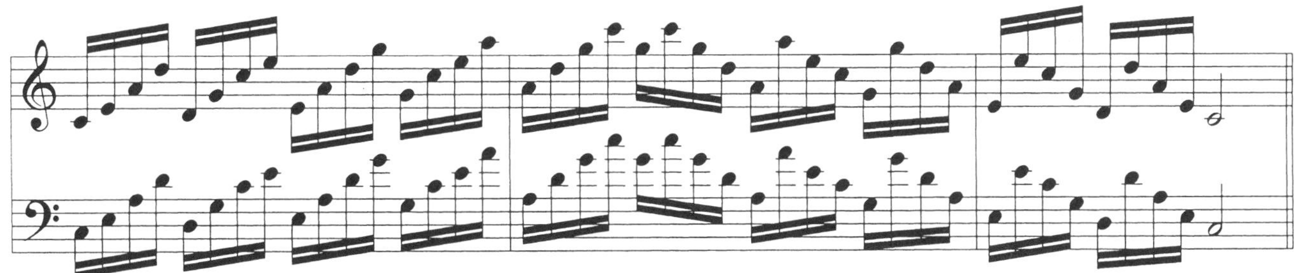

SUPERIMPOSITION FORMULAS

Patterns and melodic material derived from pentatonic scales can be superimposed over traditional harmonic progressions. Isolating melodic material from a pentatonic scale can add color to a line. Below are some formulas for superimposing pentatonic scales over chords. The colorization and function of each chord is shown.

Major pentatonic scales over Major 7 chords

C major 7 as I or IV	I or IV	IV
(1-2 [9]-3-5-6)	(5-6 [13]-M7-9-3)	(2 [9]-3-♯11-13-M7-9)
Basic Chord tones with 6 & 9	Brighter with M7 & M9	Brightest with ♯11

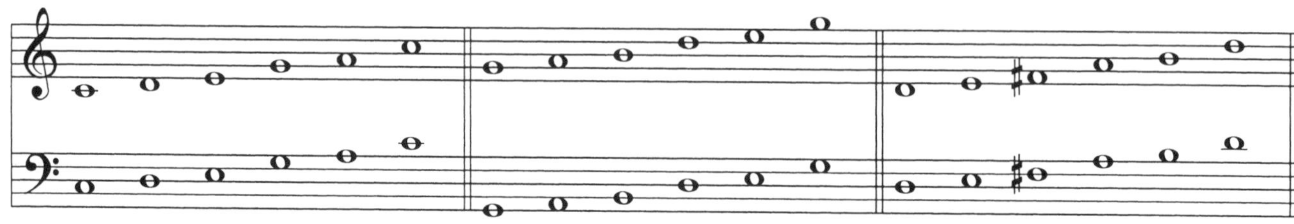

Minor pentatonic scales over Minor 7 chords

D minor 7 as ii, iii, vi or iv	ii, vi or iv	ii or iv
(1-m3-4-5-m7-1)	(5-7-1-9-4 [11]-5)	(9-11-5-13-1-9)
Basic chord tones	Brighter with M9, no 3rd	Bright with 13/ambiguous

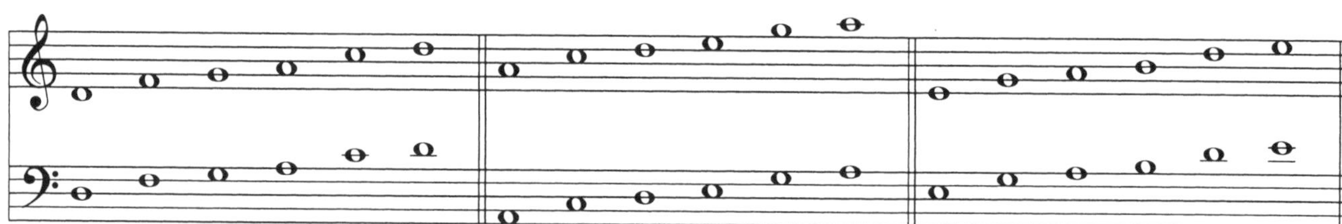

Major pentatonic scales over Dominant 7 chords

G dominant 7	G dominant 7 fully altered
R-♮9-M3-5-♮13-R	♭5[♯11]-♭13-m7-♭9-♯9-♭5[♯11]
Bright, basic chord tones ♮9, ♮13	Dark, includes all alterations

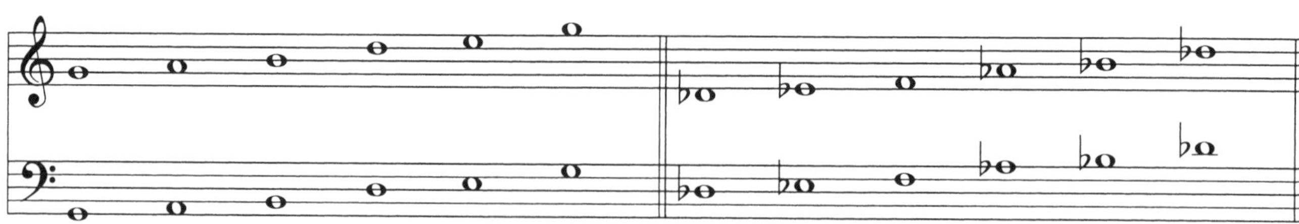

Kumoi pentatonic scales over ø7 & altered dominant chords

Dø7 as iiø7 in minor
M3-4-♭5-m7-R-m3
Basic chord tones

G7 as V7 in minor
♭9-♯9-M3-♭13-m7-♭9
Includes alterations

It would be beneficial to return to the previous exercises and apply them to harmonic progressions as shown above. For example practice:

1. Over a ii7 - V7 - I progression practice A minor pentatonic patterns over Dm7; D♭ major pentatonic patterns over G7; D major pentatonic patterns over C major; then transpose to all other major keys.
2. Over a iiø7 - V7 - i progression practice a F Kumoi pentatonic patterns over Dø7; A♭ Kumoi pentatonic patterns over G7; C Kumoi pentatonic patterns over C minor; then transpose to all other minor keys.

Not all applications of pentatonic materials fit within the key center. Pentatonic melodic patterns are often used to escape the strict and rigid domain of the tonal and key centers.

SIDE-SLIPPING & PLANING

The previous exercises have treated three and four note patterns sequentially and remained within the key center. Many contemporary composers and improvisers have used similar motives sequentially but moved outside of the established key center. Instead of using the logic of the major/minor system, they may rely on the power of motivic development for the sense of their melodic lines. If a motive is established, the listener may follow the motive as it is sequenced, even if some or all the notes have left the original key. It is the logic of the motive itself and not just the key center that explains the sensibility of the line. The melodies may seem to slip out of one key and into the next, or it may seem that the melody exists on many different planes (key centers) at the same time. When melodies move in and out of key centers it is sometimes called "side-slipping," or "planing."

The traditional tonal major/minor system is primarily based on tertian sounds. Another way of defying the gravity of strict tonality is to emphasize other intervals, particularly the interval of the perfect fourth.

QUARTAL SOUNDS

The perfect fourth is a powerful interval. The perfect fourth interval between the dominant and the tonic has been used in thousands of tunes to initially establish the tonal center. A short list would include: *Amazing Grace*, *Auld Lang Syne*, *Aura Lee*, *Do You Know The Muffin Man?*, *Farmer In The Dell*, *Hark! The Herald Angels Sing!*, *I've Been Working On The Railroad*, *Jimmie Crack Corn*, *O Come*, *All Ye Faithful*, *Old MacDonald*, *Onward Christian Soldiers*, *We Wish You A Merry Christmas*, *When Johnny Comes Marching Home*, and *You Are My Sunshine*. Traditionally, few tunes feature several perfect fourth intervals in a row. Because the perfect fourth is often use to identify tonic, use of several in a row typically blurs the tonic identification. While this may have been a deterrent to composers and improvisers in the past, it may be an incentive for contemporary composers who are looking for sounds to blur the identification of tonic and create a more ambiguous setting. Coltrane may have been attracted to *My Favorite Things* not just as a modal improvisation vehicle, but for the quartal and quintal intervalic melodic material.

Many students remember the sound of a perfect fourth by recalling one of the tunes listed above. This may not help them identify perfect fourth intervals other than the one between the dominant and tonic of major keys. There are six perfect fourth intervals available to the composer/improviser from the major scale and six others outside the key center. Often the introduction of quartal material leads the melodic material away from any key center or one specific scale. The lines may be developed by freely sequencing the intervals without regard to key center.

Here are some examples from the jazz literature where the melodic vocabulary includes an abundance of perfect fourths and sequential treatment of melodic material that is unencumbered by a key center or primary scale.

Three tunes that epitomize the use of quartal material are Eddie Harris' *Freedom Jazz Dance*, and Wayne Shorter's *Speak No Evil* and *Witch Hunt*. The *Freedom Jazz Dance* melody used quartal intervals, extended quartal arpeggios, and sequenced ideas in and out of the key of B♭. *Speak No Evil* did not slip out of the key as did *Freedom Jazz Dance*, but used a quartal arpeggio as its theme. *Witch Hunt* began with two simply stated perfect fourth intervals: 5 - 1 and 1 - 4 in the key of C minor.

Improvisers often used the quartal thematic material when improvising on tunes like those mentioned above. On *Speak No Evil* Herbie Hancock used the quartal chord D-G-C in its first inversion (see page 126) and sequenced it, first using notes from the C dorian mode, and then ignoring the key implications, transposing the motive up minor thirds, slipping in and out of the key.

Quartal chords and their inversions have fascinated more than just jazz musicians as the next few examples illustrate. In fact many jazz composers and improvisers have looked to Bartók, Holst, Hindemith, Stravinsky, Copland and others for inspiration.

Tom Harrell used quartal patterns in these excerpts to slip in and out of "Rhythm Changes" in the key of F major.

Quartal intervals are not the only intervals used to blur the key center. Kenny Dorham used a whole step pattern chromatically sequenced over this traditional harmonic progression, and Joey Calderazzo uses a simple 1-2-3 pattern sequentially over a pedal tone.

Whole-step sequential pattern

1-2-3 sequential pattern

With a glance, one can tell that the player is not thinking traditional chord changes on the B♭ blues excerpt below. Rather than the be-bop method of outlining chord tones, the player chooses four-note motives and develops them sequentially transposing them to other pitch levels. Each of the pitches could be labeled vertically as some kind of chord tone of the expected traditional blues chords, but labeling chord tones may be misleading and pointless. It would be more instructive to follow the motives independent of the underlying harmonic progression. The motives can be found in pentatonic scales and could be summarized as follows:

a. F minor pentatonic (four notes 1, ♭3 - 4 - 5). These notes comprise the 5-7-R-9 of the B♭9 chord, so the chorus begins using notes related to the harmonic progression.
b. B minor pentatonic (four notes 1 - ♭3 - 4 - 5). These notes could function as the 5-7-R-9 of an E9 chord, the tritone substitute dominant leading to the E♭7 chord. The same notes over a B♭7 are the ♭9-3-♯11-♯5 (♭13) so the solo continues with functional melodic material related to the harmonic progression.
c. B♭ minor pentatonic (three notes 1 - ♭3 - 4). These notes comprise the 5-7-R of the E♭9 chord, so the sequenced material has been consistent and tonal over the B♭7, E7 and E♭7 chords.
d. C♯ minor pentatonic (four notes 1 - ♭3 - 4 - 5). These notes have nothing to do with the underlying harmony. Tyner has left the key center for a purely motivic melodic excursion for the next few measures. The melodic material and harmonic material are at odds until m.9 of the solo.
e. F♯ minor pentatonic (four notes 1 - ♭3 - 4 - 5)
f. E minor pentatonic (four notes 1 - ♭3 - 4 - 5)
g. D minor pentatonic (four notes 1 - ♭3 - 4 - 5)
h. C♯ minor pentatonic (four notes 1 - ♭3 - 4 - 5)
i. C minor pentatonic (four notes 1 - ♭3 - 4 - 5). At this point the melodic material and the harmonic material seem to agree again. These notes correspond to the 5-7-R-9 of the F7 chord, which is harmonically identical to the beginnings of this motive. The material from mm.7-9 (e., f., g., h. & i) creates a descending step line.

B♭ Blues excerpt

Michael Brecker slipped in and around the key of F minor in this example. He used a six-note pattern sequenced down in half-steps before returning to F minor. The six-note pattern contains all the notes of these pentatonic scales: a. B minor pentatonic, b. B♭ minor pentatonic, c. A minor pentatonic, d. G♯ minor pentatonic, e. F minor pentatonic.

Pentatonic side-slipping

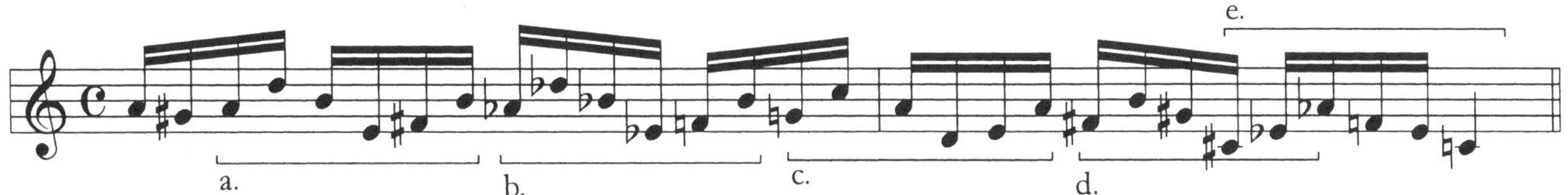

Exercises could be made from the above example taking the motive or pattern through all twelve keys. 6.14 shows the pattern in sextuplets making it easier to see and hear the six-note pattern. 6.15 shows the pattern written in sixteenth notes. The pattern is less noticeable and probably musically more interesting as it is disguised somewhat by the contradiction between the four-note rhythm pattern and the six-note melodic pattern.

6.14 Pentatonic Side-slipping Exercise no.1

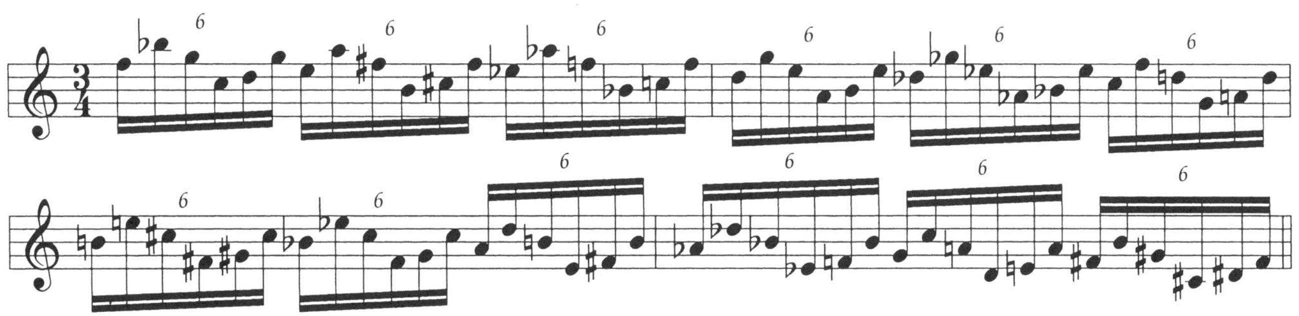

6.15 Pentatonic Side-slipping Exercise no.2

This player planes a four-note motive over a modal blues in C minor in the example below. The motive occurs earlier in the improvisation, and is shown here in an excerpt from the seventeenth and eighteenth choruses. At (a.) the pitches relate to the key center; (b.) the motive side-slips down a half-step; (c.) the motive is back to the original key; (d.) the motive side-slips up a half-step and at (e.) up another half-step; and finally at (f.) up a fourth from the original, but the motive is within the key center again.

Motivic planing or side-slipping

Gary Versace used quartal planning and rhythmic devices in developing this chorus over F blues. The motives did not necessarily outline the harmonic progression. Notice how he superimposed five and six beat rhythmic figures while superimposing interesting quartal shapes to create a musical tension.

Jonathan Kreisberg used quartal triads a major third apart on this solo break into F blues. (see exercise 6.24)

XERCISES FOR PLANING & SIDE-SLIPPING MOTIVES

The next several exercises will be based on the following three and four note motives extracted from pentatonic scales. A-C are three note motives using adjacent pitches in the scale; D-L includes motives with larger intervals. M-P are four note motives using adjacent pitches in the scale.

THREE NOTE MELODIC MOTIVES

A. B. C. D. E. F.

G. H. I. J. K. L.

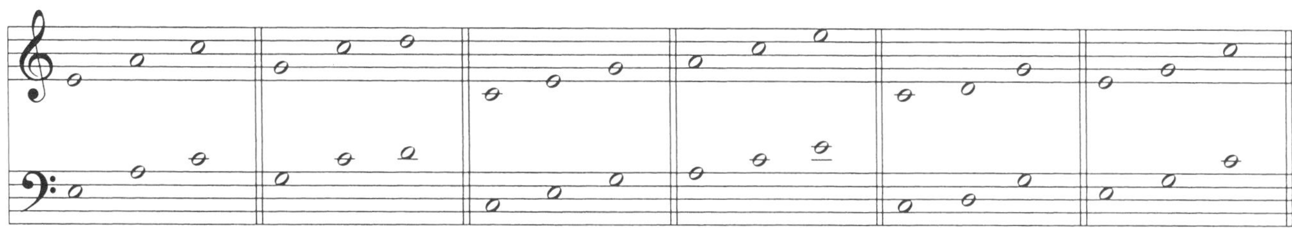

FOUR NOTE MELODIC MOTIVES

M. N. O. P.

This set of exercises takes selected motives from the above list and sequences them up minor and then major thirds.

6.16 Motive A up & down in minor thirds.

6.17 Motive E up & down in minor thirds.

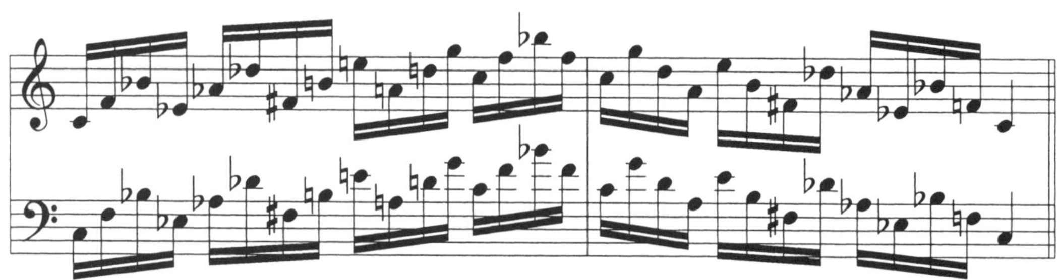

6.18 Motive K up & down in minor thirds.

6.19 Motive H inverted up & down in minor thirds.

6.20 Motive M up & down in minor thirds.

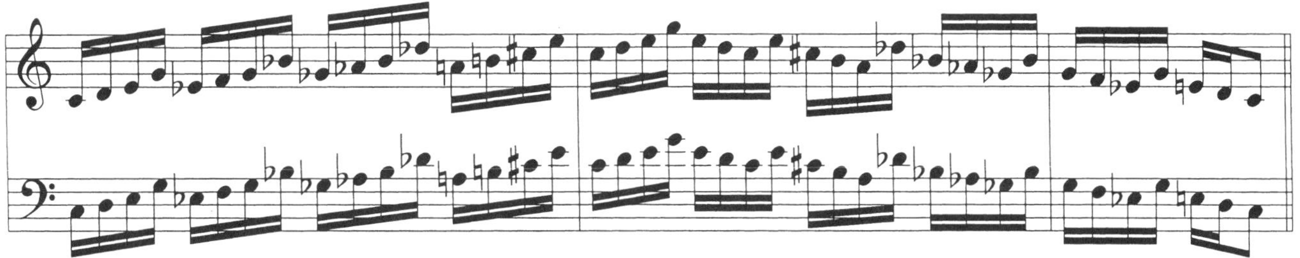

6.21 Motive N up & down in minor thirds.

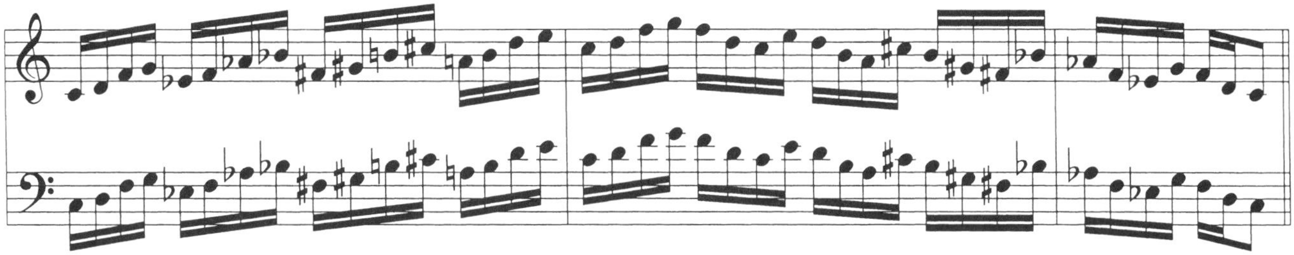

6.22 Motive O up & down in minor thirds.

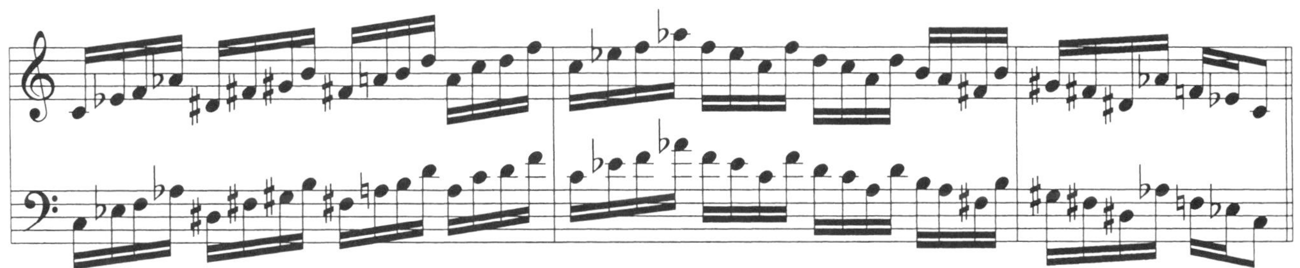

6.23 Motive P up & down in minor thirds.

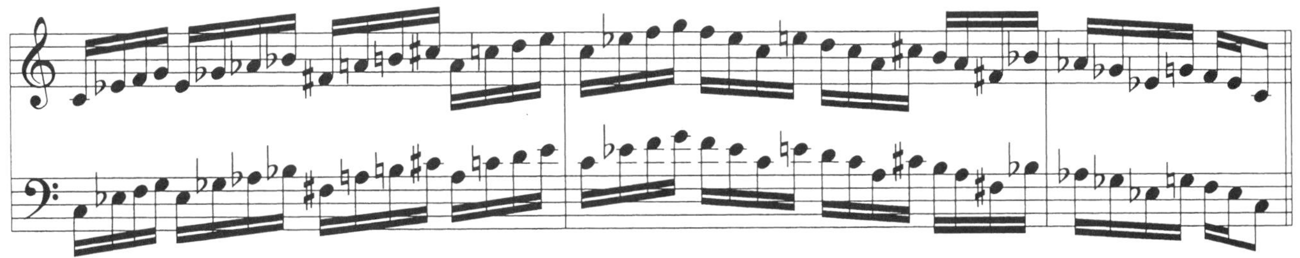

6.24 Motive E up & down in major thirds.

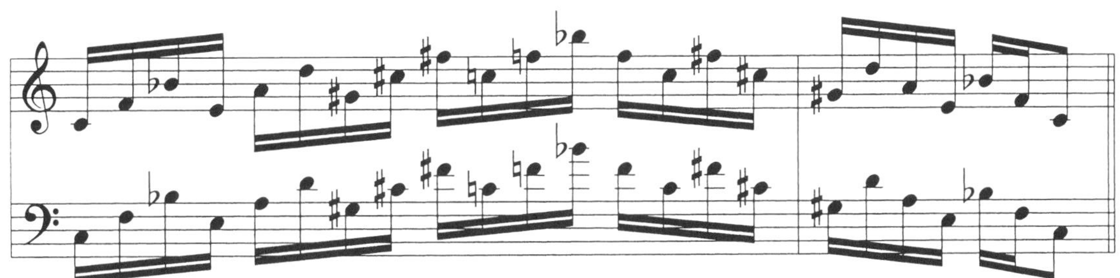

6.25 **Motive K up & down in major thirds.**

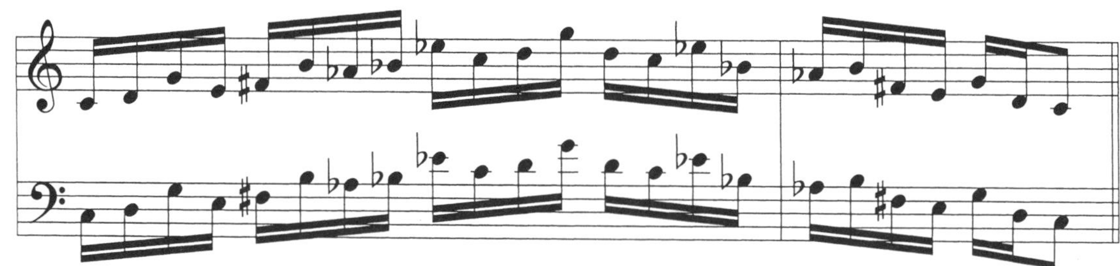

6.26 **Motive H inverted up & down in major thirds.**

6.27 **Motive M up & down in major thirds.**

6.28 **Motive N up & down in major thirds.**

6.29 **Motive O up & down in major thirds.**

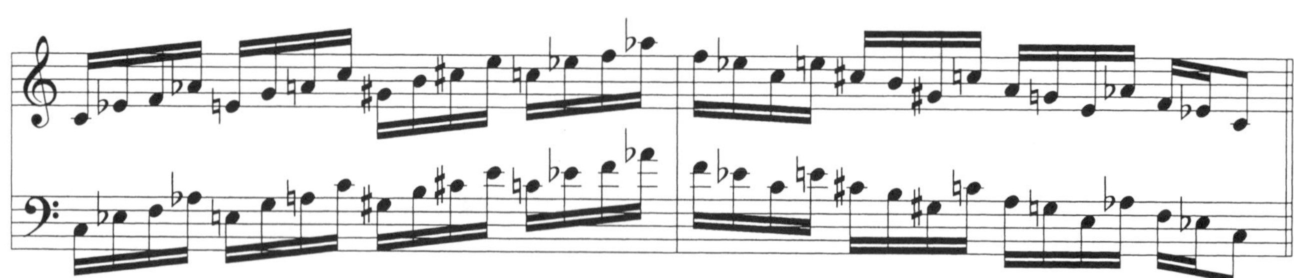

6.30 Motive P up & down in major thirds.

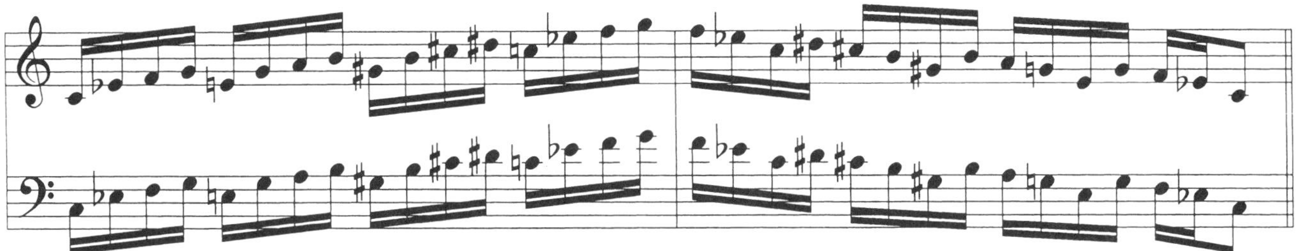

6.31 Another four-note motive up & down in minor thirds.

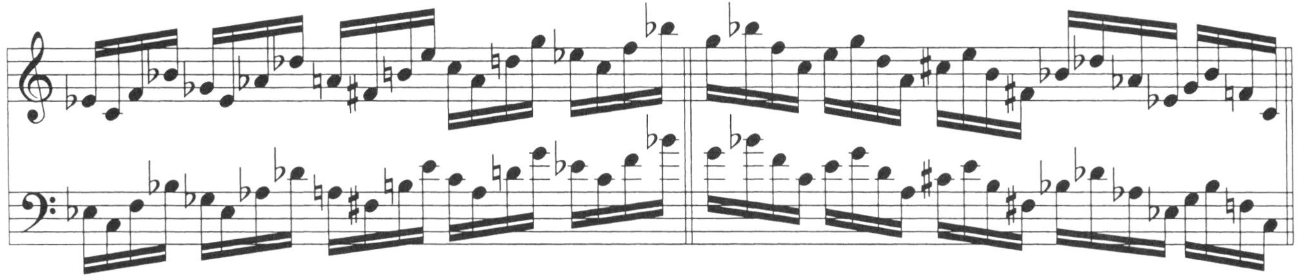

6.32 Another four-note motive up & down in major thirds.

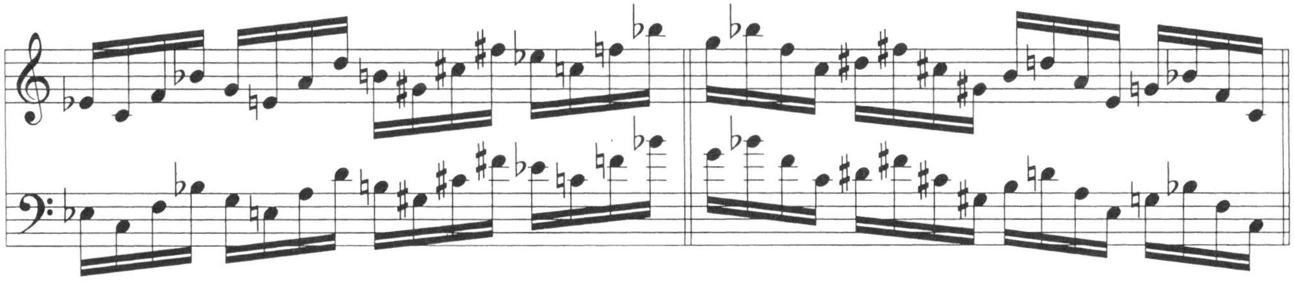

Exercises 6.16-6.32 took a few of the available motives and sequenced them up and down in major and minor thirds. Motives could be sequenced in any number of other possible intervallic combinations. The motive below is sequenced with the top note following a descending scale from A down to A in exercise 6.33; and sequenced with the top note following a descending half-whole diminished scale from A down to A in exercise 6.34.

6.33 Four-note motive following diatonic scale.

6.34 Four-note motive following diminished scale.

Exercises can be designed by using any combinations of patterns sequenced at any number of interval combinations. Any motive can be played upside down, backwards, or upside down and backwards. Any melodic shape can also be inverted by moving one or more pitches to higher or lower registers. Motives can be reordered to create new motives and patterns. When motive M (1-2-3-5 pattern in major) is inverted its mirror image becomes motive P (5-4-♭3-1 in minor). A 1-2-3-5 pattern can be reordered to 2-5-3-1 or 3-5-2-1, and then inverted to 4-1-♭3-5 and ♭3-1-4-5.

6.35 Variation of motives M and P planed at a major third interval

6.36 Variation of motives M and P planed at a major third interval. The last note of one motive becomes the first note of the second motive creating an overlap.

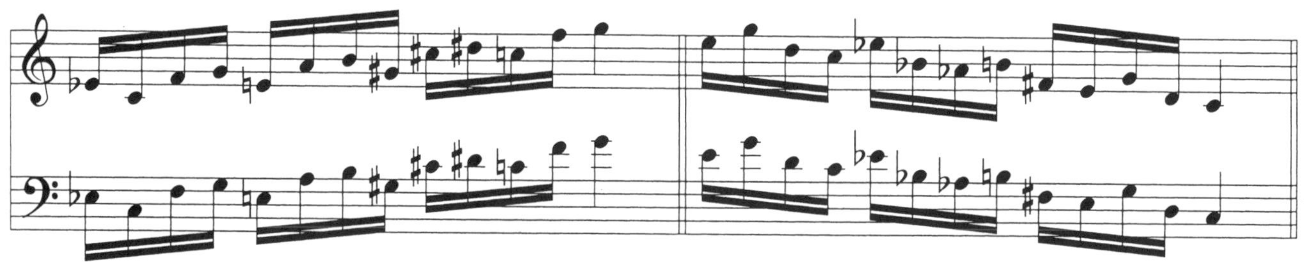

6.37 Variation of motives M and P planed at a minor third interval.

6.38 **Variation of motives M and P planed at a major third interval.**

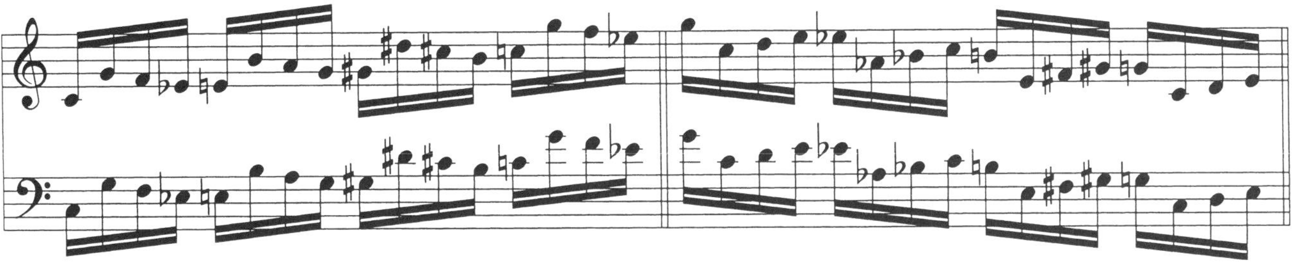

6.39 **Variation of motives M and P planed at a minor third interval. The last note of one motive becomes the first note of the second creating an overlap.**

More variations and exercises can be invented by varying the rhythmic character of the exercises.

The more inventive your practice, the more you train yourself to be inventive in a real-life musical setting. You should practice not only your physical technique, but the technique of invention.

6.40 **The four note motive N is played every five sixteenths in descending whole notes, creating an interesting polyrhythm with its five note rhythmic groupings.**

6.41 **This exercise emphasizes the four note patterns shown below.**

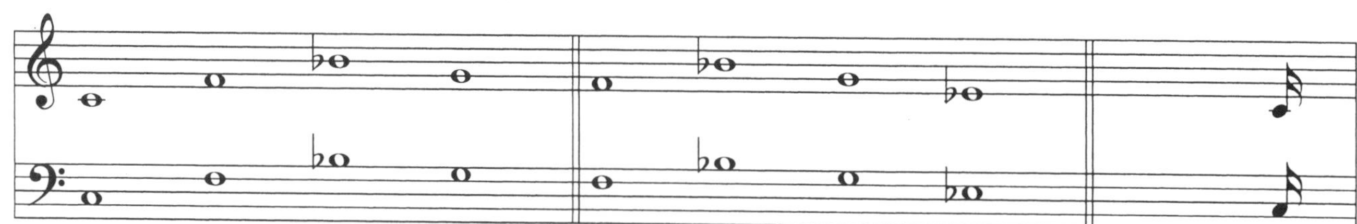

Try playing patterns back and forth between two keys.

6.42 **Side-slipping between C minor and C♯ minor pentatonic scales.**

Three note patterns:

6.43 Side-slipping between C minor and C♯ minor pentatonic scales.

Four note patterns:

Other possible key combinations include: Cm – F♯m – Cm, Cm – B♭m – Cm, Cm – A♭m – Cm. Try longer progressions moving away and returning to the original key: Cm – E♭m – F♯m – Gm – A♭m - Cm.

Zip Line is an original composition written as an illustration of composition and a vehicle for improvisation utilizing concepts from the preceding exercises. At A, theme (a.), based on motive N, recurs at different pitch levels slipping in and out of the key center. At B, theme (b.) recurs at different pitch levels. The line at B enters every five half notes making the rhythmic phrasing interesting and less predictable.

Bert Ligon: *Zip Line*

FIVE NOTE MELODIC MOTIVES

There are several five-note patterns available.

6.44 Five note pentatonic patterns in one key.

6.45 Five note pentatonic patterns sequenced up and down minor thirds.

(Fm-G♯m-Bm-Dm)

6.46 **Five note pentatonic patterns sequenced up and down major thirds.**

(Fm-Am-C♯m)

6.47 **This five note pattern (resembling an NPR News Theme) can be sequenced three times within a key center.**

6.48 **The five note pattern from 6.47 can be sequenced by transposing the group of pitches down by minor thirds. Brackets indicate the original five note pattern.**

6.49 The five note pattern from 6.47 can be inverted and sequenced by transposing the group of pitches up by minor thirds.

6.50 The five note pattern from 6.47 can be sequenced by transposing the group of pitches down and its inversion sequenced up by major thirds.

SIX NOTE MELODIC MOTIVES

6.51 This six note pattern can be sequenced by transposing the group of pitches down by minor thirds.

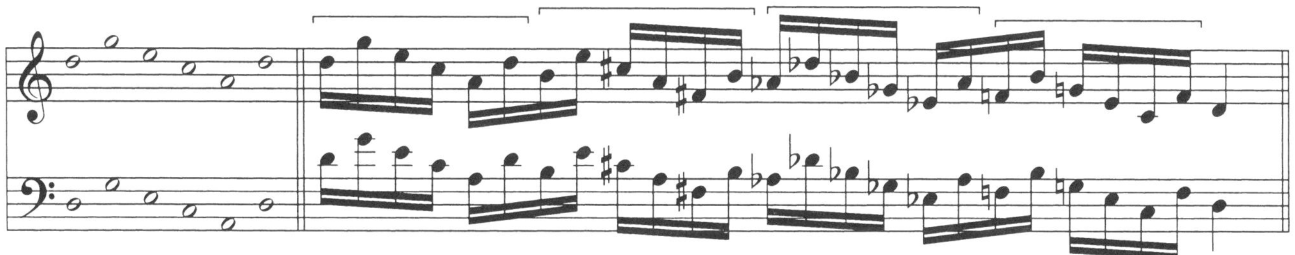

6.52 The six note pattern from 6.51 can be inverted and sequenced by transposing the group of pitches up by minor thirds.

EIGHT NOTE MELODIC MOTIVES

6.53 **This eight note pattern can be sequenced by transposing the group of pitches down by half steps.**

6.54 **The eight note pattern from 6.53 can be sequenced by transposing the group of pitches up by half steps.**

6.55 **Kenny Garret sequenced this pattern (similar to 6.51) over changes resembling** ***Yardbird Suite.***

PENTATONIC APPLICATIONS OVER TRADITIONAL HARMONY

Here are some applications of quartal/pentatonic ideas over traditional harmonic progressions.

6.56 Using Quartal/Pentatonic ideas over traditional harmonic progressions.

Exercise 6.46 uses F minor pentatonic melodic patterns over the Fm7 chord followed by E major pentatonic melodic patterns over B♭7 (creating a B♭7 with all alterations: ♯9, ♭9, ♭5, ♭13) and B♭ major pentatonic over E♭ emphasizing quartal sounds.

6.57 Using Quartal/Pentatonic ideas over traditional harmonic progressions.

Pentatonic scales can be expressed as large quartal chords. The first measures shows two quartal chords that may be useful over a Dm7 chord; the second measure shows two quartal chords that may be useful over a Cmaj7 chord.

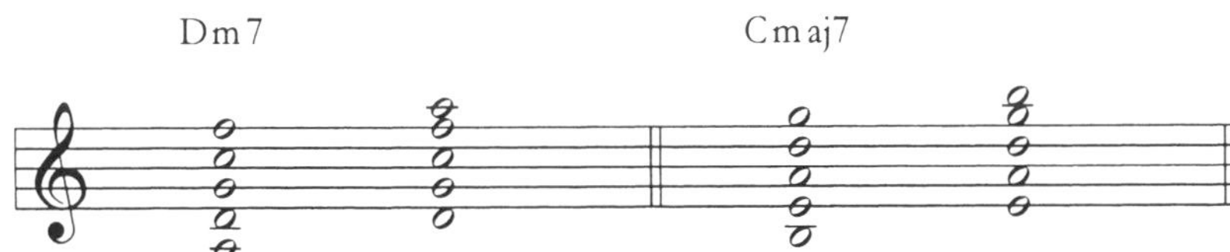

Arpeggiated lines can be created from the shapes shown above that can be applied musically over traditional ii7 – V7 – I progressions.

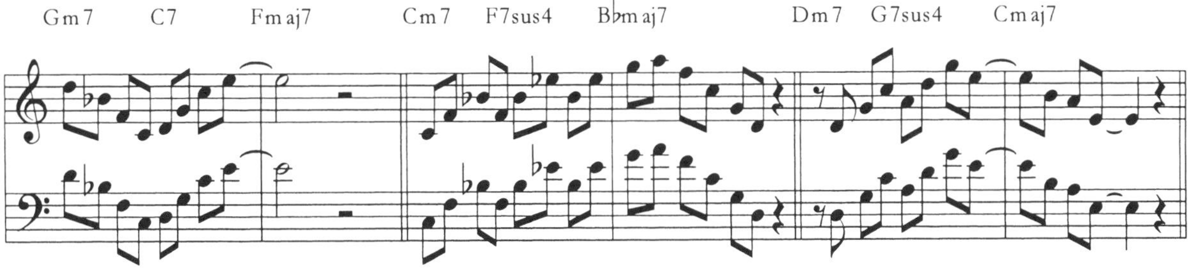

These quartal, large interval, giant step lines can add a flavor to progression like the following that is similar to Coltrane's *Giant Steps.*

The clusters below of 1-2-3-5 and 1-♭3-4-5 patterns extracted from pentatonic scales are in, out and around but finally lead to notes in F minor.

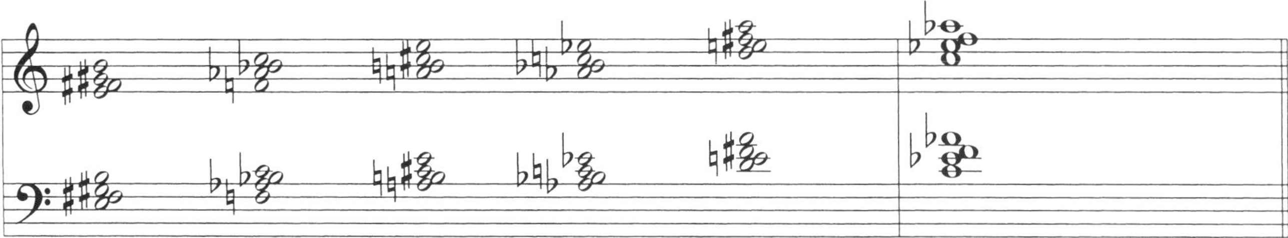

These clusters can be used to create lines that hover in, out and around F minor. The brackets show the groupings that relate to the previous example. The final Fm7 chord is split in two: two notes occur at the beginning of beat four and two more as the last notes of the line. Try developing lines like this for this and other keys.

6.58 Side-slipping in and around F minor using patterns extracted from pentatonic scales.

Here are some clusters patterns extracted from pentatonic scales that begin and end in D minor. These are the basis for the lines in exercise 6.48.

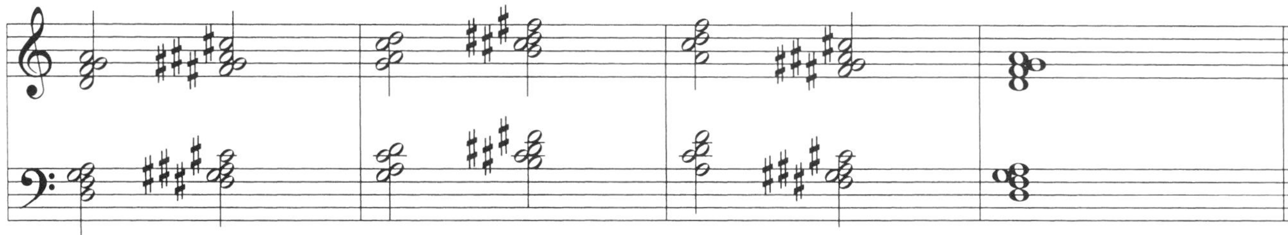

6.59 Side-slipping in and around D minor using patterns extracted from pentatonic scales.

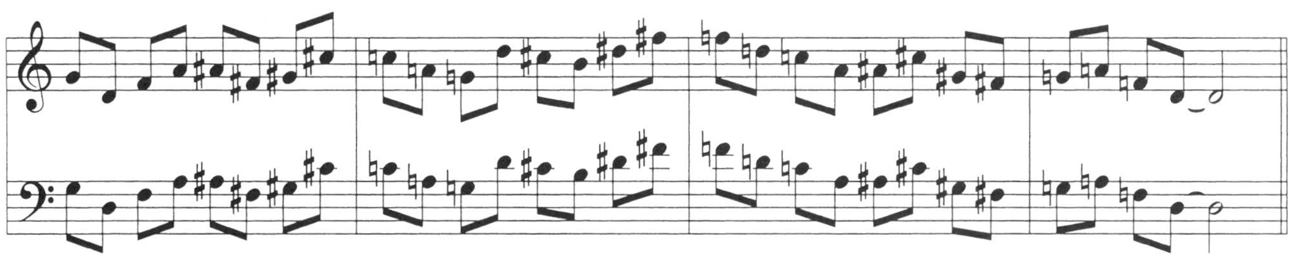

MOTIVIC DEVELOPMENT

Composers and improvisers use the following motivic and compositional development devices to stretch simple melodic germs into longer lines and structures. In order to play your instrument in the key of F it makes sense to practice scales and arpeggios in the key of F. It follows that in order to integrate the tools of compositional development, a musician should find ways to integrate the compositional concepts into daily practice Using these devices to develop your own exercises will improve the ability to apply them spontaneously in real-life musical settings. The terms and illustrations below should assist in acquiring an understanding and encourage exploration and mastery of the concepts. To understand some of the concepts of thematic development in jazz improvisations one should listen to recordings of Sonny Rollin's on *St. Thomas* and Miles Davis on *So What.*

MOTIVIC AND COMPOSITIONAL DEVELOPMENT DEVICES

Here is a simple five note melodic idea for purposes of illustration. (Motives are easier to remember and develop if they are short and are surrounded by ample silence). The intervals of this motive are: descending M2/descending m2/ascending m3/descending P5. A listener would not necessarily be expected to hear individual intervals, but it is necessary for the discussion. One may hear the motive as playing around the notes of a C major triad with one passing tone.

Simple triadic motive

A. Repetition

Obviously, repetition is the most important compositional device. If a theme does not recur it is not a theme, for something that occurs only once cannot be the basis for the development of a piece or an improvisation. So many beginning improvisers play good and interesting short melodic ideas at the beginning of an improvisation and never develop them. I have stopped them in improvisation classes after the third or fourth measure and asked them to play the first two measures again. Most of the time they cannot remember what they just played. If they do not remember, then they cannot expect the listener to remember. In order to develop logical improvisations, one skill that must be developed is musical memory.

B. Transpose

A repetition of the motive might occur in a different key.

C. Mode Change

A repetition of the motive might occur in a different mode. Here the major mode has been changed to minor.

D. Fragmentation

After hearing the motive and some repetition of the motive, development by subtraction is possible. The first part or the second part may be played and developed and still heard as a part of the original motive.

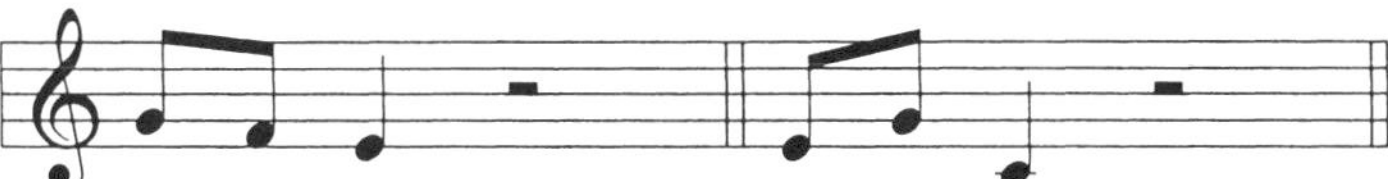

E. Addition

After hearing the motive and some repetition of the motive, development by addition is possible. Material may be added to the beginning, the middle or after the statement of the original motive.

Three notes added to the beginning of the original motive:

Three notes added to the end of the original motive:

F. Sequence

A sequence is the repetition of the motive at different pitch levels following the same or similar melodic intervals. A motive may be transposed using exact intervallic relationships or using diatonic intervallic relationships.

Sequence using diatonic intervallic relationships:

Sequence using exact intervallic relationships:

G. Embellishment or ornamentation

A repetition of the original motive may be embellished or ornamented. This differs slightly from addition. In the addition examples from above, the original motive was left intact and notes added before or after. In the example below several individual notes of the motive are embellished using various auxiliary tones. The original motive is shown with down stemmed notes.

H. Augmentation

Augmentation makes something bigger. Musical augmentation can apply to the pitch or the rhythmic content of the motive.

Rhythmic Augmentation: (basis for the embellishment example above at G).

Intervallic Augmentation

One diatonic step added One chromatic step added Freely augmented

I. Diminution

Diminution makes something smaller. Musical diminution can apply to the pitch or the rhythmic content of the motive.

Rhythmic Diminution

Intervallic Diminution

J. Inversion/Retrograde/Retrograde Inversion

To invert a motive is to turn it upside down. What intervals went up go down and what intervals went down go up. A motive played backwards is in retrograde. A motive played upside down and backwards is in retrograde inversion. These devices are central to twelve-tone music but are quite useful to any composer and improviser. Below are examples of (1.) the original motive, (2.) inversion of the motive using exact intervals, (3.) the inversion of the motive using diatonic intervals, (4.) the motive in retrograde, and (5.) the motive in retrograde inversion.

1. 2. 3. 4. 5.

Palindromes are possible when a motive is stated forwards and backwards as in this example (D-A-G-A-D):

M. Displacement

A motive may be displaced rhythmically or its pitches may be octave displaced.

Motive with octave displacement. (Octave displaced pitches are circled.)

Octave displacement can often disguise the original motive to the point where it may be no longer recognizable as in the example below.

???*

The device is still quite useful and may lead to even more interesting material than the original motive.

Motive with rhythmic displacement.

N. Combinations. A number of combinations are possible limited only by imagination. Sequencing ornamented inverted fragments of the original motive with octave and rhythmic displacement is a possibility.

*The octave displaced melody you may have recognized as *Aura Lee.*

VII. 1-2-3-5 PATTERNS

One motive (M) from Chapter 6 is so prevalent in improvised jazz it warrants a separate short chapter. A 1-2-3-5 melodic pattern in major and in minor is used in a number of ways in composition and improvisation. They may be sequenced diatonically or "planed" and used thematically to side-slip in and out of keys.

1-2-3-5 in Major 1-2-3-5 in Minor

In developing exercises, variety can be achieved by mixing up the direction and order of the pitches. 1-2-3-5, can be: 5-3-2-1, 3-5-2-1 and many other variations that may be musically useful.

MAJOR 1-2-3-5 **MINOR 1-2-3-5**

1.) 1-2-3-5 **2.)** 5-3-2-1 **3.)** 3-5-2-1 **4.)** 3-5-2-1 **5.)** 1-2-♭3-5 **6)** 5-♭3-2-1 **7.)** ♭3-5-2-1 **8.)** ♭3-5-2-1

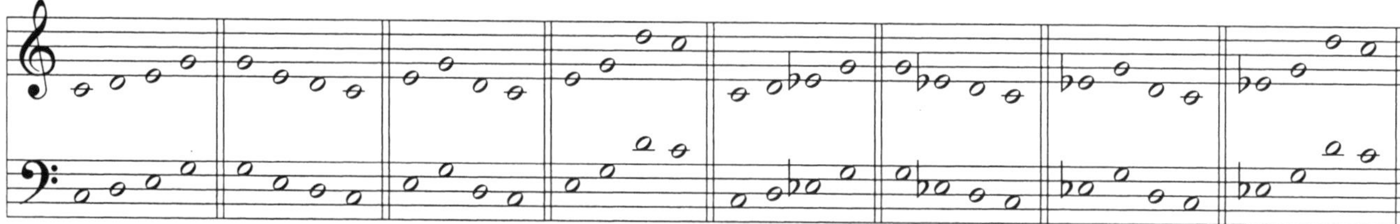

EXERCISES

Get these patterns under your fingers by practicing the four major and minor patterns shown above:

1. Around the circle of fifths.
2. Up and down the two whole-tone scales.
3. Up and down minor thirds.
4. Up and down major thirds.

PPLICATIONS TO INDIVIDUAL CHORDS

The major 1-2-3-5 pattern may begin on other steps of the scale. For a major 7th chord, a major 1-2-3-5 pattern could be played from (a.) the root yielding the triad and the second or ninth, (b.) the dominant yielding the fundamental tone 5 and the colorful tones 6 (13)-7-9, and (c.) the second degree yielding the 9-3-♯11-13 for a lydian or IV chord quality.

For a minor 7th chord a minor 1-2-3-5 pattern may be played from (d.) the root yielding the triad and the 9th, and from (e.) the 5th yielding 5, ♮13, ♭7th and 9th for a dorian sound. A major 1-2-3-5 pattern may be played from (f.) the minor 3rd yielding the ♭3-4-5-♭7, and from (g.) the ♭7 yielding the ♭7-R-9-11.

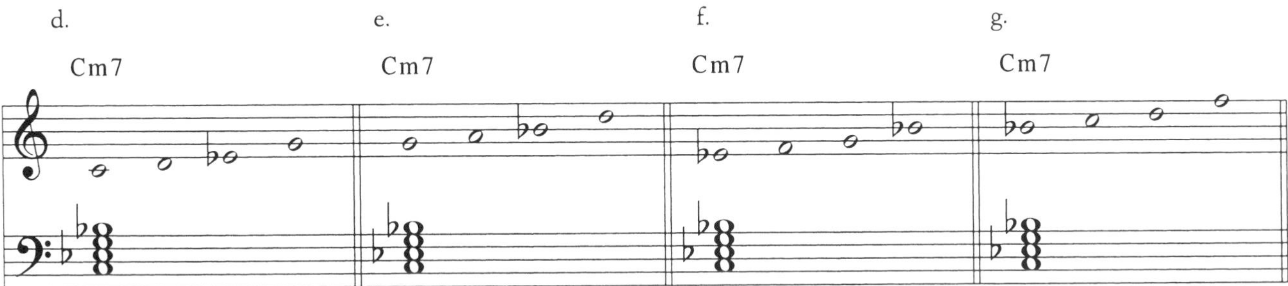

For a dominant 7th chord a major 1-2-3-5 pattern may be played from (h.) the root yielding the triad and the 9th. A minor 1-2-3-5 may be played from (i.) the 5th yielding 5-13-♭7-9. A major 1-2-3-5 pattern may be played from (j.) the minor 7th yielding the ♭7-R-9-11 (or sus4). For a lydian dominant chord a major 1-2-3-5 pattern may be played from (k.) the second yielding 9-3-♯11-13.

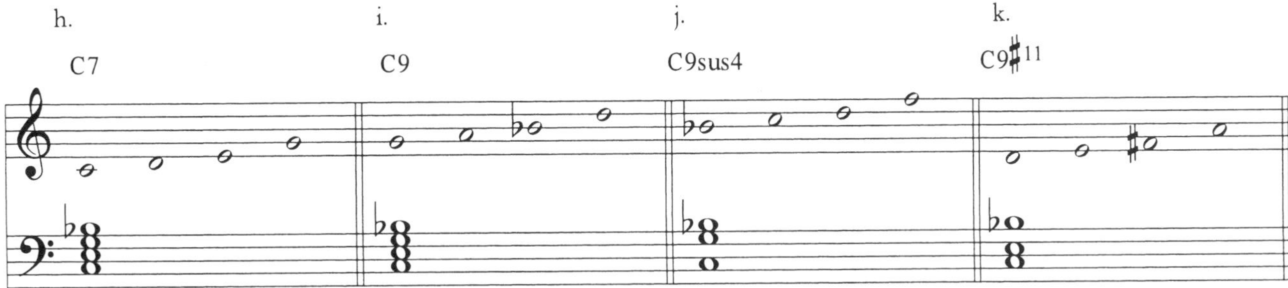

For a half-diminished chord a minor 1-2-3-5 may be played from (l.) the ♭3 yielding ♭3-4-♭5-♭7. A major 1-2-3-5 pattern may be played from the 7th of a half-diminished chord (m.) yielding 7-R-♯2-11.

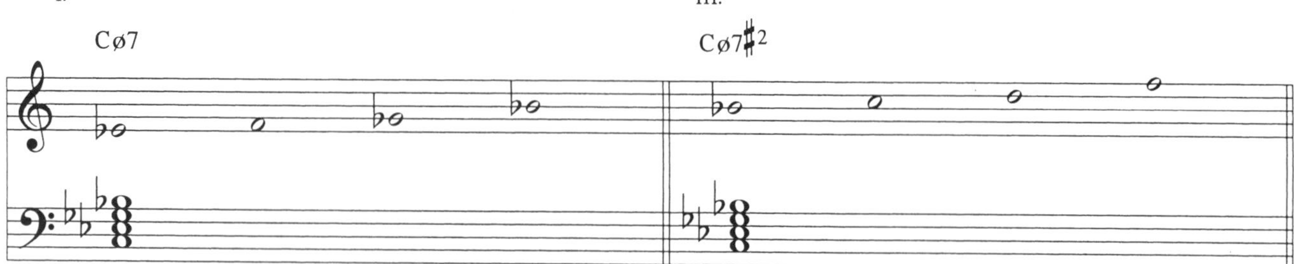

Three possible 1-2-3-5 patterns are available for altered dominants. A minor 1-2-3-5 pattern may be played from (n.) the ♭9 yielding ♭9-♯9-3-♭13. A major 1-2-3-5 patterns may be played from (o.) the ♭5 yielding ♭5-♭13-♭7-♭9 and from (p.) the ♭13 yielding ♭13-♭7-R-♯9.

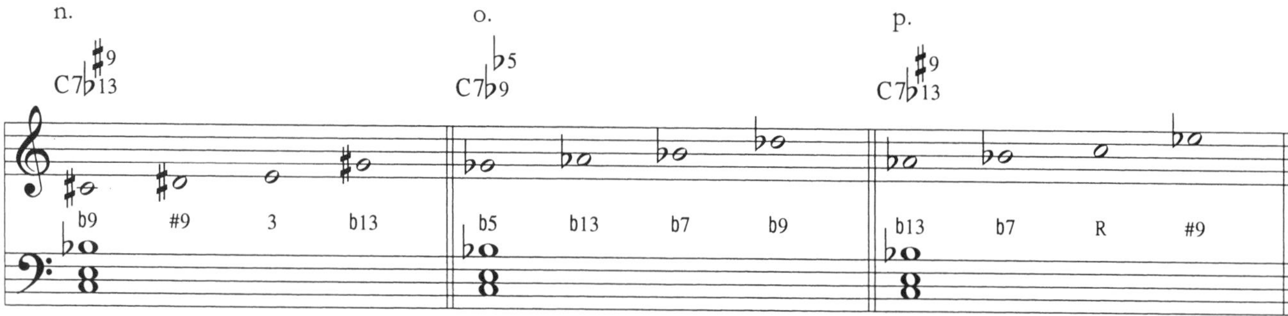

You may encounter this chord in contemporary jazz compositions. Playing a major 1-2-3-5 pattern from (q.) the 3rd yields the 3-♯11-♯5-7 of this lydian augmented chord.

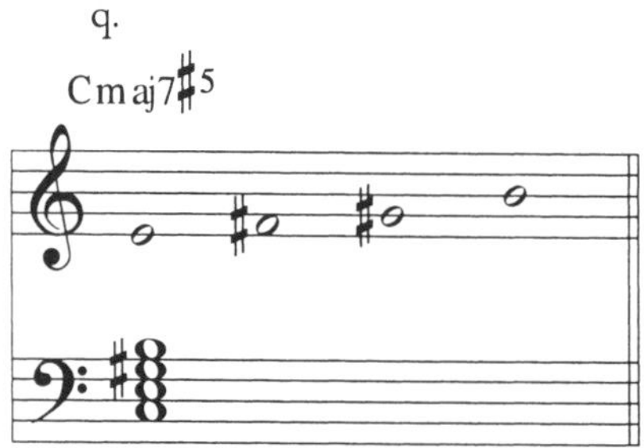

EXERCISES

1. Practice all of the patterns listed above for each chord type.
2. Practice the patterns over traditional harmonic progressions.

The following examples from jazz trumpet artists Tom Harrell, Clifford Brown, Randy Brecker and Lee Morgan may offer some insight into possible musical applications of these common patterns. The players used the 1-2-3-5 pattern from the root and the 5th of chords.

Major and minor 1-2-3-5 patterns over popular jazz progression.

This player used major 1-2-3-5 patterns to imply substitutions in this turnaround progression. The line implies the progression F - A♭ - D♭ - C7 where the A♭ chord may be a tritone substitute for the D7 and the D♭ a tritone substitute for a G7.

Major 1-2-3-5 patterns turnaround progression.

This player used the major 1-2-3-5 pattern from the root and then the ♭5 a tritone away over the G7 dominant chord, and from the roots of each the dominant chords in the next excerpt.

Major 1-2-3-5 patterns a tritone apart.

Major 1-2-3-5 patterns from the roots.

Minor 1-2-3-5 off the ♭9 of C7 (C♯m/C7)

1-2-3-5 diatonic patterns.

1-2-3-5 patterns that do not match the chords, but have a linear sensibility.

1-2-3-5 off the ♭9 of G7 (A♭m/G7)

1-2-3-5 patterns that do not match the chords, but have a linear sensibility.

1-2-3-5 pattern from the major third for Lydian Augmented chord.

1-2-3-5 patterns from the root of the Gm and Cm, and off the 5th of the B♭7 are heard in these lines from Clifford Brown.

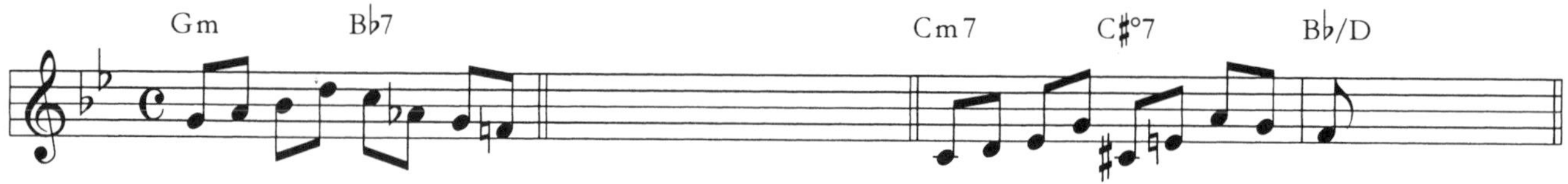

-2-3-5 EXERCISES APPLIED TO HARMONIC PROGRESSIONS

Consider that for each chord type there may be a major and a minor 1-2-3-5 pattern that could be played from up to four different positions on that chord, and that each of those 1-2-3-5 patterns may be varied in direction, order and octave placement. Then consider the combinations of these possibilities when two or more of these chords occur in a progression. The number of possible exercises becomes overwhelming. Considering all of the possibilities may help industrious musical explorers find ideas they would not have found without the thorough examination.

These exercises will give a starting point for incorporating these ubiquitous patterns into your jazz improvisations and compositions.

7.1a 1-2-3-5 Patterns over major 7 chord. Transpose for all major chords.

7.1.b Flat the 3rd and play for all minor chords.

1-2-3-5- Patterns over major ii7- V7 - I

F major, C major and D minor 1-2-3-5 patterns may be applied to a Dm7 chord. A♭ minor and E♭ major may be applied to a G7 chord. Exercises 7.2-7.7 explore a few of the possible combinations. Practice these, invent more, and transpose to all major keys.

7.2 F/Dm7 - A♭m/G7 **7.3 C/Dm7 - A♭m/G7**

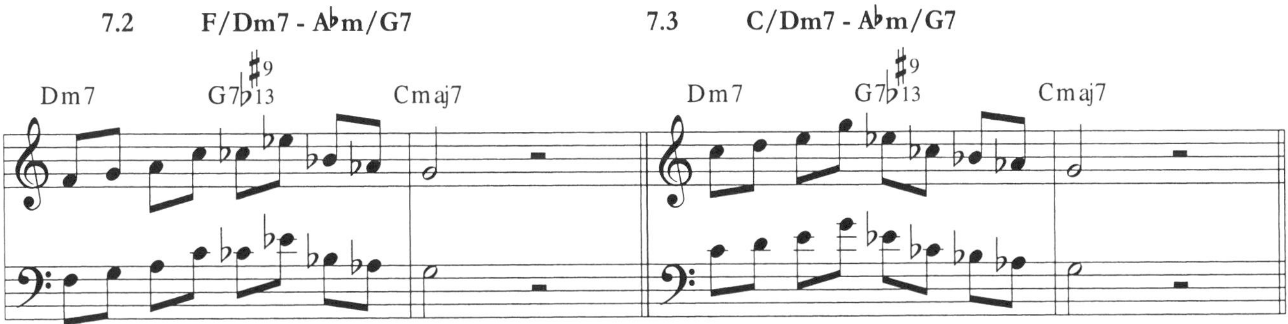

7.4 Dm/Dm7 - A♭m/G7 **7.5 F/Dm7 - E♭/G7**

1-2-3-5- Patterns in cadences to minor

F major 1-2-3-5 patterns may be played over Gø7 and C♯m and A♭ major patterns over C7. Here are two possibilities. Practice these, invent others and transpose to all minor keys.

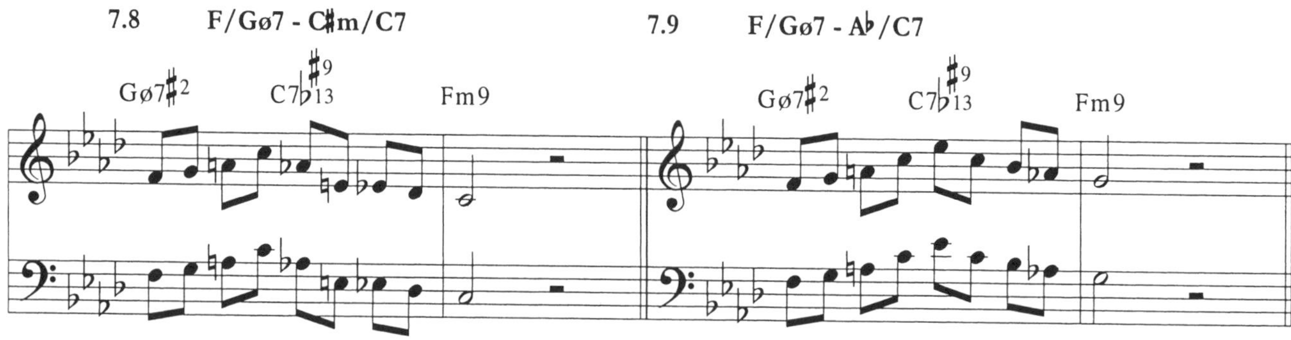

A lydian dominant on the flat sixth often substitutes for the iiø7 in a progression leading to minor. E♭ major and A♭ minor 1-2-3-5 patterns may be played over D♭9♯11 and C♯m and A♭ major patterns over C7. Here are four exercises for F minor. Invent more and transpose to all minor keys. This cadence could be practice again resolving to F major and then practice transposed to all major keys.

1-2-3-5 Patterns over Turnarounds

A typical turnaround pattern I - vi7 - ii7 - V7 may be reharmonized using secondary dominants. The new progression could be I - V7/ii - V7/V - V7. Every dominant chord also has a tritone substitute that could be used in this progression. In C the progressions would be:

Standard turnaround using diatonic chords:	C I	Am7 vi7	Dm7 ii7	G7 V7
Turnaround using secondary dominants:	C I	A7 V7/ii	D7 V7/V	G7 V7
Turnaround using tritone substitutions for all dominants:	C	E♭7	A♭7	D♭7

Turnarounds occur at the end of almost every jazz standard and blues and are the basis for progressions like "rhythm changes" and many standard tunes. The next three exercises examine a few of the possibilities incorporating the tritone substitute turnaround. Exercise 7.14 applies major 1-2-3-5 patterns from each root. Exercise 7.15 applies a major 1-2-3-5 pattern from the fifth of C, but applies minor 1-2-3-5 from the fifth of each dominant chord. Exercise 7.16 applies a major 1-2-3-5 pattern from the fifth of C and major 1-2-3-5 patterns from the 9th of the dominant chords creating lydian dominant sounds. Practice and apply to turnarounds in all keys.

7.14 Turnaround using tritone substitutions

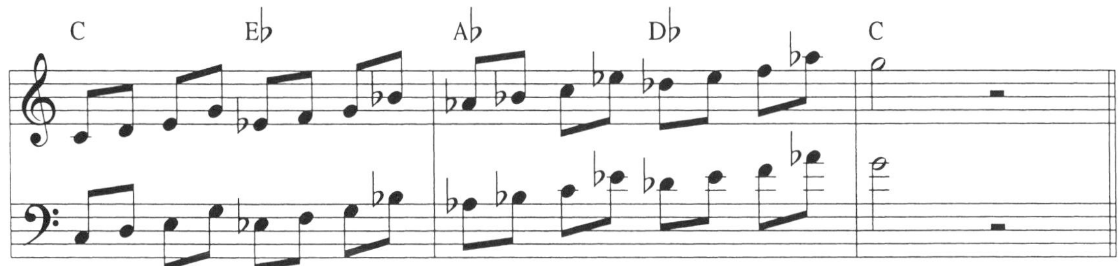

7.15 Turnaround using tritone substitutions

7.16 Turnaround using tritone substitutions

EXPLORING MATHEMATICAL POSSIBILITIES

How worthwhile or practical is it to search for every available possible combination? Choices have to be made because not every possibility is musically useful and there are too many possibilities to practice. Some time spent searching for possibilities is useful as it may lead you to musical ideas you would have never reached without exhaustive searching. Along the way you may encounter material that may not be useful, but if a good idea is hiding right behind it, the hunt my be worth the time invested. This is true not only for developing new technical and melodic studies, but particularly true when composing. I never trust a first draft. I constantly write and rewrite, think and rethink. Only after having many possibilities on the table do I actually have a choice. With only a first draft, there is no choice. Having five to ten choices in front of me I may decide the first draft is the best musical version, but without the other versions, there is no informed or educated choice.

These next exercises may show the value of exploring many mathematical possibilities when inventing exercises or music. The exercises are all over a iiø7 - V7 progression in A minor. (They could also be practiced leading to A major). Over the iiø7 (Bø7) there could be a minor 1-2-3-5 pattern and a major 1-2-3-5 pattern each with two variations of order and octave placement for six possible melodic patterns. Over the V7 (E7) there could also be a minor 1-2-3-5 pattern and a major 1-2-3-5 pattern each with two variations of order and octave placement for another six possible melodic patterns. Thirty six combinations of the two are available (6 x 6 = 36). For the sake of discussion, all 36 patterns are written down in exercises 7.19-7.54. Each pattern is labeled, so that *m1—M2* indicates minor pattern 1 is used over the Bø7 chord and major pattern 2 is used over the E7 chord. I would have guessed that not all of the exercises would have made musical sense, but they all seem to, and some that I would never have come up with without the search may be the most interesting.

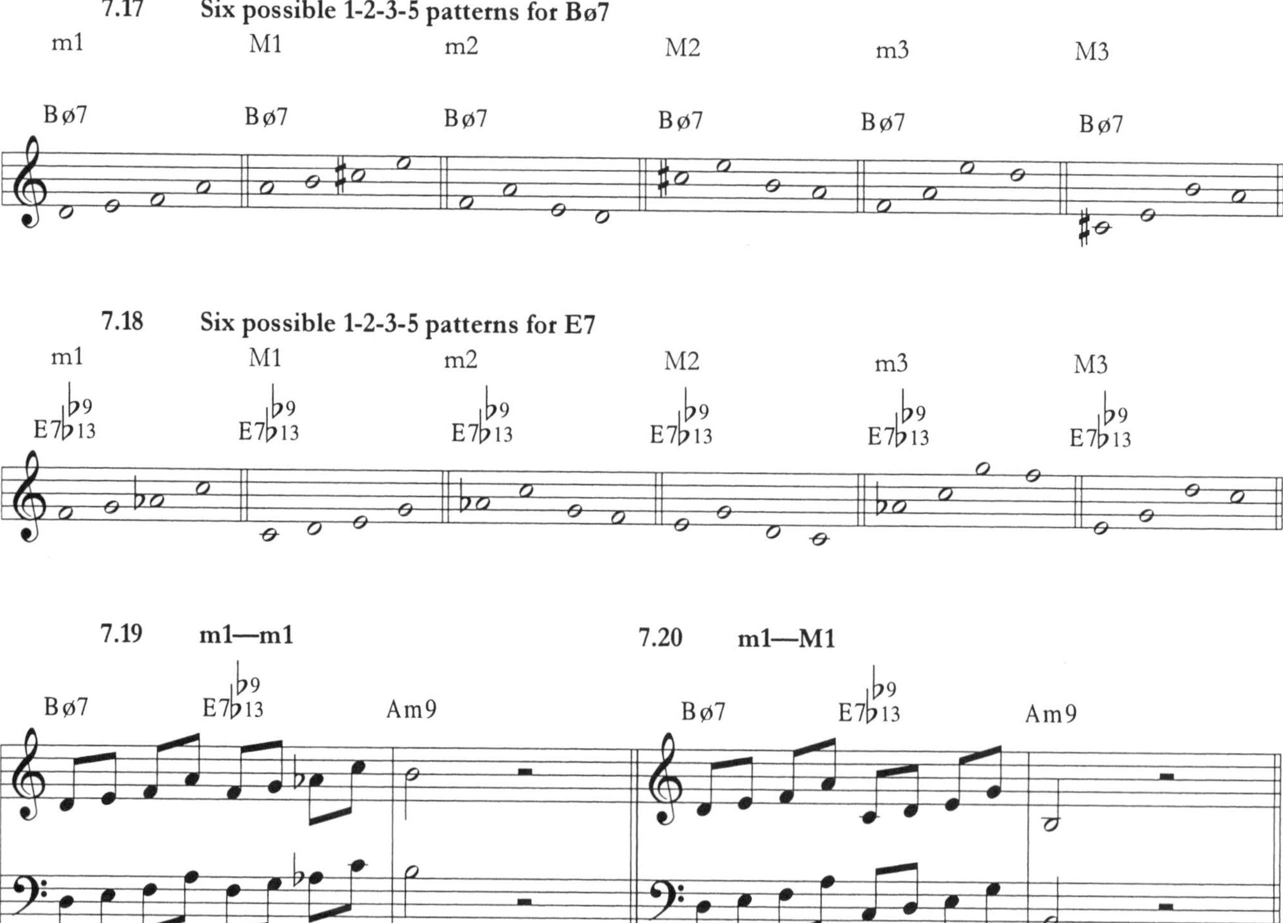

7.21 m1—m2
Bø7
E7♭9♭13
Am9
7.22 m1—M2
Bø7
E7♭9♭13
Am9
7.23 m1—m3
Bø7
E7♭9♭13
Am9
7.24 m1—M3
Bø7
E7♭9♭13
Am9
7.25 M1—m1
Bø7
E7♭9♭13
Am9
7.26 M1—M1
Bø7
E7♭9♭13
Am9
7.27 M1—m2
Bø7
E7♭9♭13
Am9
7.28 M1—M2
Bø7
E7♭9♭13
Am9
7.29 M1—m3
Bø7
E7♭9♭13
Am9
7.30 M1—M3
Bø7
E7♭9♭13
Am9

7.31 m2—m1
Bø7
E7♭9♭13
Am9
7.32 m2—M1
Bø7
E7♭9♭13
Am9
7.33 m2—m2
Bø7
E7♭9♭13
Am9
7.34 m2—M2
Bø7
E7♭9♭13
Am9
7.35 m2—m3
Bø7
E7♭9♭13
Am9
7.36 m2—M3
Bø7
E7♭9♭13
Am9
7.37 M2—m1
Bø7
E7♭9♭13
Am9
7.38 M2—M1
Bø7
E7♭9♭13
Am9
7.39 M2—m2
Bø7
E7♭9♭13
Am9
7.40 M2—M2
Bø7
E7♭9♭13
Am9

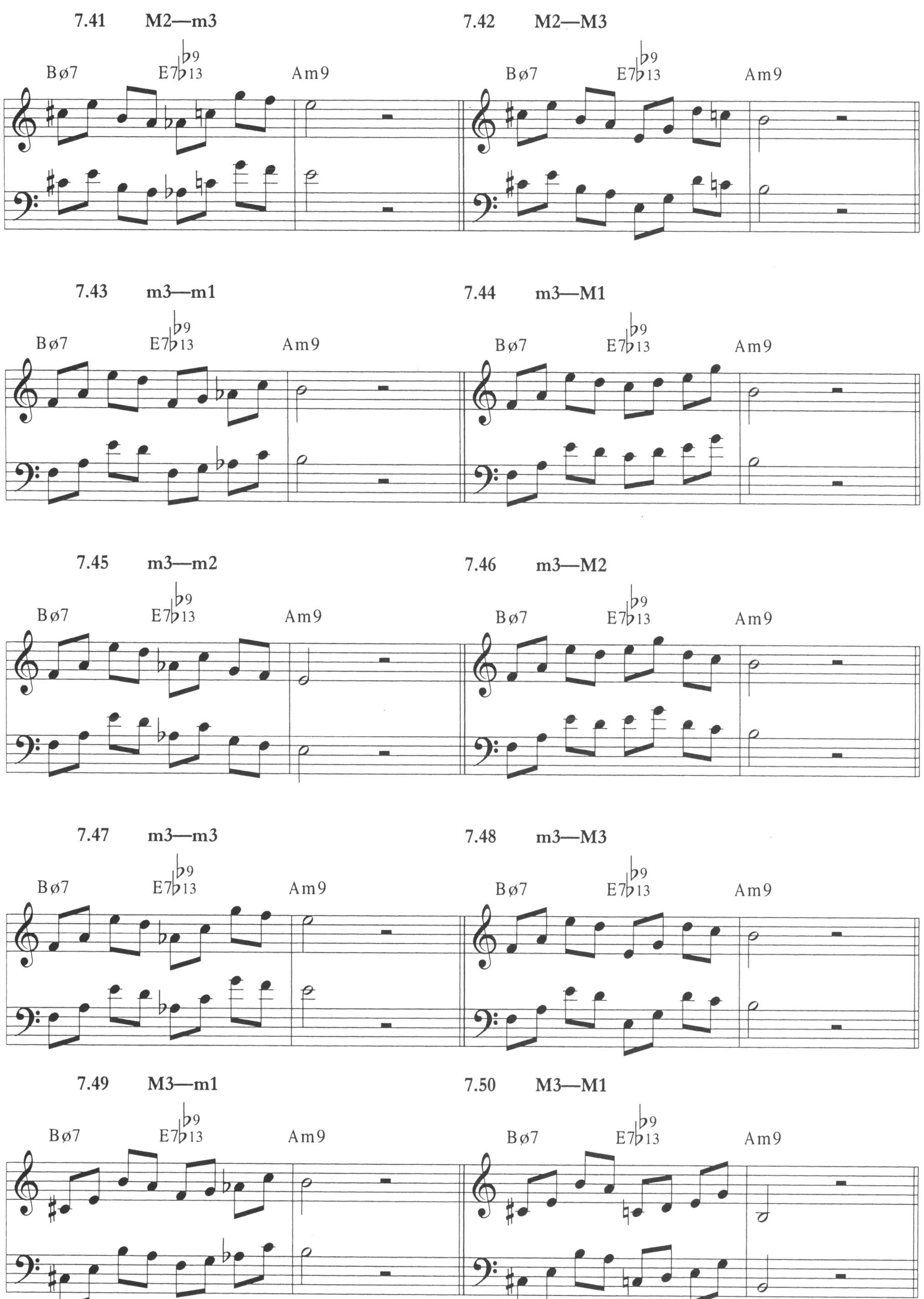
7.41 M2—m3
Bø7
E7♭9♭13
Am9
7.42 M2—M3
Bø7
E7♭9♭13
Am9
7.43 m3—m1
Bø7
E7♭9♭13
Am9
7.44 m3—M1
Bø7
E7♭9♭13
Am9
7.45 m3—m2
Bø7
E7♭9♭13
Am9
7.46 m3—M2
Bø7
E7♭9♭13
Am9
7.47 m3—m3
Bø7
E7♭9♭13
Am9
7.48 m3—M3
Bø7
E7♭9♭13
Am9
7.49 M3—m1
Bø7
E7♭9♭13
Am9
7.50 M3—M1
Bø7
E7♭9♭13
Am9

7.51 M3—m2
Bø7
E7♭9♭13
Am9
7.52 M3—M2
Bø7
E7♭9♭13
Am9
7.53 M3—m3
Bø7
E7♭9♭13
Am9
7.54 M3—M3
Bø7
E7♭9♭13
Am9

1-2-3-5 Patterns Applied to Standard Jazz Compositions

Applying any of the exercises to standard progressions is a first step to integrating the vocabulary into complete compositions. Here is an example of how the patterns may be applied to a popular jazz harmonic progression.

7.55 1-2-3-5 Exercise over popular harmonic progression.

1-2-3-5- Patterns Contradicting the Harmony

The melodic strength of the 1-2-3-5 patterns, in part due to their ubiquity and in part due to the natural strength of the triad, makes them good musical tools for slipping in and out of the key, contradicting the harmony. Some examples below, from contemporary improvisers Tom Harrell, Randy Brecker and John Scofield, illustrate 1-2-3-5 patterns that appear to have little to do with the given harmonic context. The lines are so strong and sound right in themselves that they almost make the underlying harmony sound wrong.

1-2-3-5 patterns that contradict the chords, but have a linear sensibility.

The following exercise should encourage some exploration of side-slipping using 1-2-3-5 patterns.

An A major 1-2-3-5 pattern is superimposed over the Fm7 creating tension that seems to resolve when the E is resolved to the E♭ in m.2. The E♭, however is a non-harmonic tone to the B♭7 chord, but is resolved with the typical chromatic approach to the D♮. A B minor 3-5-2-1 pattern is played over the B♭7 chord yielding the ♭13, ♯9 and ♭9 resolving to the B♭, the fifth of E♭. A brief D major 1-2-3-5 is played over the E♭ suggesting a side-slip into the key of D before resolving in the last measure using a 1-2-3-5 B♭ major pattern.

7.56 1-2-3-5 patterns side-slipping over traditional progression.

VIII. TRIADIC SUPERIMPOSITION

The triad is the backbone of thousands of melodies. The triad is the first three pitches in the overtone series and the natural laws of physics insist that the planet vibrates with these tones when the winds blow, which may explain the universal occurrence of the triad in melodies. In this century, composers and improvisers have used the triad in other contexts to create or enhance and sometimes create new sonorities. This chapter catalogs some possibilities of triadic superimpositions and suggests some exercises creating melodies using the concepts.

Superimposition of Major triads over Major 7th chord

Triads built on:

5: G/Cmaj7 2: D/Cmaj7 3: E/C (Cmaj7♯5) 7: B/Cmaj7

Cmaj9 Cmaj9♯11 Cmaj7♯5 Cmaj7♯9♯11

Superimposition of Major triads over Minor 7th chord

Triads built on:

♭3: E♭/Cm7 4: F/Cm7 5: G/Cm ♭7: B♭/Cm7

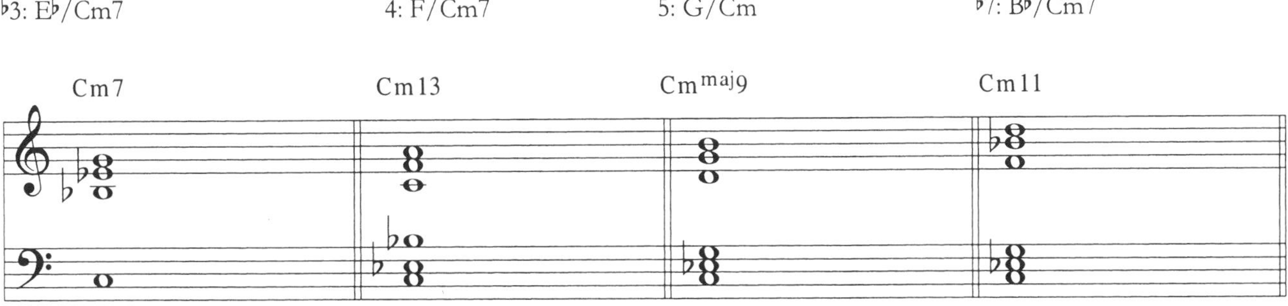

Superimposition of Major triads over Dominant 7th chord

Triads built on:

Root: C/C7 | 2: D/C7 | ♭3: E♭/C7 | ♭5: G♭/C7 | ♭6: A♭/C7 | 6: A/C7 | ♭7: B♭/C7

C7 | C9♯11 | C7♯9 | C7(♭5 ♭9) | C7(♯9 ♭13) | C13♭9 | C9sus4

Superimposition of Minor triads over Dominant 7th chord

Triads built on:

Root: Cm/C7 | ♭2: C♯m/C7 | ♭3: E♭m/C7 | ♯4: F♯m/C7 | 5: Gm/C7 | 6: Am/C7

C7♯9 | C7(♭9 ♭13) | C7(♭5 ♯9) | C13(♭9 ♯11) | C9 | C13

Superimposition of Major triads over half & fully diminished 7th chords

Triads built on:

♭7: B♭/Cø7 | 2: D/C°7 | 4: F/C°7 | ♭6: A♭/C°7 | 7: B/C°7

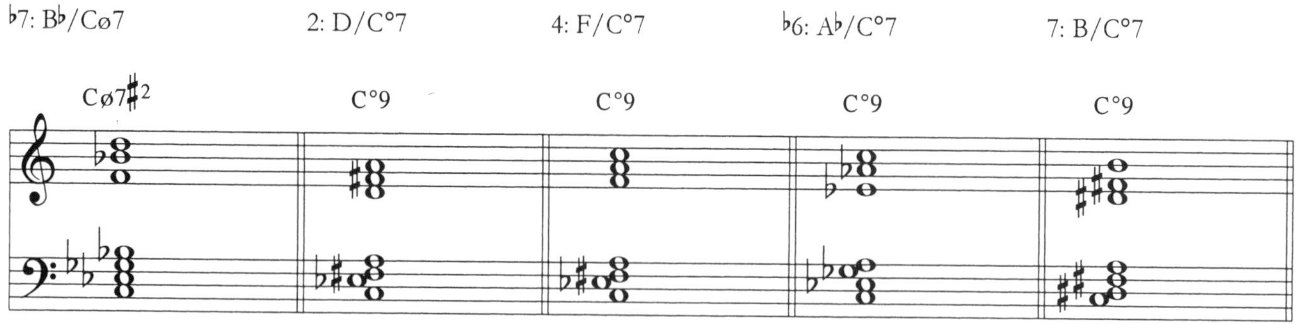

Some contemporary composers exploit the triadic superimposition concept. The following piece was written to demonstrate some of the possibilities available by superimposing various major triads over dominant seventh chords in a blues progression. Triads were used from the root, 2nd, ♭5th, ♭6th, and 6th degrees of the chords below to create this melody over a blues in F. (Accidentals shown were chosen to aid visualization of triads rather than indication of melodic direction.)

TRIAD SUPERIMPOSITION EXERCISES

In the following exercises, melodies were created using triads superimposed over traditional harmony. The original chords are shown above the music and the triadic superimposition shown above that using slash chord notation. Accidentals shown were chosen to aid visualization of triads rather than indication of melodic direction. Play and learn these combinations in all keys and then create exercises of your own using these and other triadic superimpositions.

Accidentals shown were chosen to aid visualization of triads rather than indication of melodic direction.

8.1

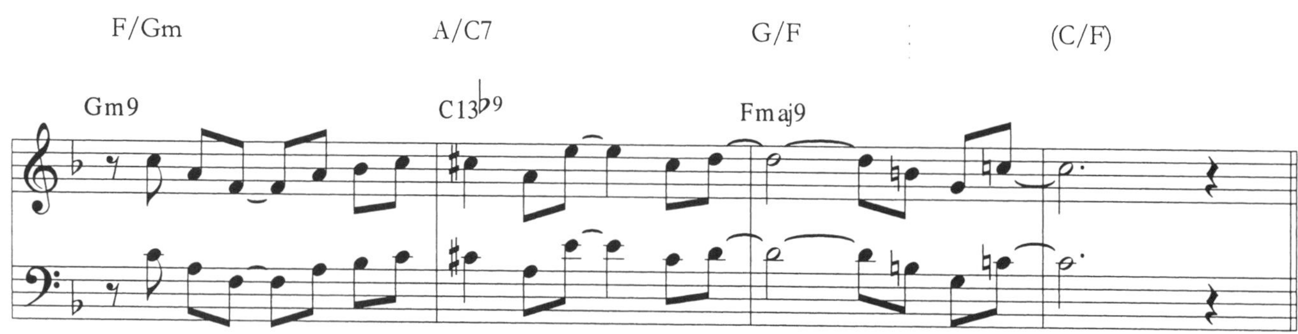

8.2

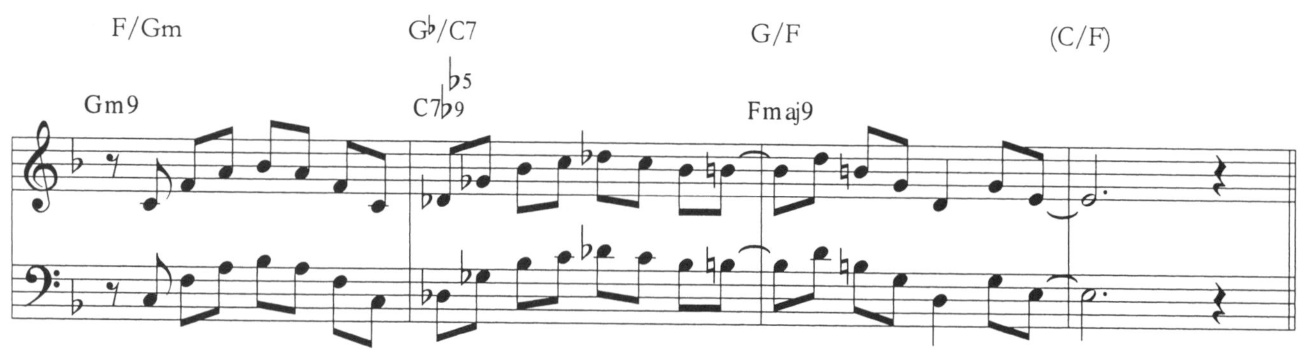

8.3

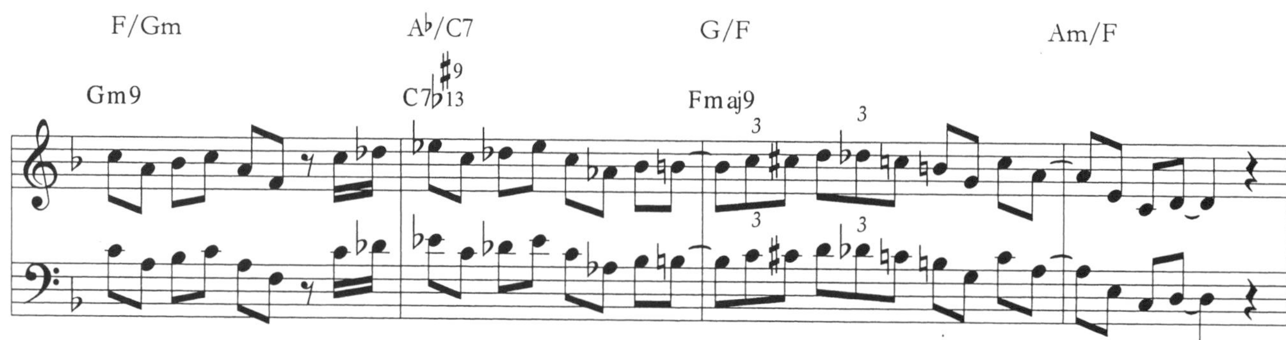

8.4

F/Gm
G♭/C7
E/F
Am/F
Gm9
C7♭5♭9
E/F
Fmaj9

8.5

F/Gm
C♯m/C7
C/F
Gm9
C7♭9♭13
Fmaj9

8.6

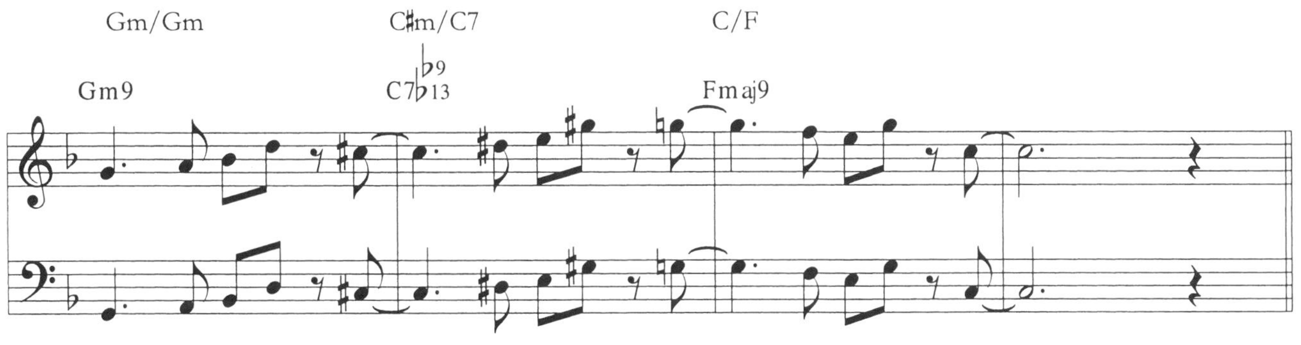
Gm/Gm
C♯m/C7
C/F
Gm9
C7♭9♭13
Fmaj9

8.7

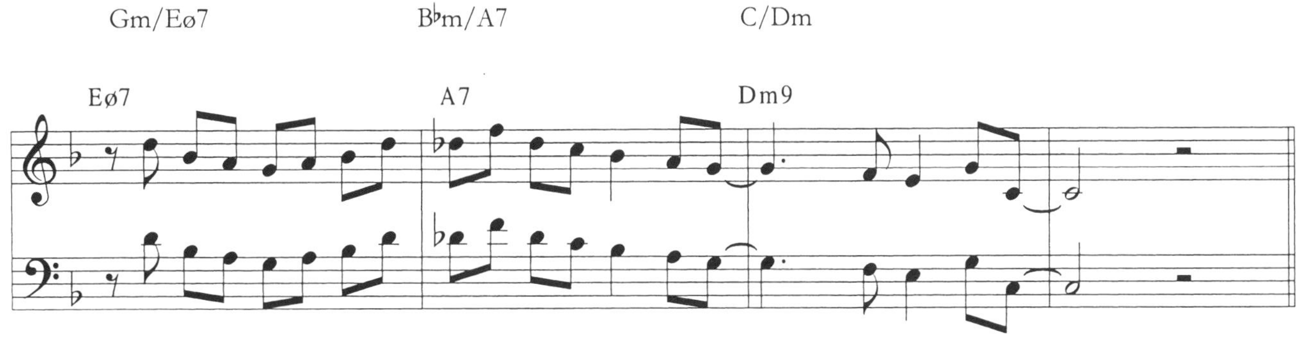
Gm/Eø7
B♭m/A7
C/Dm
Eø7
A7
Dm9

8.8

8.9

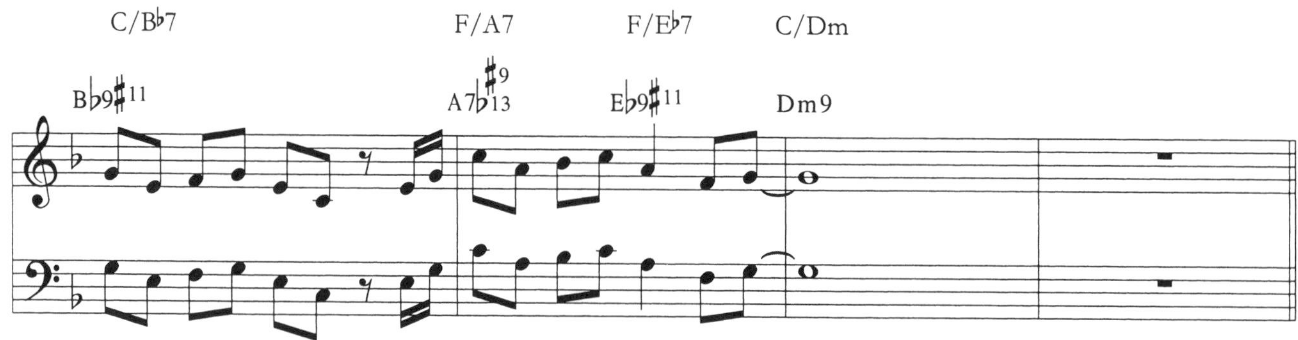

8.10 Triads superimposed over the "Rhythm Changes" B section

E/D7 = D9♯11 — E♭/G7 = G7♭13♯9 — D/C7 = C9♯11 — D♭/F7 = F7♭13♯9 & C♭/F7 = F7♭5♭9

8.11 Triads superimposed over the "Rhythm Changes" B section

E/D7 = D9♯11 — E♭/G7 = G7♭13♯9 — D/C7 = C9♯11 — D♭/F7 = F7♭13♯9 & C♭/F7 = F7♭5♭9

8.12 Triads superimposed over the "Rhythm Changes" B section

B♭/D7 = D7♭13♯9 — A/G7 = G9♯11 — A♭/C7 = C7♭13♯9 — G/F7 = F79♯11 & B/F7 = F7♭5♭9

TRIAD SUPERIMPOSITION APPLIED

The progression below is a popular jazz progression. Triads were chosen out of the possible triadic superimpositions and are shown below for each chord in the tune. These are not chord voicings but triad shapes shown in both clefs from which melodies may be created. Remember that no single approach to improvising over a progression is necessarily recommended. Great improvisers vary the types of approaches. However, singling out individual approaches and practicing applying them over individual tunes is the way to master distinct concepts.

Triadic superimpositions for melodic invention applied to an entire tune.

This etude is based on the triadic superimpositions outlined before. Compare the basic triad shapes and the melodic material created from them.

MORE EXERCISES

1. Invent your own exercises and etudes based on the possibilities shown in this chapter.
2. Combine the triadic imposition approach with other melodic approaches in your practice and improvisations.

IX. LINEAR IMPLICATIONS of HARMONY

Great melodies can exist in total independence of harmonic implications, but they often are inextricably related. So often taught as if it were a strictly vertical entity, harmony is historically a result of melodic lines. The essence of voice leading is that the individual voices lead somewhere, that each voice has a linear implication. As soon as a line begins or stresses a chord tone, there is a linear expectation connected with that note. Melodies do not always have to continue to follow their expected harmonic path, or all melodies would be so predictable that no one would listen. Composers and improvisers are aware of the natural tendencies and expectations connected to voice leading. They are also aware that the audience will respond to these principles intuitively whether or not the audience is musically educated. The composers and improvisers will give the listener at times what is expected and at other times set them up for a surprise. The only way the surprise works is that the listener on some level has an expectation about where notes should resolve. Most melodies create a balance between a melody line following the expected resolutions dictated by voice leading principles and a departure and independence from those expectations. The ability to understand and hear the lines suggested by individual notes of the harmony is a necessary skill in order to successfully negotiate the harmonic progressions in jazz literature.

Below is a typical progression found in music from the baroque, classical and present day pop and jazz. The harmony is voiced in five-parts more typical of jazz. The progression is a key center cycle: ii7 - V7 - I - IV - iiø7/vi - V7/vi - vi7. The roots consistently move down in fifths. The progression includes the two most common progressions in jazz: ii7 - V7 - I in major and iiø7 - V7 - i in the relative minor. Each voice has a linear implication throughout the progression. One voice does not leap around, but follows a smooth linear path to a logical conclusion.

The voice leading principles can be simply stated:

- 3rds resolve to 7ths
- 7ths resolve to 3rds
- 5ths resolve to 9ths
- 9ths resolve to 5ths
- With dominant chords, 13ths can be substituted for 5ths and resolve as 5ths normally would resolve to 9ths.
- 5ths, 9ths or 13ths following the voice leading principles regardless of any alterations. All combinations of resolutions are possible:

♮9 – ♭5	♭9 – ♭5	♯9 – ♭5
♮9 – ♮5	♭9 – ♮5	♯9 – ♮5
♮9 – ♭13	♭9 – ♭13	♯9 – ♭13
♮9 – ♮13	♭9 – ♮13	♯9 – ♮13

ii7 - V7 - I - IV - iiø7/vi - V7/vi - vi7 progression voiced in five parts

Dm7 G7 Cmaj7 Fmaj7 Bø7 E7 Am7

Practice singing through the progression one voice at a time to hear the individual lines suggested by the harmony. The individual lines are separated for study on the following pages. Practice singing them individually and in the pairs indicated to get familiar with the basic motion and direction of each line. Play on your instruments in every key. Begin adding to and elaborating on the basic structure of each line. Add these new ideas to your toolbox of compositional devices and melodic arsenal. Learn to recognize the lines when you hear them in all styles of music.

A line beginning on the third creates a line with harmonic clarity. There is no doubt about what the chord qualities are when the third is played over the root in the bass. The following exercise isolates the line starting on the third of the ii7 chord. This line is the basis for many melodies.

9.1 Implied line with 3rds resolving to 7ths

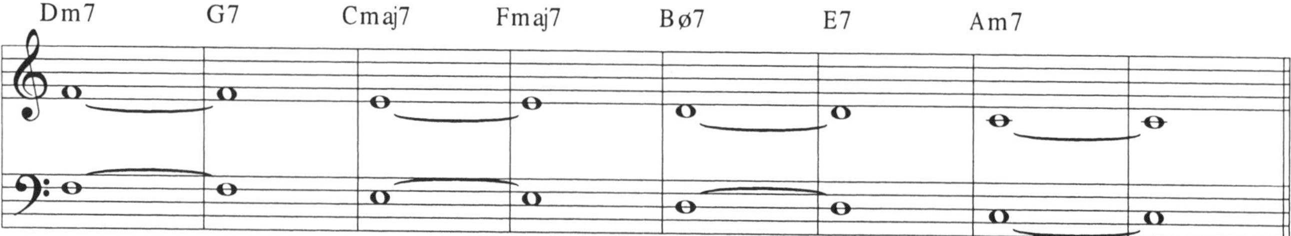

The following line begins on the seventh of the ii7 chord. The term dissonance is not a term measuring aesthetic attractiveness, but a term defining perceived instability. The seventh is a dissonant, unstable, restless note, wanting to resolve down to the third of the chord that follows. The pattern in 9.2 is the reverse of 9.1. These two lines provide the most harmonic clarity of any implied single line because they rely on thirds and sevenths, fundamental identifying notes of the harmony. The pitches in 9.2 move at opposite times than the pitches shown in 9.1, the stable pitch becomes the unstable pitch while the unstable pitch resolves. Try singing 9.1 while someone else sings 9.2 to hear the alternating voice resolutions. Note: this line begins on the last pitch of the previous example; combining the two creates a sixteen measure line that loops back into itself. This line is also the basis for many melodies.

9.2 Implied line with 7ths resolving to 3rds

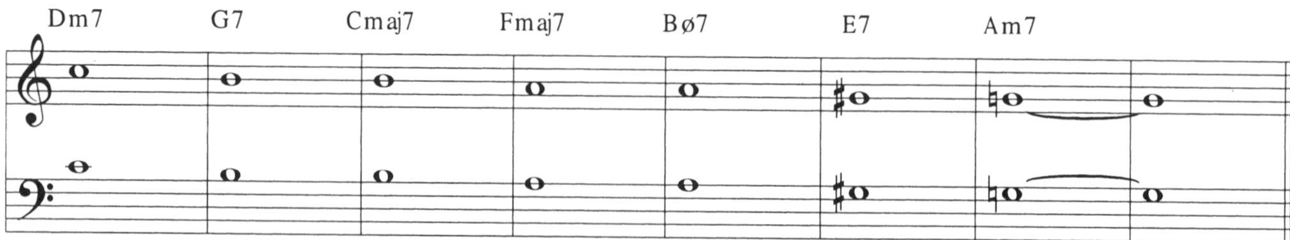

Starting on the ninth of the first chord creates a colorful line, though not as harmonically clear as a line including thirds and sevenths. Ninths resolve to fifths (or thirteenths), fifths to ninths. This line works well especially if other instruments are providing more of the fundamental parts of the harmony. This line is also the basis for many melodies.

9.3 Implied line with 9ths resolving to 5ths (or 13ths)

Dm9 G7 Cmaj7 Fmaj7 Bø7 E7 Am7

9 13 ♭13 9 5 9 ♭13 9

Starting on the fifth creates a line opposite to that in 9.3. These two lines can be combined as the last pair creating and endless loop.

9.4 Implied line with 5ths resolving to 9ths

Dm9 G7 Cmaj7 Fmaj7 Bø7 E7 Am7

5 ♮9 ♯9 9 5 9 9 ♭9 ♯9 ♭9 5

COMPOUND MELODIES

Single lines may sometimes be created which suggest two or more individual lines. There are excellent examples from all style periods, with some of the best known found in Bach's compositions for solo cello and solo violin. Suggesting two or more of the previous lines can create compound melodies. The distinction of the two lines is more evident if the two lines are separated by an interval of more than a third. Any smaller interval and it is difficult to distinguish two independent lines.

The line shown in 9.5 is very satisfying harmonically as each third is followed by a seventh, which is resolved over the bar line. The interval between the two lines is a fourth or fifth.

9.5 Structure for compound melody beginning with 3rds & 7ths

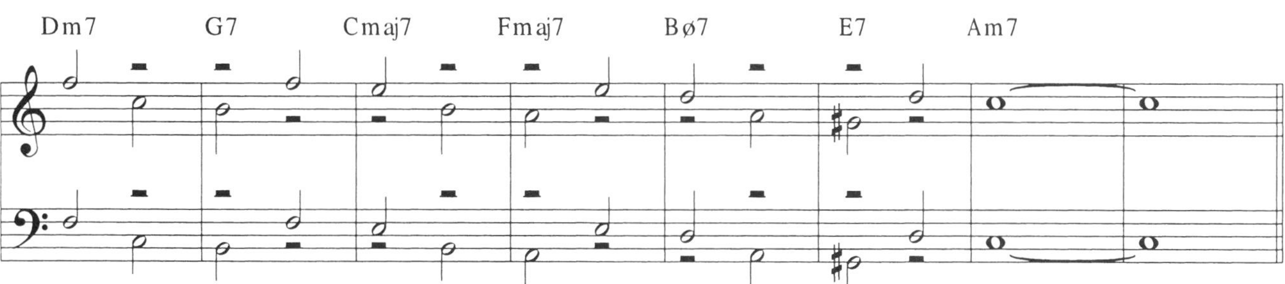

Exercise 9.6 was created using the simple structure shown in 9.5. Internalize the simple structure first by singing and playing the voice leading in order to create lines like this. The significant pitches often occur on the upbeats helping the line to swing and are approached with a number of diatonic and chromatic leading tones.

9.6 Compound melody beginning with 3rds & 7ths

A compound melody using the following structure relies on the 3rd-7th for harmonic clarity and the 5th-9th for harmonic color. The interval between the two lines is a sixth.

9.7 Structure for compound melody beginning with 3rds & 5ths

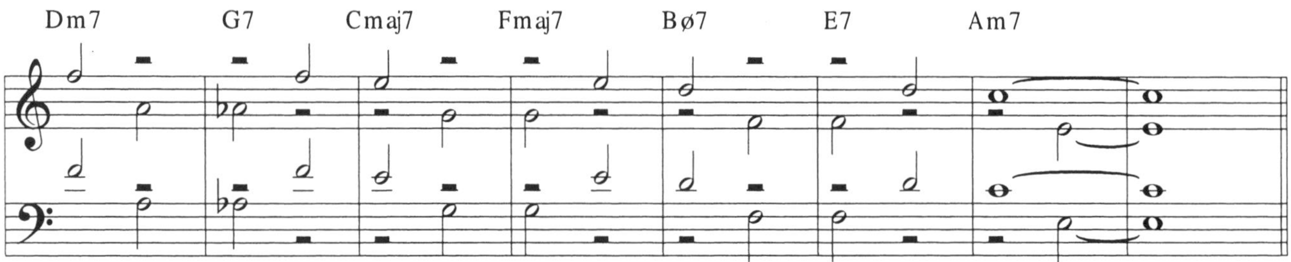

Exercise 9.8 follows the structure of 9.7. The clarity of the thirds is obscured somewhat by preceding each with a suspended fourth. The suspended fourth resolving as expected to the third makes this melody more interesting. There are many great melodies from every era and musical style that use a 4-3 suspension. Jazz improvisation students should not be taught to "avoid the fourth," but should be taught to hear and complete the resolution to the third.

The large interval between the two parts of this compound melody make the two individual lines are easier to hear. The lower part sounds like an answer to the upper part. Try singing the two parts separately. The top line works very well without the lower line and the lower line works well as an independent accompaniment line. If these two lines were in the same octave by transposing the top part down an octave, the melody would still be pleasant, but the distinction of two separate parts would be obscured.

9.8 Compound melody beginning with 3rds & 5ths

A compound melody based on the structure of 9.9 assumes the fundamental 3rds and 7ths will be heard in the accompaniment or be inferred by the listener. Melodies created from this structure can be very colorful and at the same time be harmonically ambiguous with the absence of 3rds and 7ths. You can hear similar structures in the bridge to tunes like Brounislau Kaper's *Invitation*. The interval between the two lines is a fifth.

9.9 Structure for compound melody beginning with 9ths & 5ths

Exercise 9.10 follows the structure of 9.9.

9.10 Compound melody beginning with 9ths & 5ths

The fifth to ninth resolutions provide the color while the seventh to third provide harmonic stability in this compound melodic structure. This structure can be heard in Toots Theilman's *Bluesette.* The interval between the two lines is a sixth and seventh.

9.11 Structure for compound melody beginning with 5ths & 7ths

The 7ths resolving to 3rds provides harmonic clarity and provides an answer to the upper part of the melody in the following exercise.

9.12 Compound melody beginning with 5ths & 7ths

Lines created using the three basic outlines (discussed in more detail in the *Connecting Chords with Linear Harmony*, Chapter 10 of *Jazz Theory Resources*, and in Chapter 15 of this book) can suggest compound melodies.

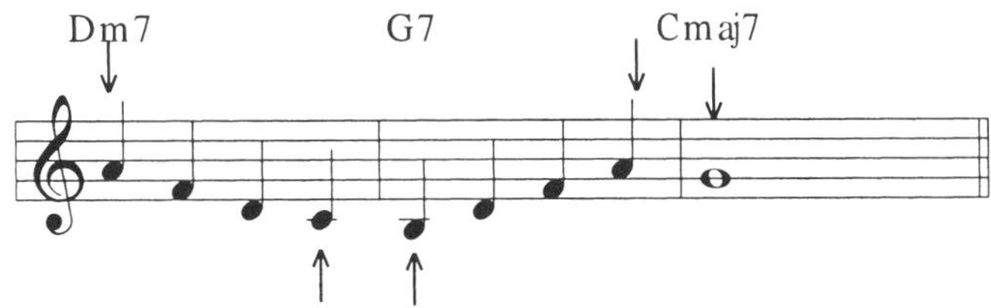

X. EXTENSIONS & CONNECTIONS

Most of the music that is studied in music theory and history classes uses the tertian triad, three note chords built in thirds, as the basic building block for harmony and melody. Jazz and contemporary music often uses extended tertian sonorities. Four, five, six and seven note sonorities can be created by stacking intervals of thirds over a root tone. In this discussion scale positions will be referred to by the numbers 1-2-3-4-5-6-7; chord tones will be referred to by the numbers 1-3-5-7-9-11-13. The second, fourth and sixth scales tones become the 9th, 11th and 13th chord tones.

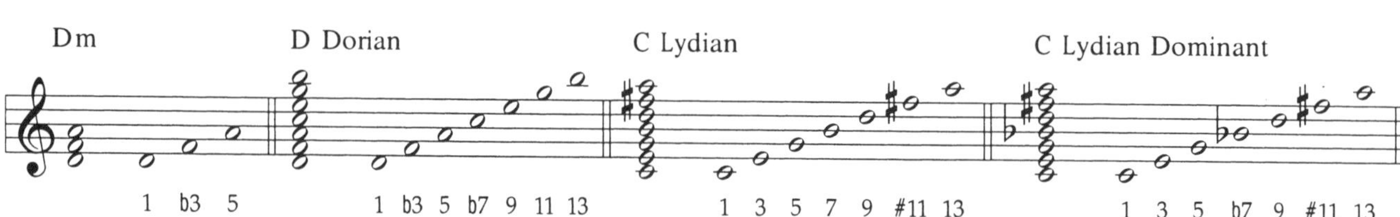

Upper tertian extensions must be added to the jazz student's aural and theoretical vocabulary, but study should include the understanding of the connections between subsequent chords with upper tertian extensions. Lines involving extended tertian extensions can create a more colorful and dense ambiance. Improvisers will often maintain the density introduced by these upper extensions by linking the upper structure of one chord to the upper structures of the next.

Sonny Rollins is known for his use of motivic development in his improvisations. In these two examples he displayed his understanding of voice leading and upper extensions. In the first excerpt the F-A-C-E in the m.1 could be heard as the 7-9-11-13 of the G7 or as the 3-5-7-9 of a implied Dm7. The E resolves to the E♭, the C to the B, and the A to the A♭. The F would be expected to stay the same over the G7 and resolve to the E over the C chord, but Rollins moves it chromatically up to F♯ and then to G. In the second excerpt he appears to imply a D9 chord before resolving to the G7. Notice how the upper three voices move down in half steps: E-E♭, C-B, and A-A♭. The chords to the right show voicings implied by these excerpts.

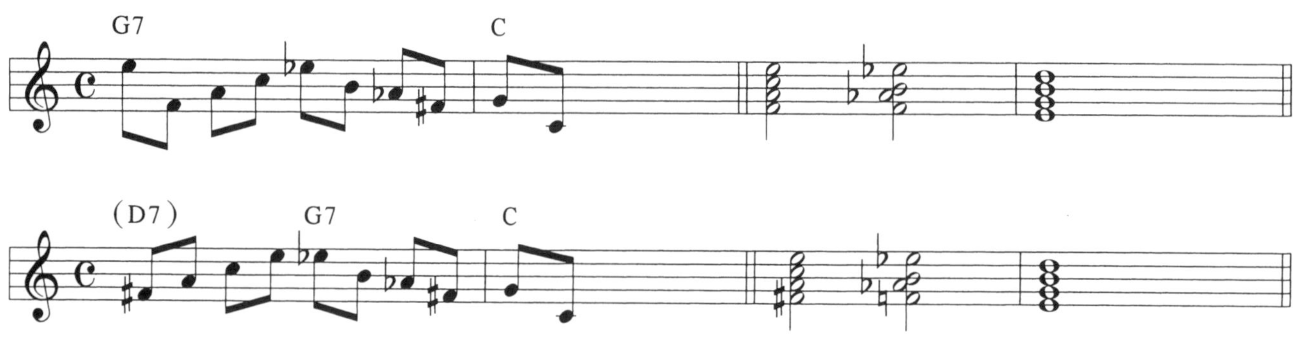

Hank Mobley arpeggiated the upper structures in this excerpt. The 5th of Dm (A) resolves to the ♭9 of G (A♭). All three pitches over the G7 resolve down a half step to the notes over the Cm7. The resolutions follow voice leading principles. The 9th of G7 (A♭) resolves to the 5th or Cm (G); the enharmonically spelled 3rd of G7 (C♭) resolves to the 7th of Cm7 (B♭); the ♭13th (E♭) of G7 resolves to the 9th of Cm (D) and then moves to the ♭13th (D♭) of F7. Notice that the F-A♭-C♭-

E♭, the 7-♭9-3-♭13 of the G7 chord are identical to the 3-5-7-9 notes of the tritone substitute dominant chord D♭9. The chords to the right show voicings implied by these passages.

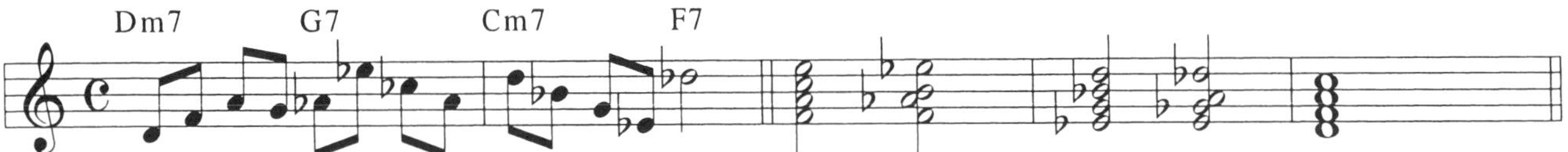

Bill Evans created a chromatic line (illustrated with circled notes) using voice leading principles in this passage. Consider that the D♭7 is a substitute dominant for the G7. The voice leading is consistent: E-E♭-D-D♭-C = 9-♭13-9-♭13-9.

Kenny Dorham clearly arpeggiated each chord in these two excerpts from the same improvisation. It may be easier to think of the second chord in the first excerpt as a D♭9 rather than a G7; then the notes are just the descending arpeggio 9-7-5-3. The same may be true for the F7 chord: these notes are the 3-5-7-9 arpeggio for the tritone substitute dominant B9. The two arpeggios in the second excerpt may suggest that Dorham is thinking the 3-5-7-9 arpeggios of C9 - B9 - B♭. The chords to the right show voicings implied by this passage.

It appears that Joe Pass and Dorham practiced the same arpeggios. Joe Pass played the inversion of the second Dorham excerpt in this line from a blues improvisation. Is it easier to hear and think of the second chord as F7 or B7?

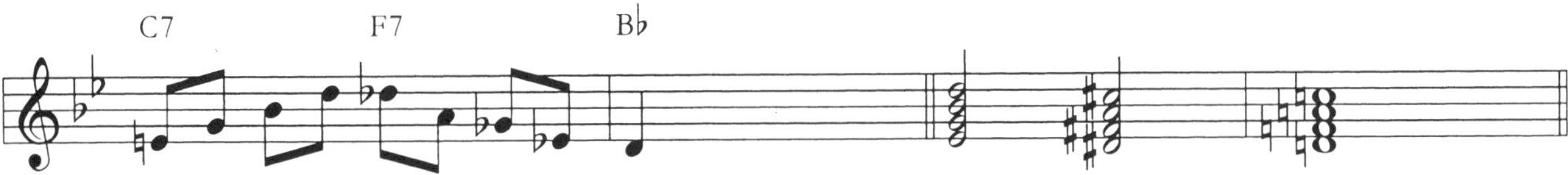

Here are two illustrative examples that may be familiar. In the first one, the B♭m7 is arpeggiated 1-3-5-7-9-11. The B♭m is again arpeggiated (3-5-7-9) over the E♭7 chord. A descending line is created at the top of the line (shown with circled notes). Several other voices are resolved internally: the F ultimately resolves to E♭; the A♭ resolves to the G, the D♭ to the C. The second excerpt implies similar voice leading. The 9th (F) of E♭m resolves to the ♭13 (E) of the A♭7 chord and then to the 9th of the D♭ chord. The chords to the right show voicings implied by these passages.

Kenny Barron used the descending arpeggios of these chords making the voice leading easy to see and hear in these three excerpts. The chords to the right show voicings implied by these passages. Listen to the chromatic resolution of the top three voices.

Listen to the upper structure connections in this excerpt from Bill Evans. If the B7 chord is considered an F7, the tritone substitution, then Evans melodically arpeggiates the 5-7-9-11 of each of the three chords. Evans may have been imagining different harmony for this passage. These extended lines fit with the common progressions: iiø7 – V7 – i (F♯ø7 – B7 – Em), VI – V7 – i (Cmaj7 – B7 – Em), and VI – Tritone Sub.7 – i (Cmaj7 – F9♯11 – Em).

The next four excerpts are based on the following framework. The second chord may be considered C7 (♭13, ♭9) or its tritone substitution G♭9 (3-5-7-9-♯11).

In the first two excerpts from this blues improvisation, Tete Montoliu played the ascending 3-5-7-9-11 Gm arpeggio into the C7 measure. The A is lowered to A♭ suggesting the C7♭13, the A♭ resolving to the G. The use of extended arpeggios lifted the melodic line into several registers. In the third excerpt, Montoliu played the descending Gm9 arpeggio and then an extended arpeggio over C7. The notes in the final measure are the ♭7-♭9-3-♭13-root-♯9 of C7 but may be easier to hear and comprehended as the 3-5-7-9-♯11-13 of the G♭9♯11, the tritone substitute dominant for C7.

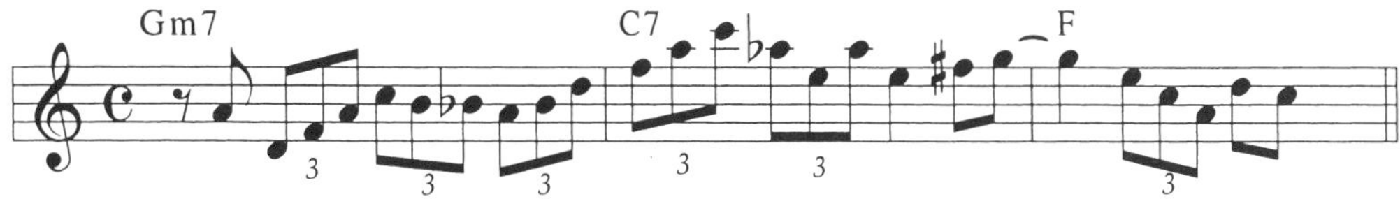

Bill Evans suggested another chromatic line dictated by voice leading principles in this excerpt. The A-A♭-G is the 9-♭13-9 voice leading.

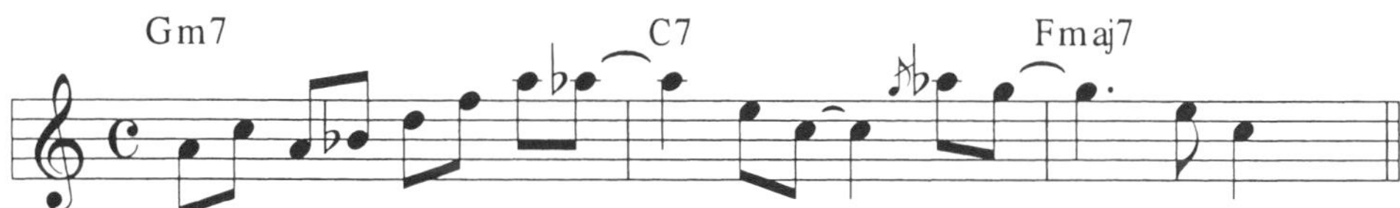

After seeing how the extended arpeggios lift the lines into several registers, many would think this type of approach would be limited to piano players. Tom Harrell seems to have played these excerpts effortlessly on trumpet showing a 1-3-5-7-9-11 arpeggio in one and a 3-5-7-9-11 arpeggio in two different octaves in the second example below. The ease at which these artists play these excerpts is probably due to hours and hours of focused practice.

Bill Evans chromatically resolved every voice in this extended tertian example. The voicings to the right show the basic voice leading framework. The tertian chord D-F-A♭-C-E is at once the ♭7-♭9-3-♭13-root of E7 or the 3-5-7-9-♯11 of the tritone substitute dominant B♭7.

Tom Harrell used similar extended tertian arpeggios and resolutions to the ones used by Bill Evans in this passage from the same passage in the same tune, though from a different recording session. The upper notes of the Bm9 (F♯A-C♯) are lowered over the E7 (F-A♭ [G♯]-C). Note the use of the F minor 5-3-2-1 pattern over the E7 chord supplying the ♭13-3-♯9-♭9.

EXTENDED TERTIAN EXERCISES

Isolate specific chord types and practice some common melodic arpeggios.

10.1 Common elaboration for Cmaj7, Cm7 and Cm^{maj}7

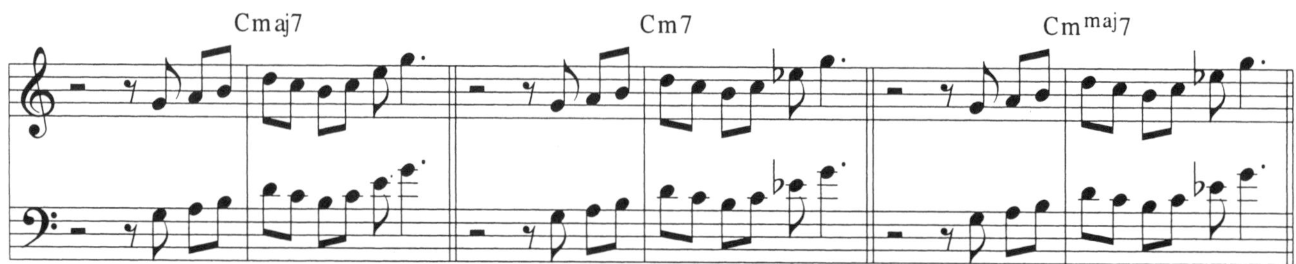

10.2 Another common elaboration for Cmaj7, Cm7 and Cm^{maj}7

10.3 Another common elaboration for Cmaj7, Cm7 and Cm^{maj}7

ARPEGGIO EXTENSIONS EXERCISES

10.4 **Basic arpeggio extensions for ii7 - v7 - i in major.**

10.5 **Basic arpeggio extensions for iiø7 - V7 - i harmonic minor for V7.**

10.6 Basic arpeggio extensions using modes of melodic minor.

Accidentals shown are chosen to aid visualization of triads rather than indication of direction. For example: the G7 chord may contain a C flat rather than a B natural to help distinguish from the B flat as in the extended chords below.

Learn to think of these chords with tertian extensions. Learn them for each chord and then learn to play them in the context of specific harmonic progressions.

10.7

The remaining exercises place extended upper structure arpeggios in harmonic contexts. Practice these in all twelve keys. Rework and invent your own exercises and practice in all twelve keys.

10.8 Practicing four part voice leading

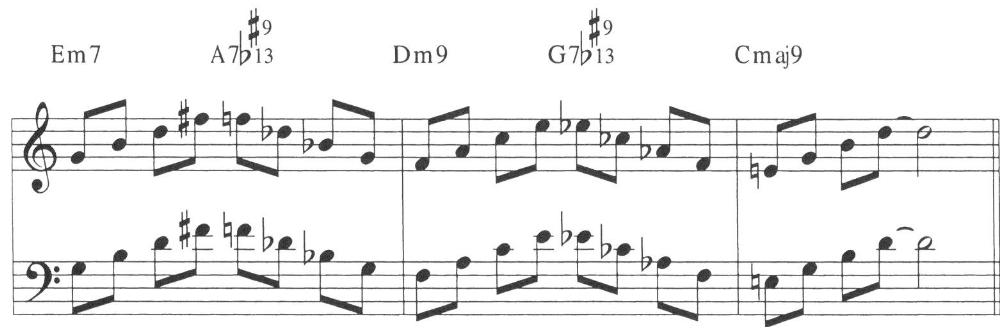

10.9 Four part voice leading in minor

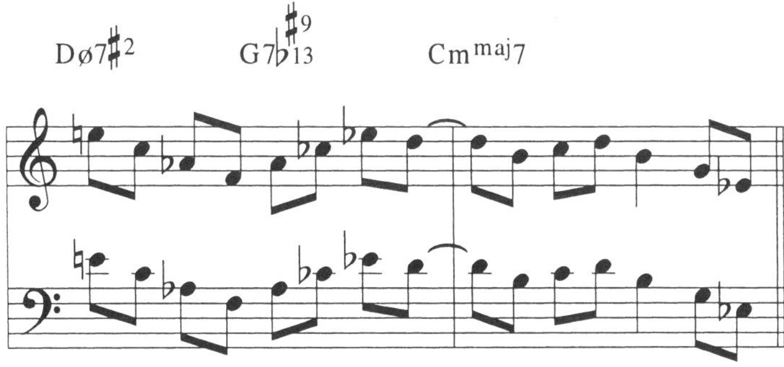

10.10 Exploring the full range of tertian arpeggios

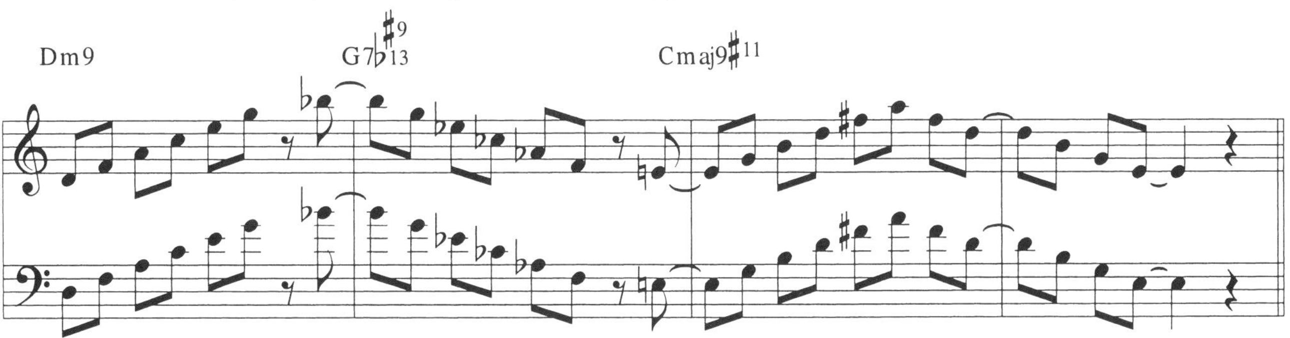

10.11 Exploring the full range of tertian arpeggios

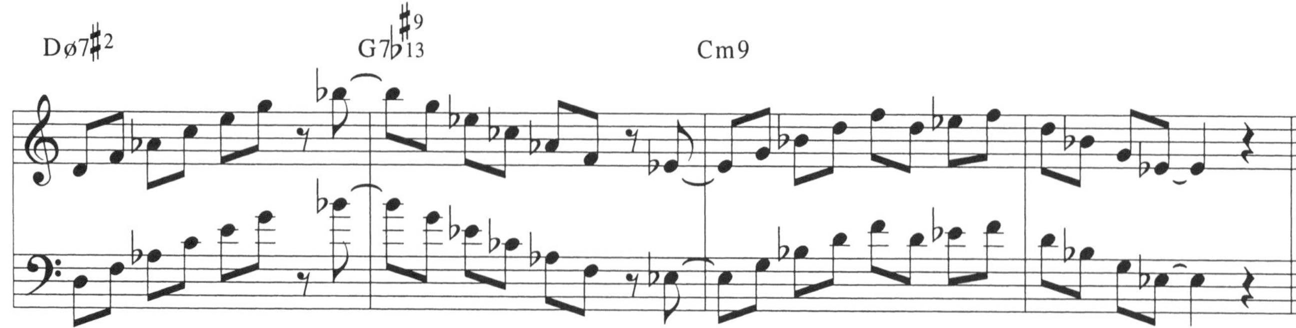

10.12 Wide range lines using extended arpeggios

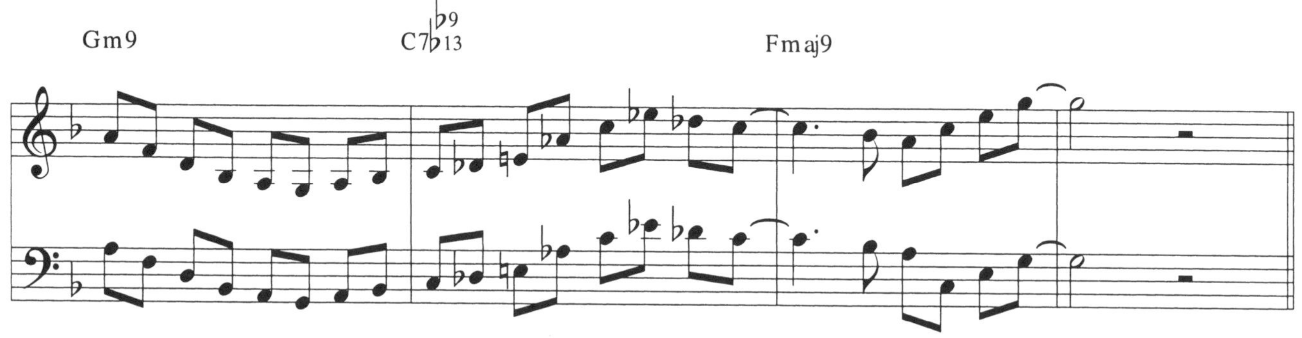

10.13 Three part upper extension voice leading

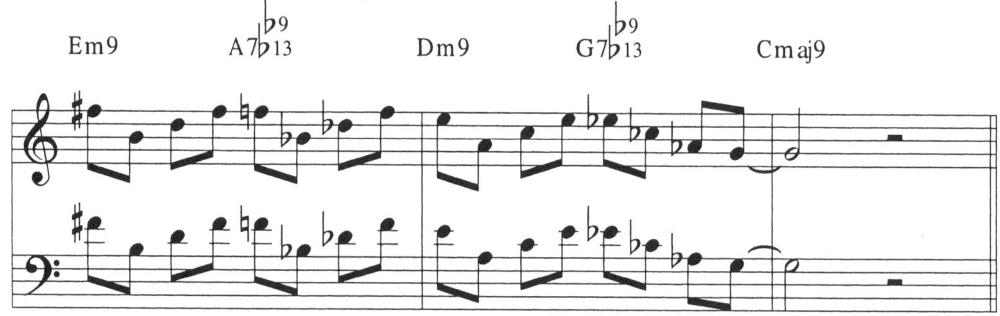

10.14 Isolating and following colorful upper voices

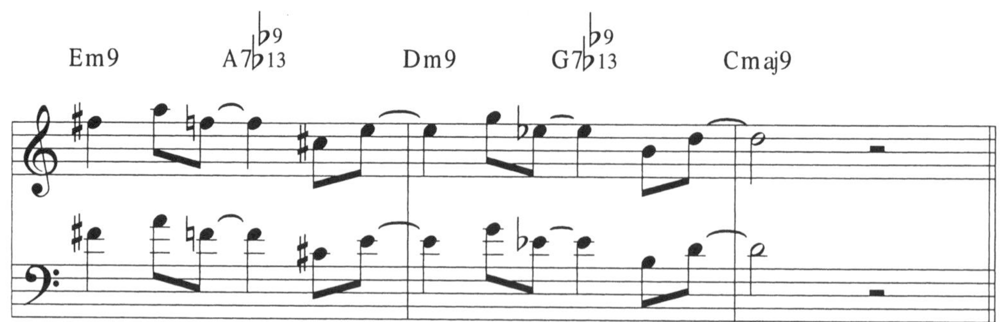

10.15 Three part upper extension voice leading including passing tones

10.16 Extended tertian arpeggios in progression

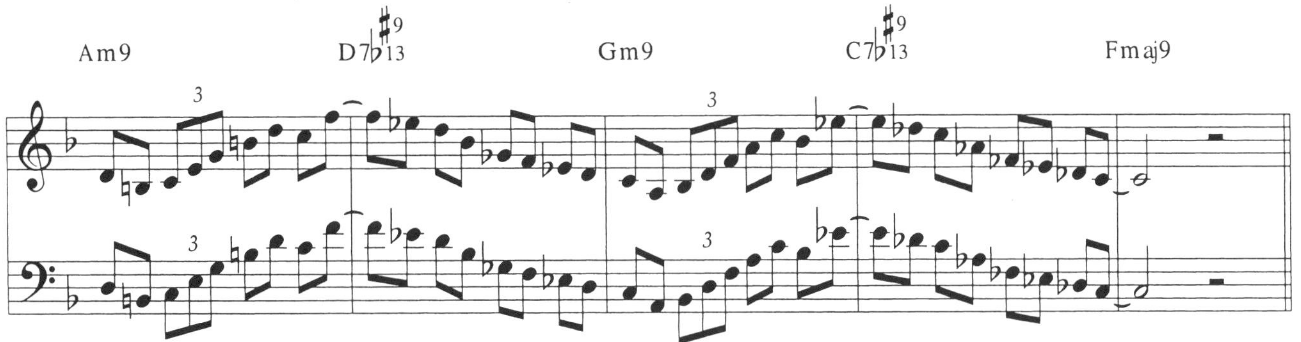

10.17 Four part voice leading with combinations of directions

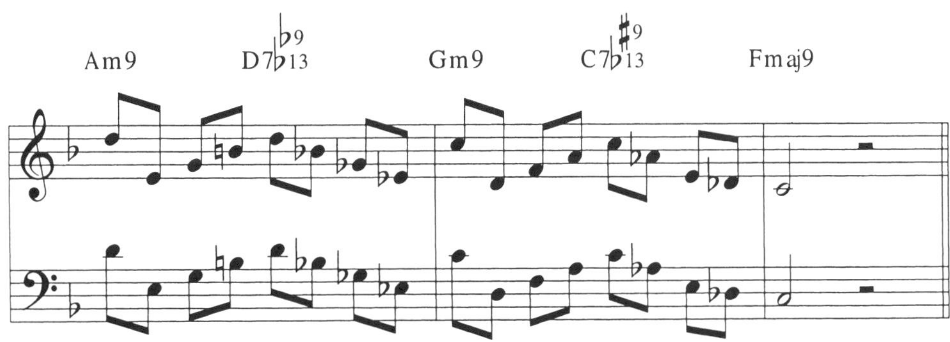

10.18 Extended tertian arpeggios

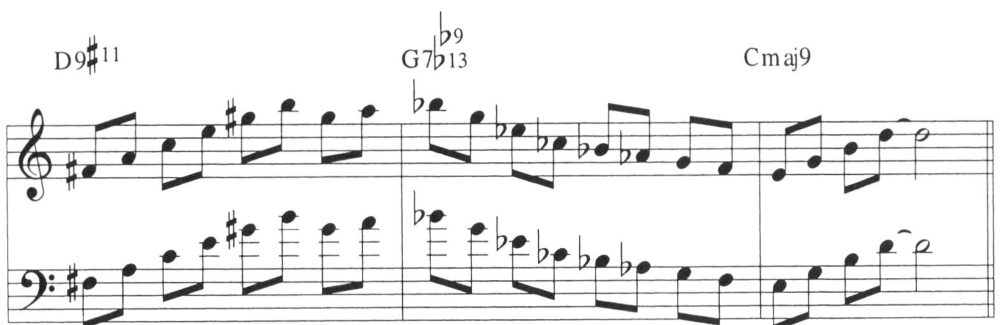

10.19 Three part voice leading

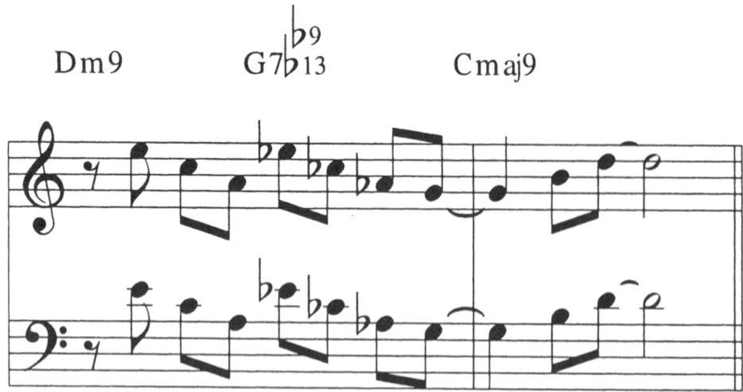

10.20 Four part voice leading with combinations of directions

10.21 Extended tertian arpeggios ignoring the V7 chord

10.22 Diatonic 7th chords arpeggios leading to four part voice leading resolution

10.23 Wide angled broken chords and voice leading. Within the large leaps and color tones, the 7ths resolved to 3rds.

The large intervals between the voices can create lines that suggest compound melodies—single line melodies that sound like two or more melodies at once. If you are attracted to wide range melodies like these, you should study the solo literature for violin and cello by J. S. Bach. The first of the next three examples are from Bach. The third example is from John Scofield, who seems to be pursuing similar ideas if not directly influenced by Bach.

J. S. Bach: Suite No. 1 for Cello Solo, Menuet II

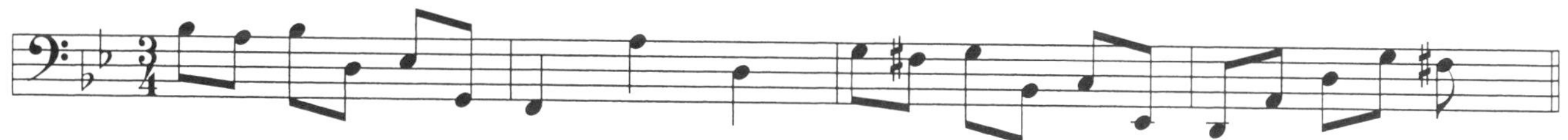

J. S. Bach: Partita No. 1 for Violin Solo, Courante

Wide interval lines from guitar solo

Create some exercises like the following to add a wider range of voice leading to your improvisation vocabulary.

10.24 Open position voice leading

Extended arpeggios can help when negotiating seemingly unrelated or distant adjacent chords like one might find in pieces by composer Chick Corea and others. B♭m9, Dm9 and Bm9 are from three different keys, but they share several of the same basic letters in their chord spellings (D-F-A-C-E). Knowing arpeggios like those shown below can lead to some very interesting lines. A line over the B♭m9 may be aiming for an E♭, but at the arrival, that note becomes the bright sounding E♮ over the Dm9. That same E♮ will change its character completely when it changes from the 9th of Dm9 to the 11th of Bm9. Begin by finding the basic arpeggios and look for common tones, look for how those tones change chromatically through a passage.

10.25 Distantly related m9 chord arpeggios

Lines can then be created calling attention to the pitches that stay the same and pitches that change chromatically. The following progression is similar to a passage from Chick Corea's *Humpty Dumpty*.

10.26 Challenging harmonic progression

The following passage includes major 7 chords that plane: E♭ moves down a half step to D, up an enharmonic minor third to G♭, then down a half step to F. Step lines can be created with the upper extensions. The triadic 1-2-3-5 pattern on the root of E♭ can transpose down to the 1-2-3-5 pattern on the root of the D chord. The same 1-2-3-5 built on the 5th of the G♭ chord is available down another half-step that then transposes down to the same 1-2-3-5 pattern off the 5th of the F chord. Finding these voices that move in half steps provides contrast the root movement. The rest of the exercise is designed to learn the arpeggios and their connections, relations, similarities and differences.

10.27 Challenging harmonic progression

The arpeggio below over the E♭ and D chords provides the 3rd, 5th, M7th, and 9th. In the third and fourth measures over G♭ and F chords the arpeggio provides the M7th, 9th, ♯11th, and 13th. The arpeggios in the second four measures of the phrase call attention to the common tones D, F, A and C. The C and F are natural for each of the chords. The D is D♭ for the A7 and B♭m7, but is D♮ for the B♭maj7 and Dm9. The A is A♮ for the A7, B♭maj7 and the Dm9, but A♭ for the B♭m7.

10.28 Challenging harmonic progression

XI. AUGMENTED SCALE EXERCISES

The augmented scale is an unusual scale of limited transposition. It is constructed with the intervals: m3-m2-m3-m2-m3-m2. The unusual construction limits its use in traditional settings. Improvisers and composes who use this scale and sonorities from this scale may superimpose it over traditional settings for effect or create new music suited for these sounds. I discovered the augmented scale for myself by reasoning that if the diminished scale was constructed by adding a leading tone to the diminished chord tones then an augmented scale could be created by adding leading tones to an augmented chord.

Diminished Scale =
°7 chord with leading tones

Augmented Scale =
Augmented chord with leading tones

As with many of my early "discoveries" I later found many musical explorers preceded me.

Béla Bartók:

Because of its symmetry there are only two modes of the augmented scale. The scale can only be transposed to four different pitch sets as shown below.

Augmented Scales:

C-E-A♭　　A♭-F-A　　D-F♯-B♭　　E♭-G-B

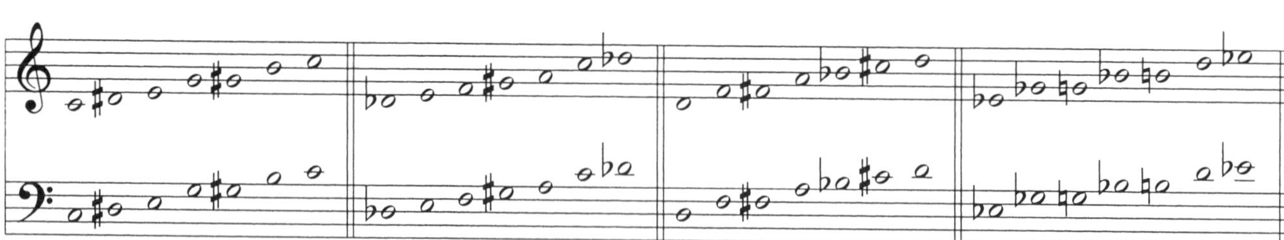

The most common chords derived from the augmented scale are a major 7 chord with a ♯5 and a minor chord with a major seventh. Some unusual chords may be created that may be difficult and misleading to name in the traditional sense.

Chords derived from the C-E-A♭ Augmented Scale

AUGMENTED SCALE EXERCISES

Transpose these exercises for all augmented scales.

11.1 Exercise emphasizing the m2 interval

11.2 Exercise emphasizing the m3 interval

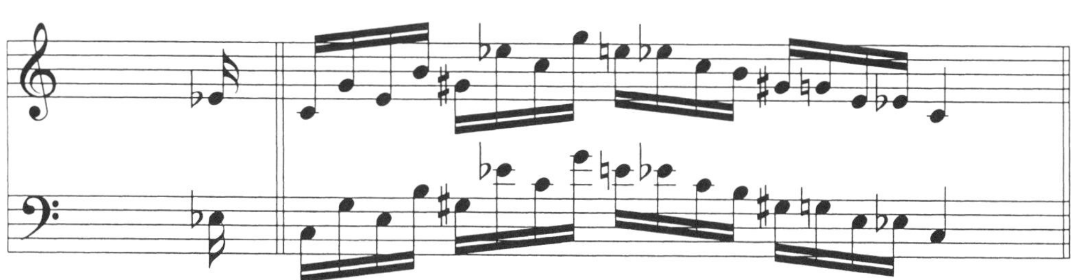

11.3 Exercise emphasizing the m2 interval as LNT

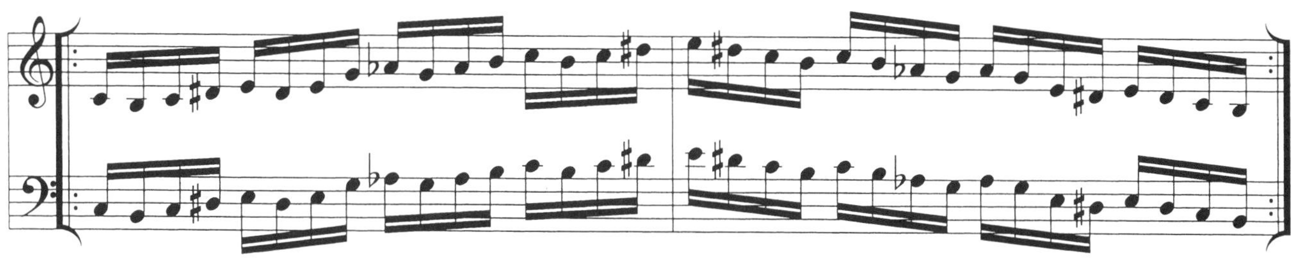

11.4 **Exercise emphasizing ascending and descending augmented triads**

11.5 **Exercise emphasizing ascending and descending augmented triads**

11.6 **Exercise emphasizing descending and ascending augmented triads**

11.7 **Exercise emphasizing the three major triads and the intervallic inversion emphasizing the three minor triads**

11.8 **Exercise: five-note pattern emphasizing major third intervals**

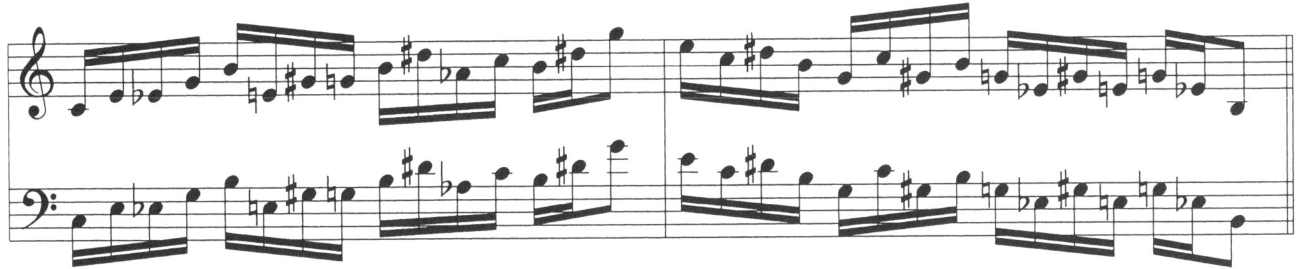

11.9 **Exercise: five-note pattern emphasizing major third intervals**

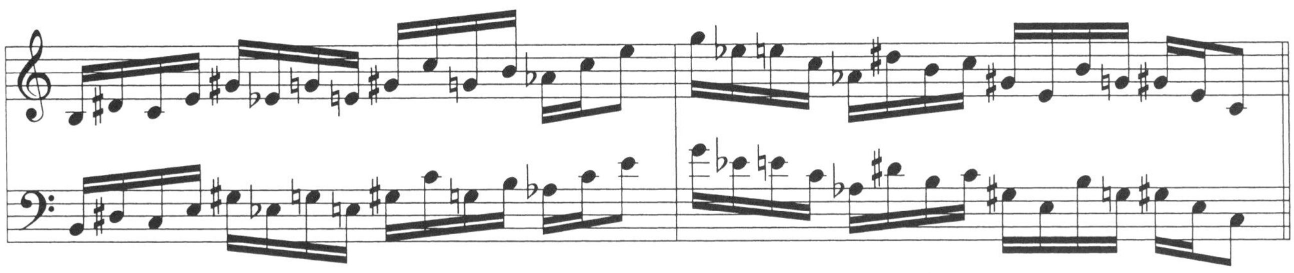

11.10 **Exercise emphasizing major/minor duality**

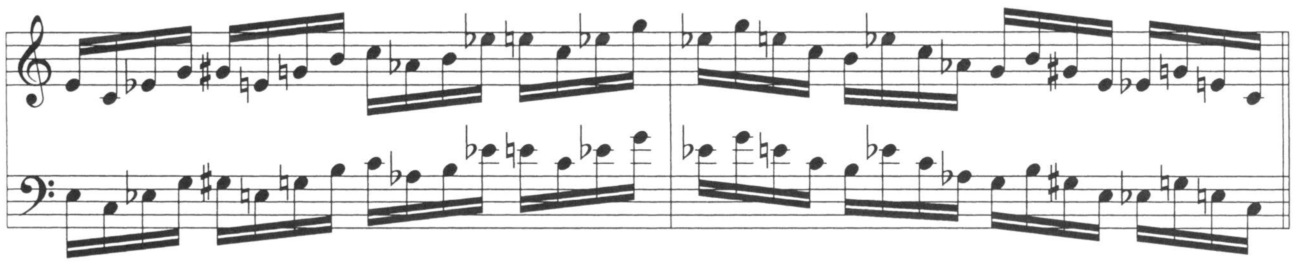

11.11 **Exercise emphasizing perfect fourths**

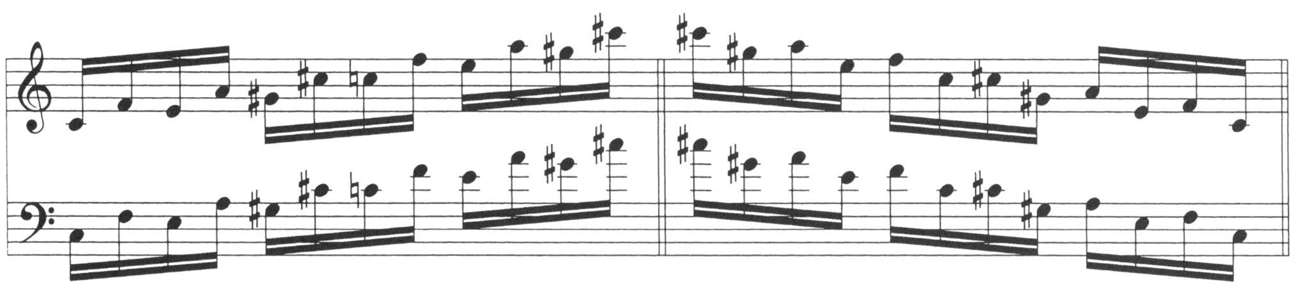

11.12 Exercise emphasizing perfect fourths in a cycle

11.13 Exercise emphasizing perfect fourths in a cycle

XII. QUARTAL EXERCISES

This chapter explores the extended arpeggio concept applied to tertian chords in chapter 10 as applied to some quartal chords discussed in chapter 6. There are three quartal chords from the pentatonic scale as discussed in chapter 6. Stacking thirds creates extended tertian chords. Stacking fourths can create large, extended quartal chords. These chords can be combined and superimposed over traditional chords and traditional harmonic progressions. These extended quartal chords can be melodically connected in a way similar to that of extended tertian chords.

The chart below separates the three quartal chords found in a D minor pentatonic and then combines them into large structure chords. The first combined chord is spaced in perfect fourths; the second and third chords include many clusters. The exercises will be based on these combinations of the three quartal chords found in pentatonic scales. As with all exercises, practice for all keys and at anytime invent your own variations of the exercises.

Quartal Chords = Combined   Quartal Chords = Combined   Quartal Chords = Combined

The D minor/F major pentatonic scale works with a number of chords including: Dm, Gm, F major, B♭ major, E♭ major, F7 and B7alt. (see pp.130-131, chapter 6.)

EXTENDED QUARTAL ARPEGGIOS FROM D MINOR/F MAJOR PENTATONIC

12.1 **Quartal chords P4 apart** **Quartal chords P4 & M2 apart**

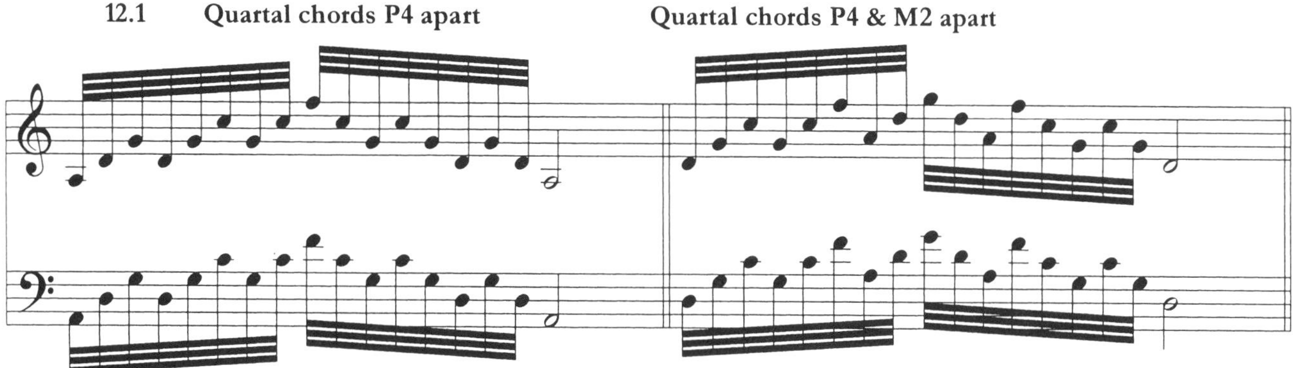

12.2 **Quartal chords M2 & P4 apart** **Quartal chords P5 apart**

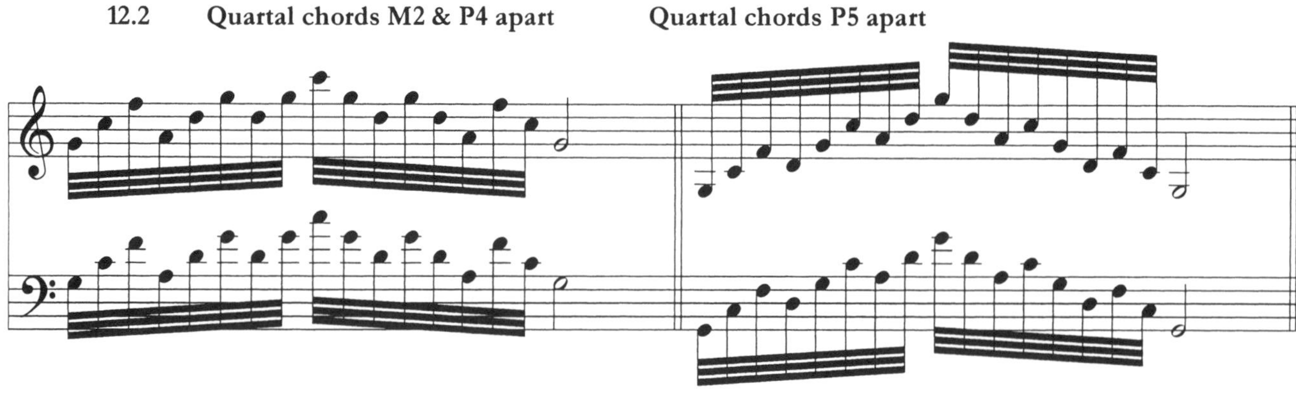

Lowering the fifth of a D minor pentatonic creates the following quartal and large chords. These tones are the same as the F Kumoi pentatonic scale. This pentatonic scale works with many chords including: Dø7, B♭9, E7alt., Fm, and G7sus♭9. The chart below shows combinations of the three quartal chords from this altered pentatonic. The quartal chord from the lowered fifth includes the intervals of a augmented fourth and a perfect fourth.

Quartal Chords = Combined Quartal Chords = Combined Quartal Chords = Combined

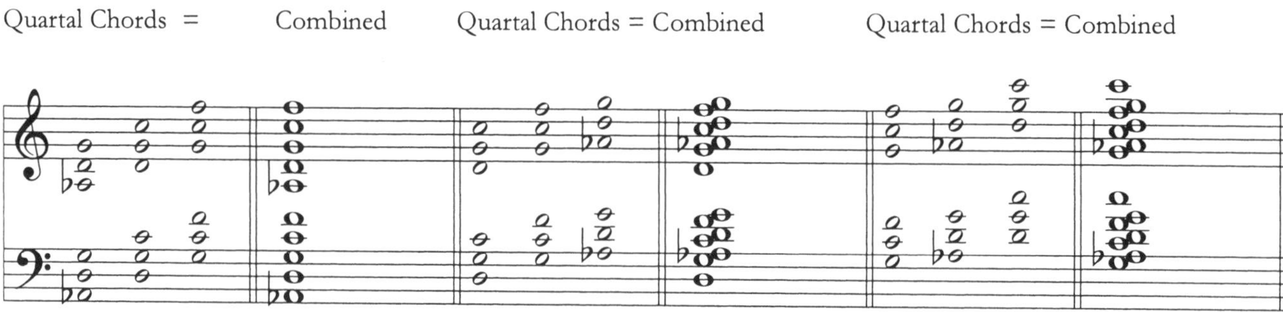

EXTENDED QUARTAL ARPEGGIOS FROM F KUMOI PENTATONIC

12.3 **Quartal chord arpeggios**

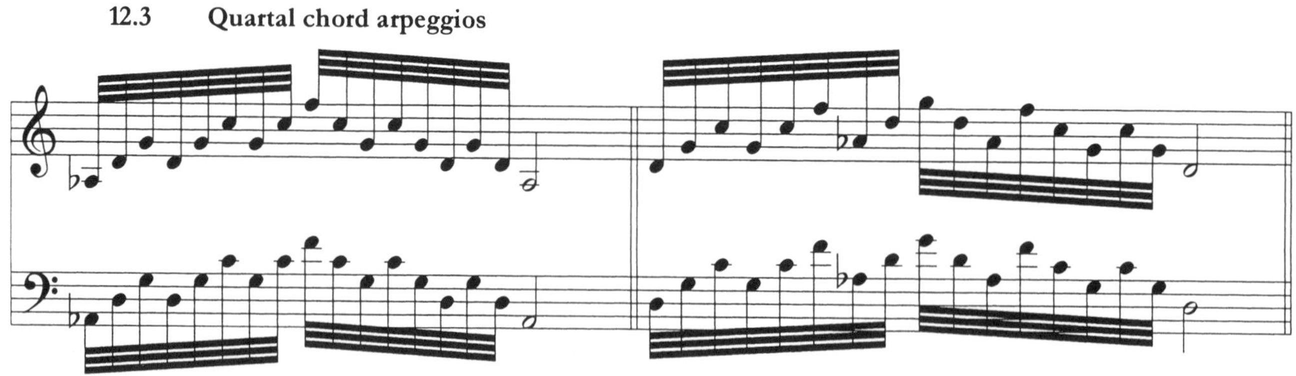

12.4 Quartal chord arpeggios

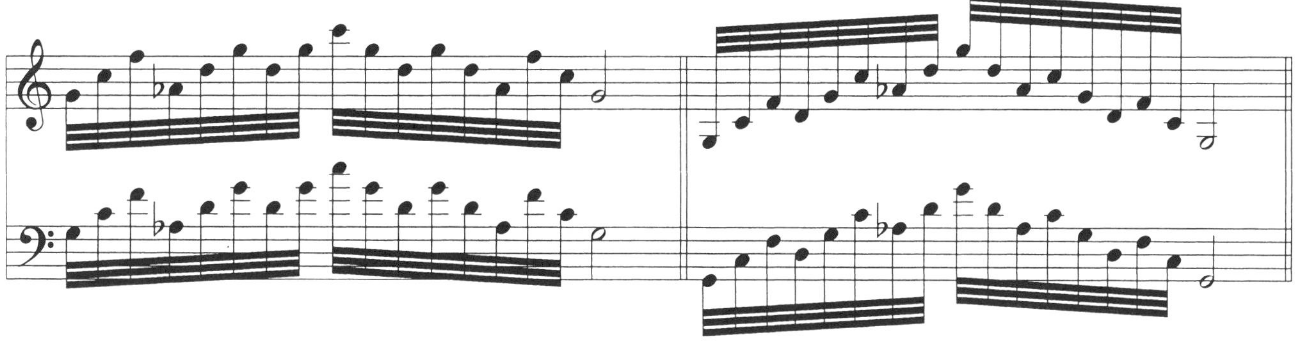

EXTENDED QUARTAL ARPEGGIOS APPLIED TO HARMONIC PROGRESSION IN MAJOR

These quartal voicings are from the first combination of the three quartal chords. The D minor pentatonic scale is the source for the Dm7 chord; the A♭ Kumoi scale is the source for the G7; an E minor pentatonic scale is the source for the Cmaj7 chord. Exercise 12.6 shows these large quartal structures as arpeggios. Each voice below moves smoothly through the progression.

12.5 Large quartal structures

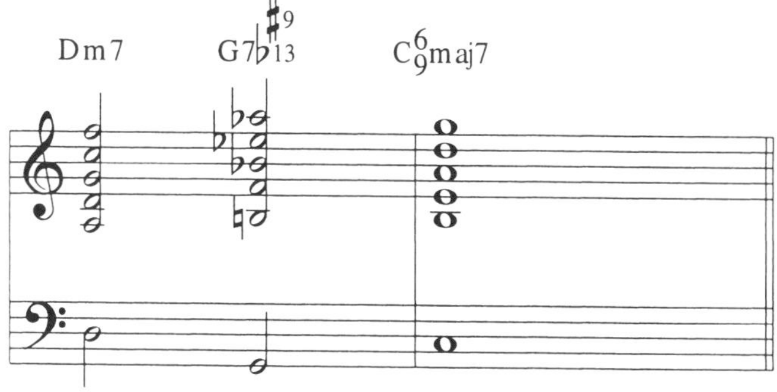

12.6 Quartal arpeggios from 12.5 applied to ii7 - V7alt. - I

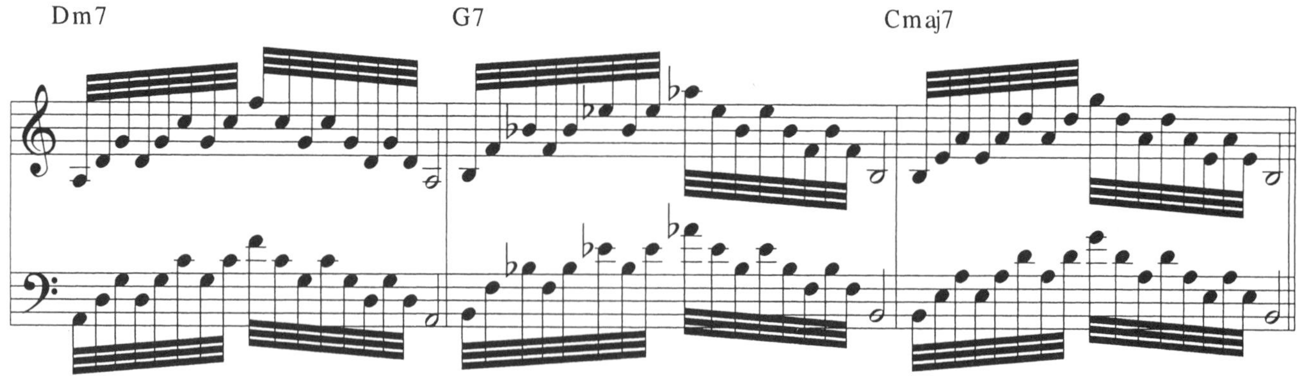

12.7 Large quartal structures

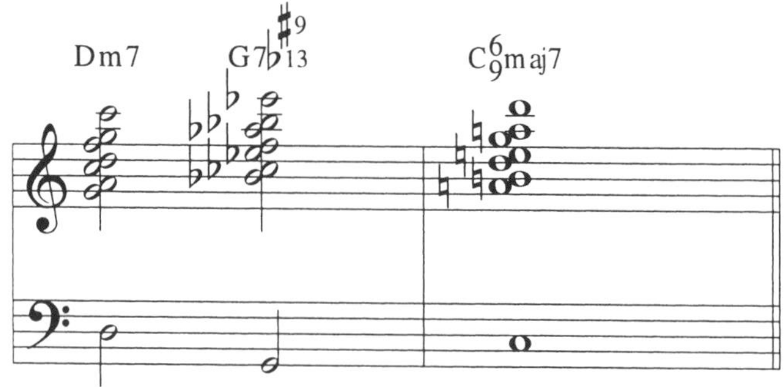

12.8 Quartal arpeggios from 12.7 applied to ii7 - V7alt. - I

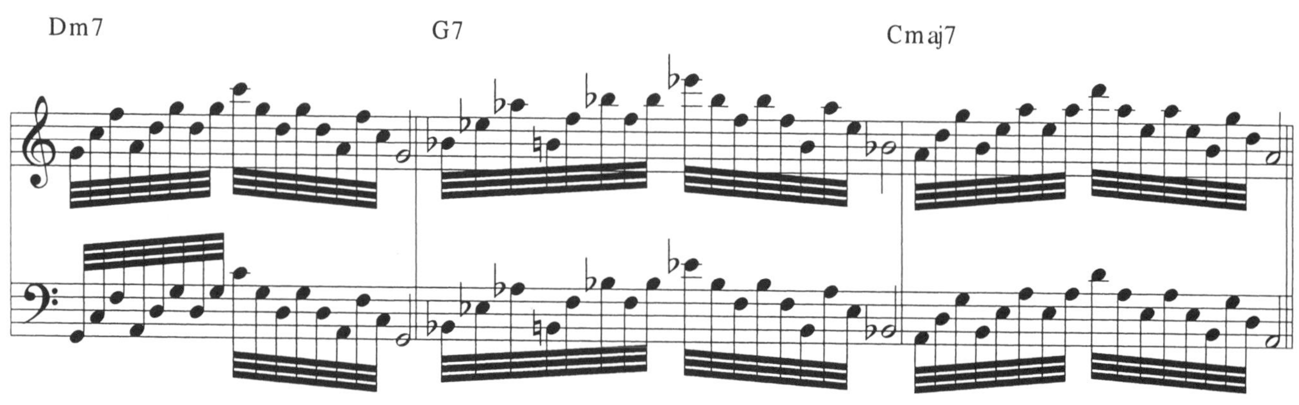

12.9 Large quartal structures

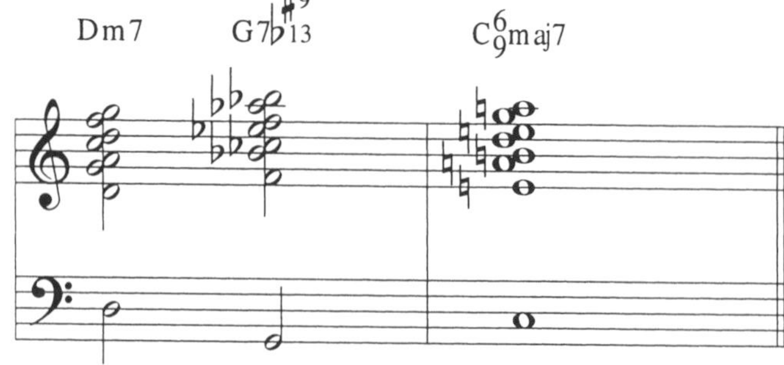

12.10 Quartal arpeggios from 12.9 applied to ii7 - V7alt. - I

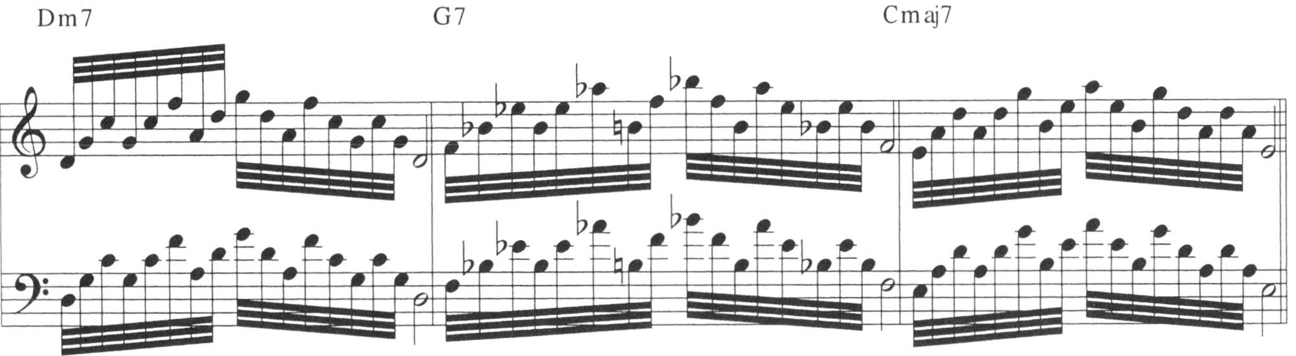

12.11 Large quartal structures

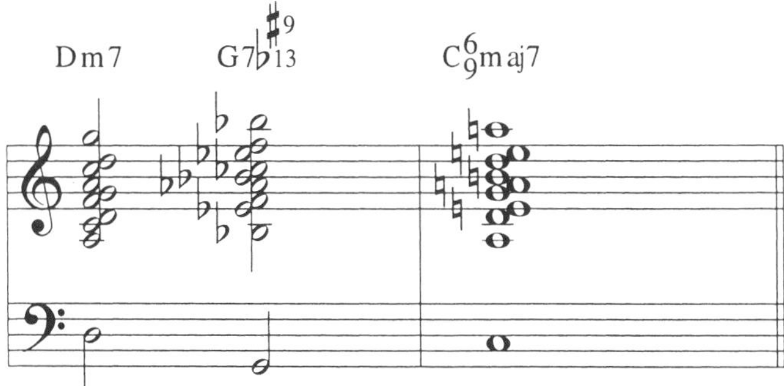

12.12 Quartal arpeggios from 12.11 applied to ii7 - V7alt. - I

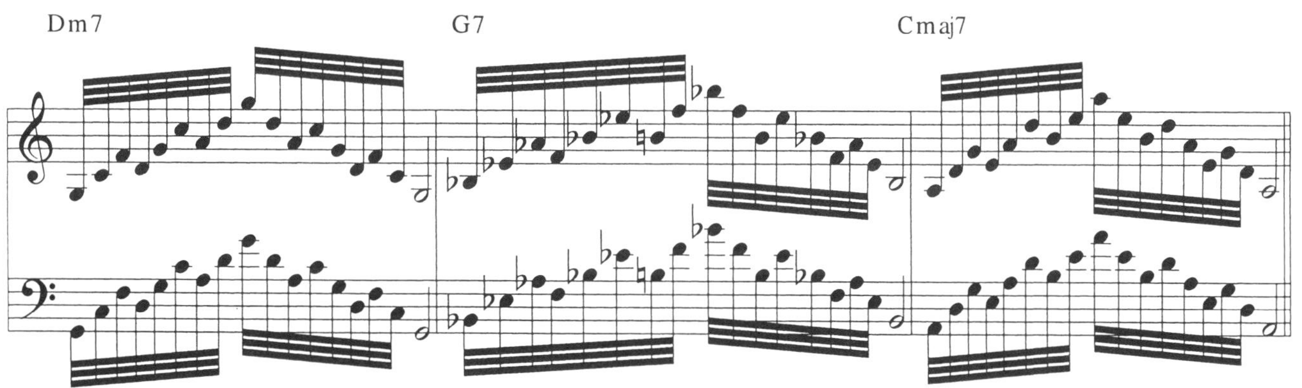

EXTENDED QUARTAL ARPEGGIOS APPLIED TO HARMONIC PROGRESSION IN MINOR

The next few exercises use the F Kumoi pentatonic over the Dø7, the A♭ Kumoi pentatonic over the G7, and the C minor pentatonic for Cm7.

12.13 **Large quartal structures**

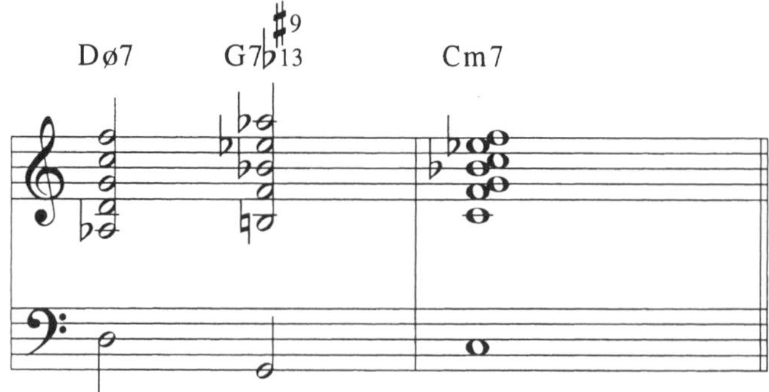

12.14 **Quartal arpeggios from 12.13 applied to Dø7 - G7alt. - Cm7 chord**

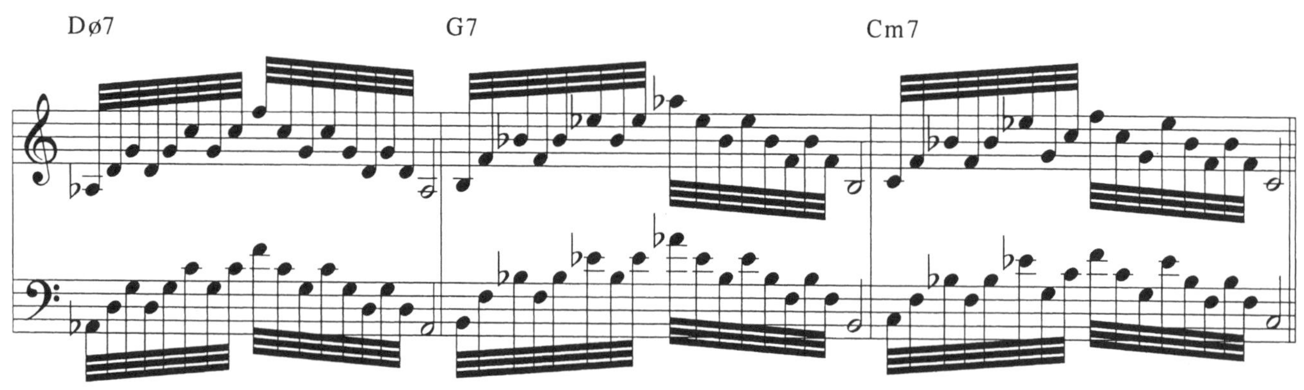

12.15 **Large quartal structures**

12.16 **Quartal arpeggios from 12.15 applied to Dø7 - G7alt. - Cm7 chord**

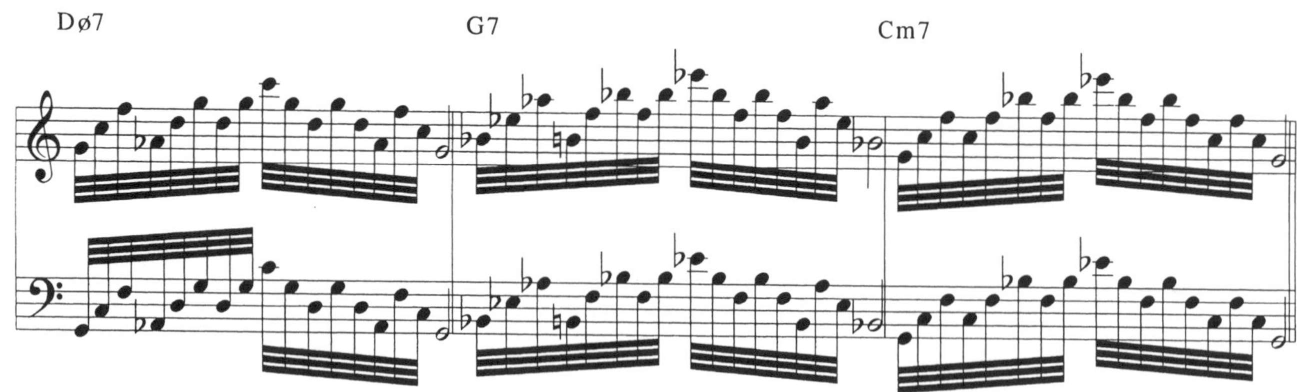

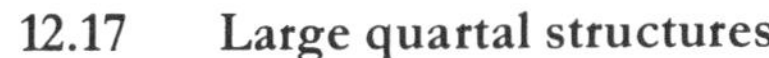

12.17 **Large quartal structures**

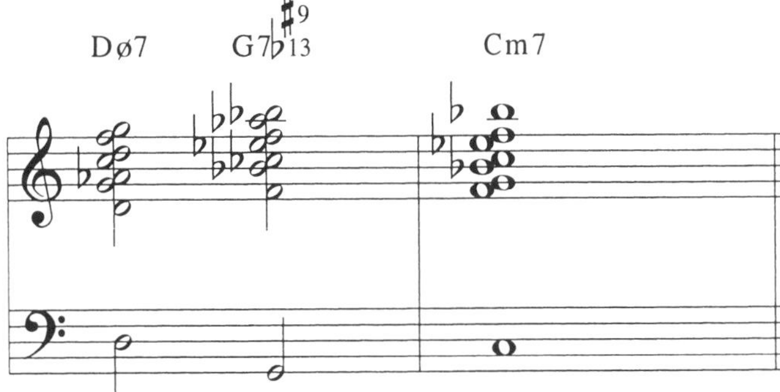

12.18 **Quartal arpeggios from 12.17 applied to Dø7 - G7alt. - Cm7 chord**

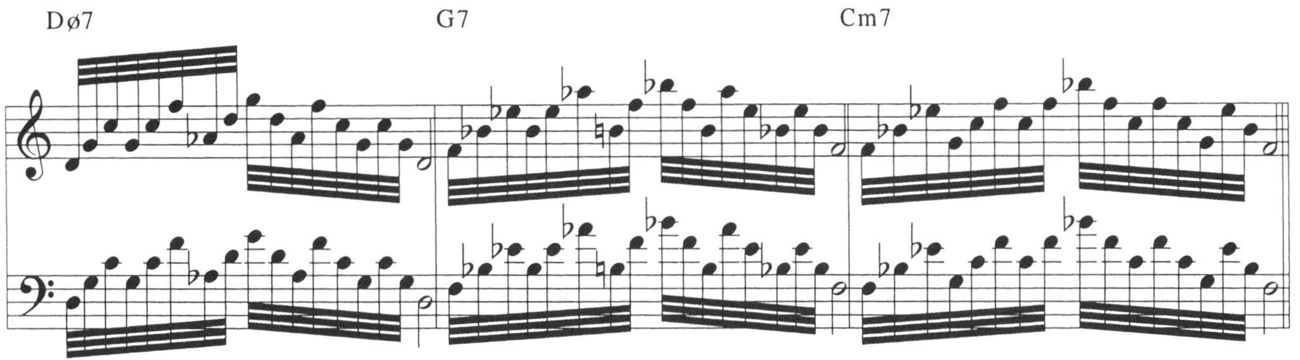

12.19 **Large quartal structures**

12.20 **Quartal arpeggios from 12.19 applied to Dø7 - G7alt. - Cm7 chord**

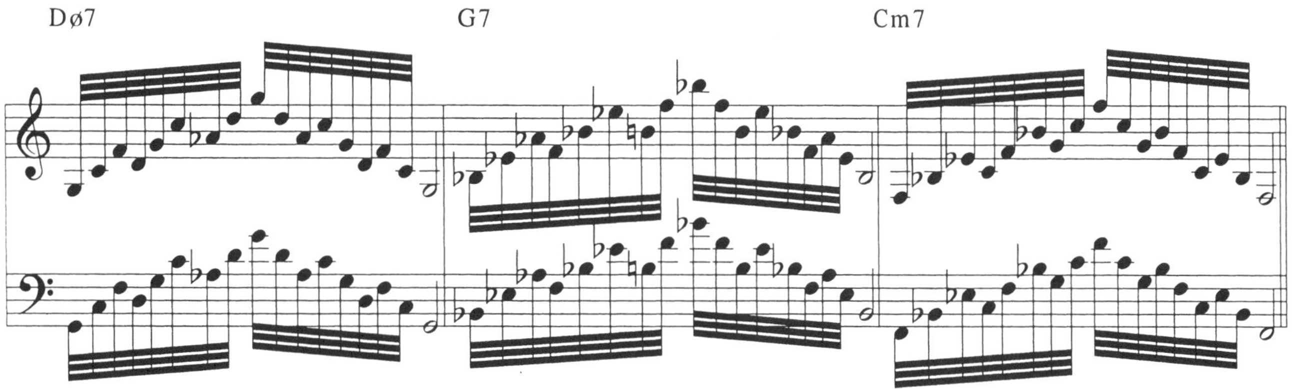

XIII. DOMINANT CHORD CYCLES

A jazz improviser will on occasion encounter harmonic progressions consisting of nothing more than a cycle of dominants never staying in one key for more than two beats. An example is shown below where eight different dominants occur in rapid succession within an eight measure phrase. These exercises are designed to prepare for those progressions.

13.1 Outline no.1: descending scale steps from 3rd of chord

This line moves step wise from third down to third. The line may be octave displaced by making a leap after arriving at the third. The treble clef line alternates between descending steps and the octave displacement. This exercise should be repeated beginning with the octave displacement as shown in the bass clef.

13.2 Outline no.2 & outline no.1

Practice this cycle two ways; first as shown, beginning with the broken chord outline no. 2 followed by the descending outline no. 1; secondly, beginning with the descending outline no. 1 followed by the broken chord outline no. 2.

13.3 Outline no.3 & 3-5-7-9 arpeggio

Practice this cycle two ways; first as shown, beginning with outline no. 3 line followed by the ascending 3-5-7-9 arpeggio; secondly, beginning with the ascending 3-5-7-9 arpeggio followed by outline no. 3.

13.4 Broken 3-5-R-7

Practice this cycle two ways; first as shown in the treble clef, a broken arpeggio followed by an ascending arpeggio, then as shown in the bass clef beginning with the ascending arpeggio followed by the broken arpeggio.

13.5 Broken 3-5-R-7 followed by outline no. 1

Practice this cycle two ways; first as shown with a broken 3-5-R-7 arpeggio followed by outline no. 1; then outline no. 1 followed by a broken 3-5-R-7 arpeggio.

13.6 Chromatic Approach to the 3rd

Be sure to practice this two ways: alternate leaping up or down from the 3rd to the root of each chord.

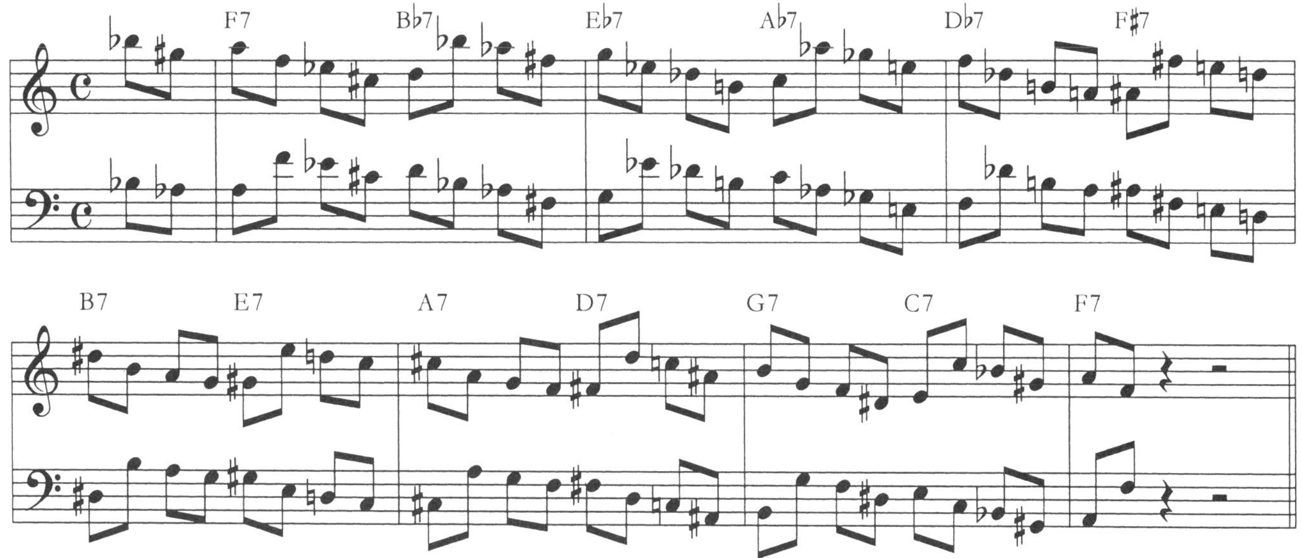

13.7 3-5-7-9 & Chromatic Approach

This exercise is valuable not only for dominant chord cycles, but for any chord moving down a fifth to any chord.

13.8 3-5-7-♭9 Arpeggio with common turn at the top

This line is in just about every jazz musician's vocabulary. It occurs several times in the melody to *Donna Lee*, both ascending (as shown in the treble clef m.1) and inverted (as shown in the treble clef m.2, where the 3rd leaps down to the 5th of the chord.)

These cycles can be useful for other progressions with fast harmonic rhythms. If you ignore the accidentals and imagine other key signatures, any of these cycle exercises will work as key center cycles. The progression for exercise 13.9 is: iii7 – vi7 – ii7 – V7 – I – IV – iiø7/vi – V7/vi – vi, etc.

13.9 Exercise 13.5 Applied to Key Center Cycle

XIV. DEVELOPING JAZZ EXERCISES

It would be an interesting experiment to take one CD, or maybe one solo on one CD and give it to a group of people to have them identify the phrase that intrigues them the most. Probably all of the responses would be different. What intrigues one would not interest the next as much. One may be drawn to a syncopated rhythmic figure, another to a fast and furious display of technique, others to a well placed color note. If they were asked to develop exercises from their favorite phrase completely different sets of exercises would be created. If they meticulously practiced the individualized exercises, they would certainly each develop different styles. The style they would develop would be their own, even though initial material might have been borrowed from someone else.

Throughout this book I hope you have been thinking of exercises that have been left out. If you are imagining other things to do, then you should follow your inspirations and add them to the exercise inventory. I hope that some sense has been made of the development of each series of exercises that will help you develop your own. I hope that by this point you can see the connection between the musical examples from each chapter and the exercises developed from them. The more you can imagine creating your own exercises and lines from musical ideas you hear in the air, the better equipped you will be to create your own voice as an artist. Do not depend on someone else to tell you what to hear and what to practice. Practice playing the things that interest you and you will develop your own voice and style.

I once overheard a student desperately trying to play a Charlie Parker solo. I use the word desperate meaning both frantic and hopeless. In no way was he prepared to play the solo, yet he wasted hours trying. I am not suggesting that the solo or playing other transcriptions is not worth the investment of time, just that there were other things he could have practiced first to better prepare himself. I do not recommend reading Goethe in German as a place to begin studying German. No one faces a major league pitcher with out having spent some time in the minors. This student would have spent his time better just examining the possibilities within the first few measures, developing exercises that would have prepared him for attempting to play and understanding Parker's entire improvisation.

This chapter will examine the first few measures of a typical Charlie Parker solo as a way of illustrating how musical material may be extracted and developed into melodic exercises. The recognition, extraction and developing process trains and strengthens the mental aspects of improvisation.

Below are the first three measures of the solo.

Begin by analyzing the first idea. Parker encircled the root of the chord with upper and lower neighbor tones and then played a descending arpeggio. This concept could then be applied to all major chords.

14.1 Isolating the first measure and playing it exactly for all major triads

If the line works for all major chords, conclude that it would work for all minor triads by lowering the third.

14.2 Isolating the first measure and playing it exactly for all minor triads

Would the line be useful if rhythmically displaced? Any rhythmic displacement that you invent could then be practiced for all major and minor chords.

14.3 Rhythmic Displacement

Examine the concepts in the first measure. The line begins by encircling the root of the B♭ chord with this pattern: lower neighbor tone - chord tone - upper neighbor tone - lower neighbor tone (LNT-CT-UNT-LNT). What follows the encircling is a descending arpeggio. Would that same pattern work musically when transposed to other parts of the chord? Practice these new concepts for all major and minor chords.

14.4 LNT-CT-UNT-LNT & descending arpeggio transposed to other parts of the chord:

Around the 3rd of B♭ major **Around the 5th of B♭ major**

The direction of the arpeggio could be changed from descending to ascending. Apply to all parts of all major and minor triads.

14.5 LNT-CT-UNT-LNT & ascending arpeggio transposed to other parts of the chord:

Around the root, 3rd, & 5th of B♭ major.

Develop exercises using subtraction: take away part of the idea. The next exercise uses a fragment of only the first six notes applied to the root, 3rd and 5th of the B♭ major triad. Practice for all major and minor chords.

14.6 Fragment of the idea

Around the root, 3rd, & 5th of B♭ major

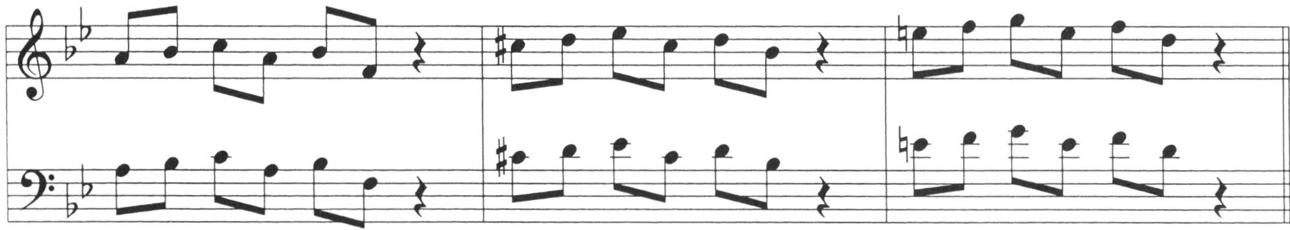

Use the fragments to create longer lines. The six note figure creates a syncopated figure over this B♭ passage in exercise 14.7. As always, if it works in B♭ major, it works in all major and minor keys.

14.7 Longer lines created out of a fragment of the original line

Here is another fragment from the original measure that can be developed by applying to other parts of the chord and transposed to all major and minor keys. This fragment, the fourth through the seventh notes of the first measure, begins with a leading tone to the root followed by an arpeggio.

14.8 Other fragments shown for B♭

Any of these triadic fragments could be applied to all diatonic chords. The last fragment show above in exercise 14.8 begins with the leading tone to the 5th followed by a descending arpeggio. This fragment is shown below in exercise 14.9 for all the diatonic chords in the key of B♭ major.

14.9 Other fragments shown for diatonic chords in B♭ major

Look back to the original solo. Parker played the pattern shown on beat two of exercise 14.9 at the start of m.2. If exercise 14.9 is musically useful with these triads in root position, practice them in other inversions for the diatonic triads.

14.10 14.8 shown for diatonic chords in inversion in the key of B♭ major

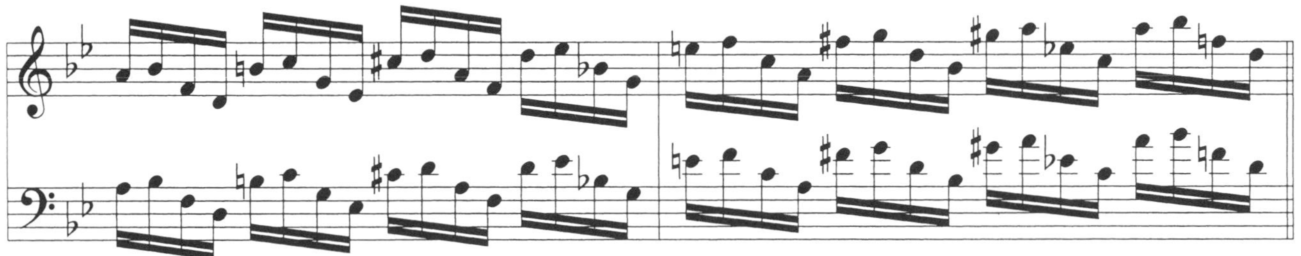

14.11 14.8 shown for diatonic chords in inversion in the key of B♭ major

How would the exercise sound turned upside down? Exercises 14.9-14.11 begin with a leading tone approaching a chord tone followed by a descending arpeggio. Exercises 14.12-14.14 begin with a upper neighbor tone approaching a chord tone followed by an ascending arpeggio.

14.12 UNT and ascending arpeggio for diatonic chords in the key of B♭ major

14.13 UNT and ascending arpeggio for diatonic chords in inversion in the key of B♭ major

14.14 UNT and ascending arpeggio for diatonic chords in inversion in the key of B♭ major

All of these exercises can and should be applied to all major and minor triads.

OTHER IDEAS TO EXPLORE

- Are there other fragments worth examining?
- Are there other exercises to develop using neighbor tones and arpeggios?
- Are there ways to combine any of the above exercises?
- Apply these and other concepts to develop exercises from other excerpts of your choice.
- Apply these idea to specific chord progressions and compositions.

Teachers open the door, but you must enter by yourself.
—Chinese Proverb

XV. OUTLINE EXERCISES

There are three common patterns used by composers and improvisers to connect the harmony in a linear way that this book refers to as outlines. An outline is typically the skeleton framework, the general contour and shape of an object. I have found that thousands of musical lines have the same basic framework and yet can sound completely unique. This is comparable to discovering that thousands of doors are rectangular, but can be finished in many styles from simple to ornate. Example of outlines can be found in any musical style period that uses traditional harmonic progressions. The outlines are plentiful in the be-bop vocabulary. There are entire solos by Clifford Brown based on nothing but outline no.1. There are hundreds of examples, explanations and exercises in my books, *Connecting Chords With Linear Harmony* and in chapter 10 of *Jazz Theory Resources.* In order to make this book a complete set of exercises, I have included several outline exercises not included in *Connecting Chords With Linear Harmony* and *Jazz Theory Resources.*

The three common outlines connect the chords using linear harmony. The harmony is a result of linear motion. The lines include the most important harmonic notes and follow the basic voice leading principles.

Outline no.1 begins on the third of a chord and moves down the scale to the seventh. The seventh, a dissonant tone, resolves to the third of the chord that follows. Outline no.1 can be sequenced through a progression where chord roots continue to move down in fifths. Outline no.1 is shown below connecting the ii7 to the V7 chord in C major and the iiø7 to the V7 chord in C minor.

Outline no.2 begins with the 1-3-5 arpeggio and then adds the dissonant seventh. The seventh resolves as expected to the third of the chord that follows. Because the seventh resolves to the next third, outline no.2 is often followed by outline no.1 that begins on the third. Outline no.2 is shown below connecting the ii7 to the V7 chord in C major and the iiø7 to the V7 chord in C minor.

Outline no.3 begins with the descending arpeggio 5-3-1 and then adds the dissonant seventh. The seventh resolves as expected to the third of the chord that follows. Because the seventh resolves to the next third, outline no.3 is also often followed by outline no.1 that begins on the third. Since the seventh resolves to the third of the chord that follows a 3-5-7-9 arpeggio also may follow outline no.3. Outline no.3 is shown below connecting the ii7 to the V7 chord in C major and the iiø7 to the V7 chord in C minor.

Practice the following outlines over ii7 - V7 - I and iiø7 - V7 - i in all major and minor keys.

OUTLINES OVER ii7 - V7 IN MAJOR

15.1 Outline no.1 **Outline no.2** **Outline no.3**

Dm7 G7 Dm7 G7 Dm7 G7

OUTLINES OVER ii7 - V7 IN Minor

15.1 Outline no.1 **Outline no.2** **Outline no.3**

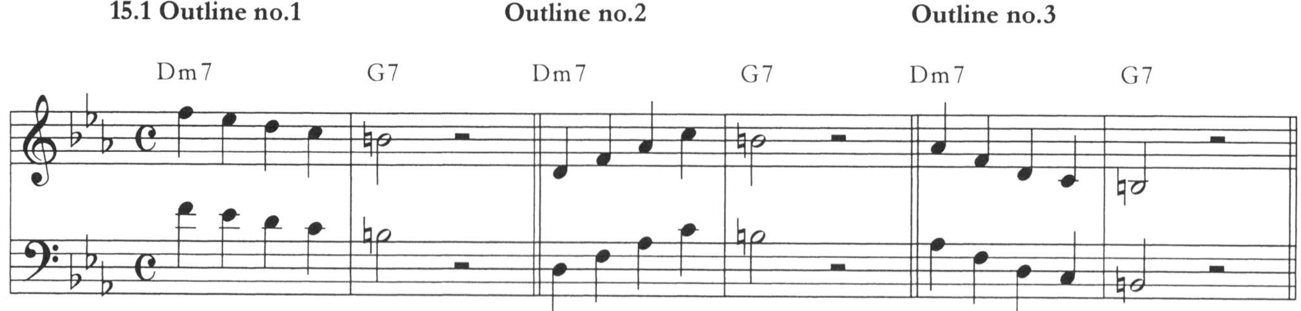

There are hundreds of examples shown of outlines in the books, *Connecting Chords With Linear Harmony*, and *Jazz Theory Resources*, with various degrees of difficulty and complexity. A few examples should be included here for clarity. Tom Harrell used outline no.1 to connect the ii7 to the V7 and the V7 to the I chord in the first example below. Miles Davis played the same outline in the key of B♭. The 3rd in both examples is approached chromatically from above.

Simple outline no. 1 for ii7 – V7 – I in F   for ii7 – V7 – I in B♭

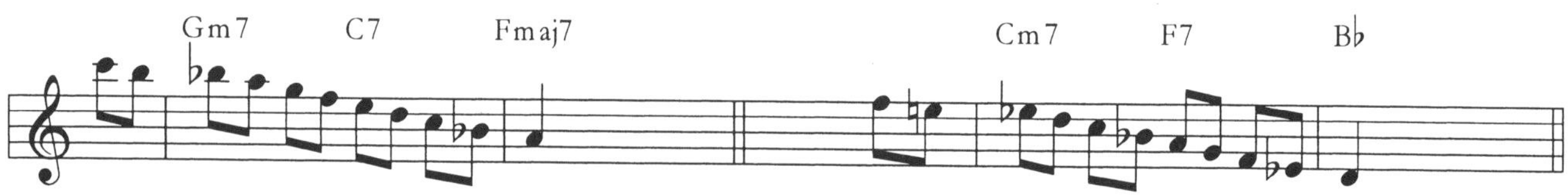

Charlie Parker used the same outline that Harrell and Davis used, but here the passage is in F minor.

Simple outline no. 1 for iiø7 – V7 – i in F minor

Roger Pemberton played outline no.1 over the ii7 - V7 - I in F major in a more elaborate fashion. Pemberton began with an arpeggio, encircled the G with upper and lower neighbor tones, approached E chromatically from below, and flats the ninth (D♭) on the way to the third of F. The important tones are in significant places and the dissonances resolve where expected.

Elaborate outline no.1 over ii7 - V7 - I in F major.

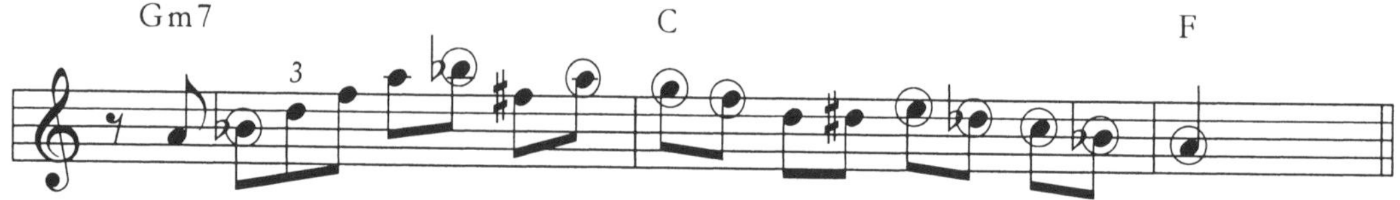

Erroll Garner may not have been able to read music, but he used outline no.2 and outline no.1 in the following excerpt.

Outline no.2 followed by outline no.1.

Joe Pass used outline no.2 with passing tones and follows it with a C triad encircled by upper and lower neighbor tones. Outline no.1 occurs in the last measure connecting C7 to F.

Outline no.2

Clifford Brown included lower neighbor and passing tones for outline no.2 connecting Dm7 to G7 and a 3-5-7-9 arpeggio as part of outline no.1 to connect G7 to C in the following example.

Outline no.2 followed by outline no.1.

Outline no.3 is often followed by outline no.1 as illustrated by the first excerpt from John Coltrane, and outline no.3 is also often followed by a 3-5-7-9 arpeggio as illustrated by the second excerpt from Jimmy Guiffre.

Outline no.3. followed by outline no.1 for D7 - G.

Outline no.3. followed by 3-5-7-9 arpeggio

Roger Pemberton used outline no.3 followed by the 3-5-7-9 arpeggio in the following example. The harmonic rhythm in this excerpt is different from the previous two. The longer values for each chord allow more time for and sometimes demand more elaboration. He used a stop and go rhythm and encircles the Bb and the G using upper and lower neighbor tones. The common practice is for upper neighbor tones to be from the diatonic scale and for lower neighbor tones to be chromatic.

Outline no.3 encircling and 3-5-7-9 arpeggio

OUTLINE EXERCISES

Here is a collection of melodic ideas in major and minor keys over standard ii7 - V7 - I and iiø7 - V7 - i progressions based primarily on the three common outlines. These progressions and outlines are the building blocks for much of the jazz literature and vocabulary. Learning to play these lines will get your fingers moving in the right directions connecting the chords, train your ears to hear these connections, and acquaint you with traditional embellishment and figuration devices. All of these can and should be systematically transposed into all twelve major and all twelve minor keys. Remember: difficult keys become less difficult with practice. There are tips on how to learn these outlines in all twelve keys beginning on page ???. Try to memorize several lines each week. As the weeks go by, the next ones to memorize will become easier. Take some of these lines and compose "improvisations" over standard jazz tunes and use these solos as etudes. Try composing one or more etude every week. Add several thousand of your own outline idea to this collection. Take the exercises that are here, find new ones from performances of other jazz musicians and search for different outcomes. When you practice, make them swing. Swing feel is achieved not only from the eighth note feel, but by accenting the tops of lines and various dynamic shadings to bring out the rhythmic character of the line. Keep the metronome clicking!

Remember: difficult keys become less difficult with practice.

OUTLINES OVER KEY CENTER CYCLE:
ii7 - V7 - I - IV - iiø7/vi - V7/vi - vi - V7/ii

Play outlines for connecting all the chords in this key center cycle. This key center cycle is used in many Baroque and Classical compositions, and dozens of jazz standards.

15.3 Outline no. 1 through key center cycle

15.4 **Inserting a 3-5-7-9 arpeggio connects the first and second notes of exercise 15.3.**

Try some variations on exercise 15.4 by adding a leading tone before each 3rd as in 15.5, or chromatic approaches as in 15.6

15.5 The 3-5-7-9 arpeggio outline no.1 exercise leading tone to the 3rd

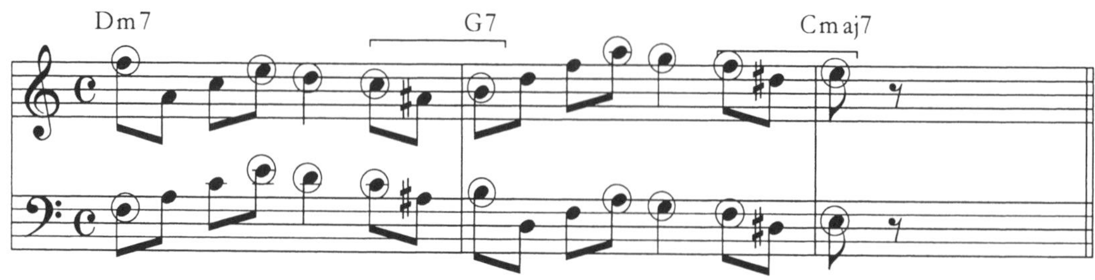

15.6 The 3-5-7-9 arpeggio outline no.1 exercise with the addition of the chromatic approaches

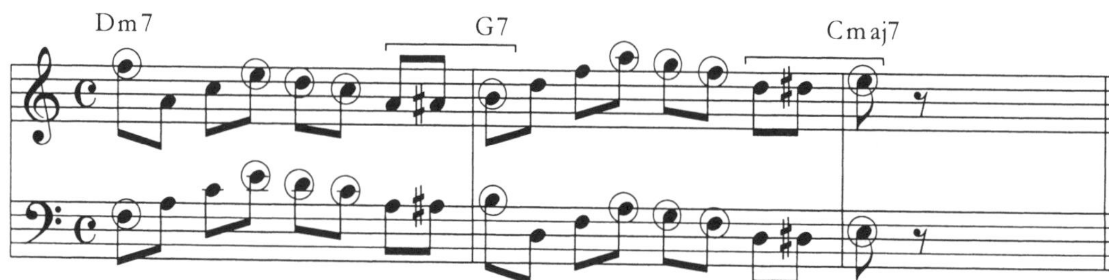

15.8 **Play outline no.2 connecting all the chords in this key center cycle (ii7 - V7 - I - IV - iiø7/vi - V7/vi - vi - V7/ii). The pattern is actually outline no.2 followed by outline no.1, and then the reverse on the second half of the exercise.**

15.9 Play outline no.3 connecting all the chords in this key center cycle (ii7 - V7 - I - IV - iiø7/vi - V7/vi - vi - V7/ii). The pattern is actually outline no.3 followed by a 3-5-7-9 arpeggio, and then the reverse on the second half of the exercise.

OUTLINES IN COMBINATIONS

Outlines often occur in combinations. With the three outlines, nine combinations may be used and should be practiced for ii7 - V7 - I and iiø7 - V7 - i progressions in all major and minor keys.

15.10 Outline no.1 followed by outline no.1

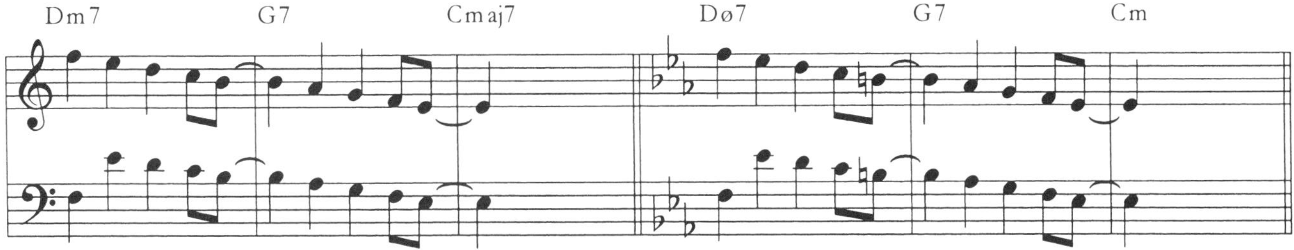

15.11 Outline no.1 followed by outline no.2

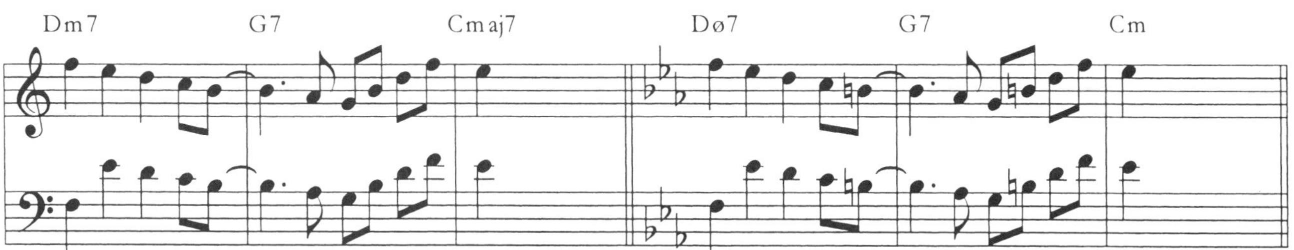

15.12 Outline no.1 followed by outline no.3

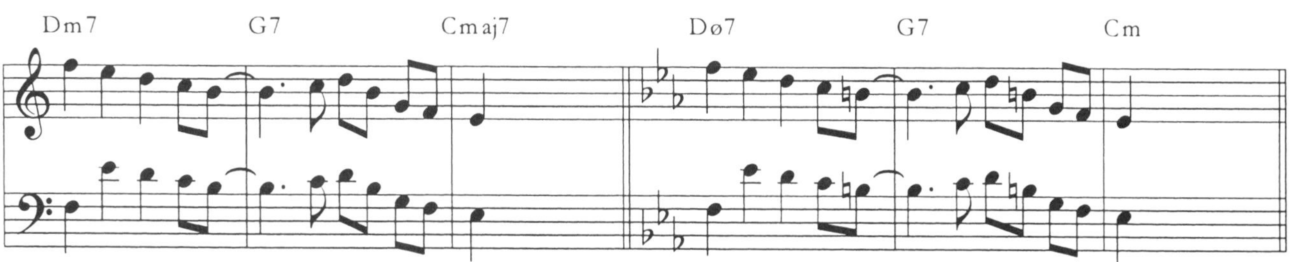

15.13 Outline no.1 followed by outline no.1

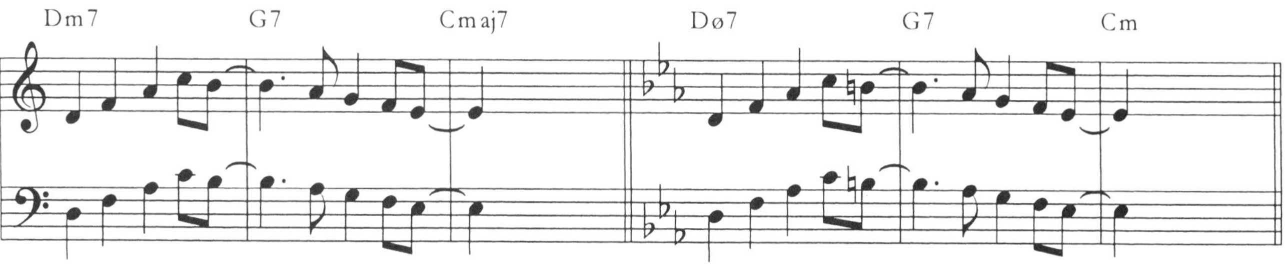

15.14 Outline no.2 followed by outline no.2

15.15 Outline no.2 followed by outline no.3

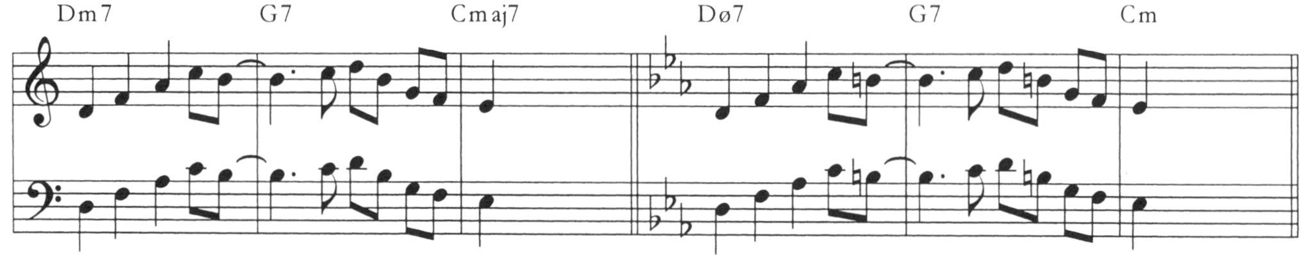

15.16 Outline no.3 followed by outline no.1

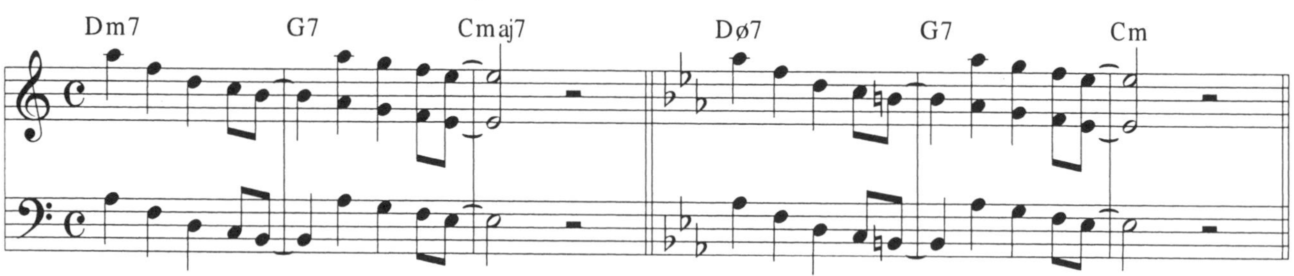

15.17 Outline no.3 followed by outline no.2

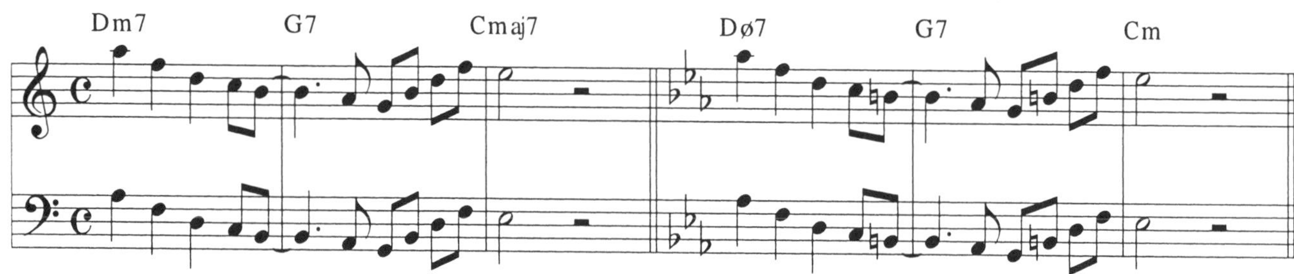

15.18 Outline no.3 followed by outline no.3

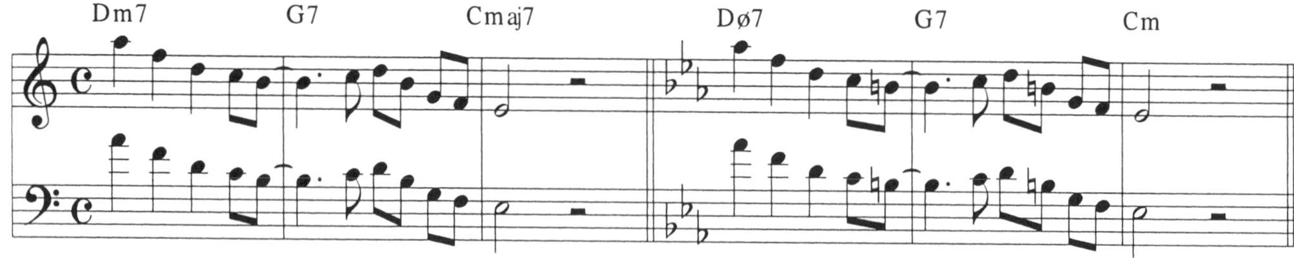

COMMON CHROMATIC APPROACHES

Common chromatic approaches were discussed beginning on page 31. Clifford Brown used several in the following sequences.

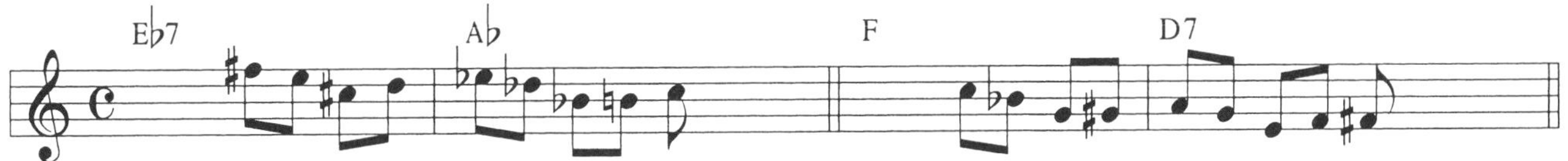

Add the following common chromatic approaches to the outline vocabulary.

15.19 **Chromatic approaches added to outline no.1 exercises. Major thirds are approached from below and minor thirds from above.**

15.20 **Chromatic approaches added to outline no.1 exercises. This is the same line as the previous example, but rhythmically displaced. The resolution of each chord is delayed until beat three.**

15.21 Chromatic approaches added to outline no.2 exercises.

15.22 Outline no.3 with chromatic approaches and encircling chord tones using diatonic and chromatic neighbor tones.

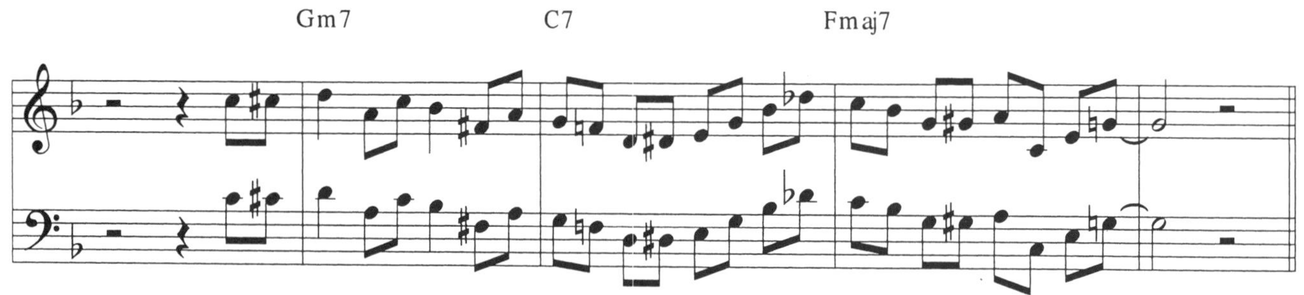

15.23 Outline no.1 encircling thirds of each chord.

15.24 Outline no.2 with third of tonic chord approached with leading tone (LT).

15.25 This exercise begins the same as the previous exercise, but on the downbeat of beat one. A lower neighbor tone (LNT) is added before outline no.2 begins.

15.26 This outline no.2 exercise begins the same as the previous two exercises, but on the downbeat of beat four as a pickup. D is followed by a LT and there is a chromatic approach leading to the third of the tonic chord.

15.27 Outline no.3 with scalar & chromatic approaches.

15.28 Outline no.3. Begins LT, includes chromatic encircling. The musical shape in the first measure is echoed in the last.

15.29 **Outline no.1 in G minor. The third of the iiø7 is encircled with UNTs & LNTs, the third of the tonic chord is approached chromatically from above.**

15.30 **Outline no.2 in D minor. Scalar approach, 3-5-7-9 arpeggio on the dominant.**

15.31 **Outline no.1 in D minor. Third of iiø7 chord is encircled with UNTs & LNTs, 3-5-7-9 cliché on the dominant, and delayed resolution to the tonic.**

15.32 **Outline no.2 cycle on turnaround progression: ii7 - V7 - I - V7/ii. Starting the exercise in the third measure creates another typical turnaround progression: I - V7/ii - ii7 - V7. The arpeggiated dominant figure occurs over both dominant chords with octave displacement.**

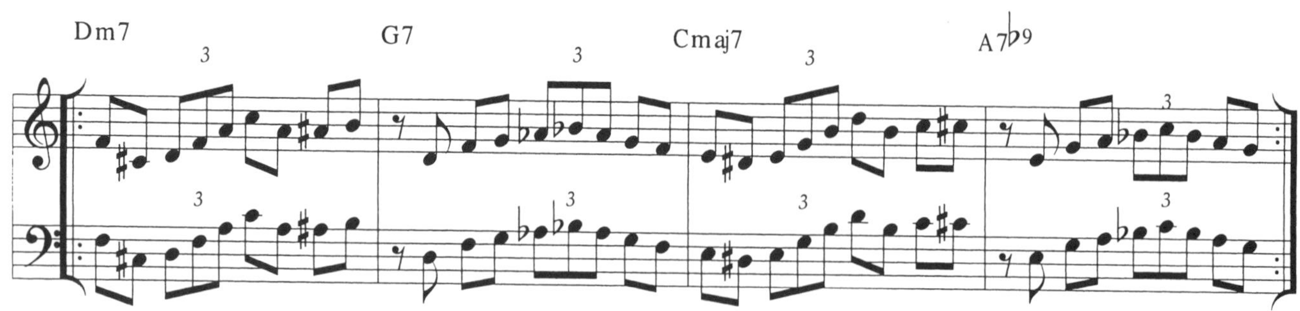

15.33 **Outline no.2 cycle on turnaround progression: ii7 - V7 - I - V7/ii. Starting the exercise in the third measure creates another typical turnaround progression: I - V7/ii - ii7 - V7. Practice this exercise with a mixture of octave displacement over the dominant chord measures.**

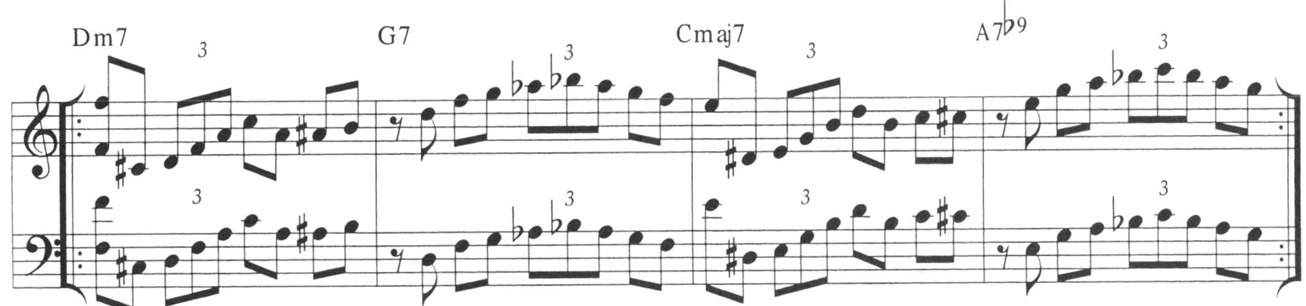

15.34 **Outline no.1 cycle on turnaround progression: ii7 - V7 - I - V7/ii. Starting the exercise in the third measure creates another typical turnaround progression: I - V7/ii - ii7 - V7. The arpeggiated dominant figure occurs over both dominant chords with octave displacement.**

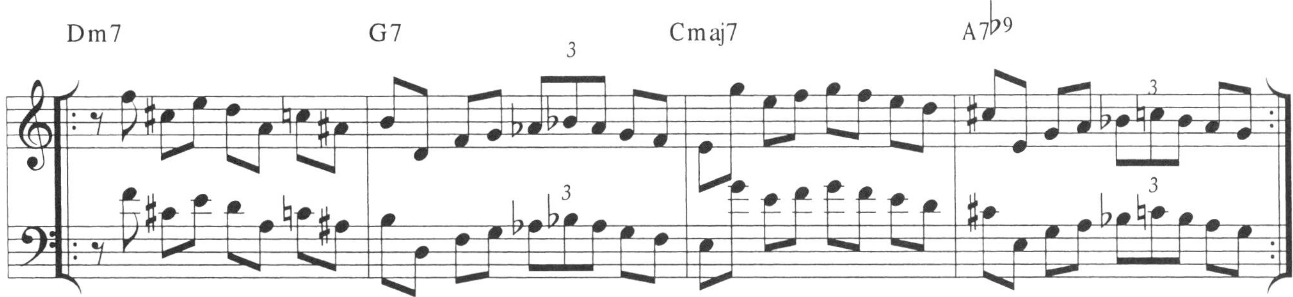

15.35 **Outline no.3 cycle on turnaround progression: ii7 - V7 - I - V7/ii. Starting the exercise in the third measure creates another typical turnaround progression: I - V7/ii - ii7 - V7. Practice this exercise with a mixture of octave displacement over the dominant chord measures.**

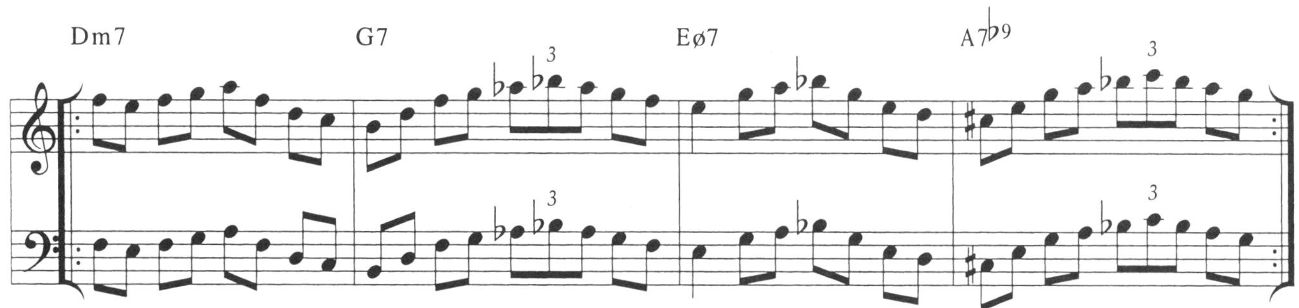

15.36 **Outline no.3 cycle on turnaround progression: ii7 - V7 - I - V7/ii. Starting the exercise in the third measure creates another typical turnaround progression: I - V7/ii - ii7 - V7. The arpeggiated dominant figure occurs over both dominant chords with octave displacement.**

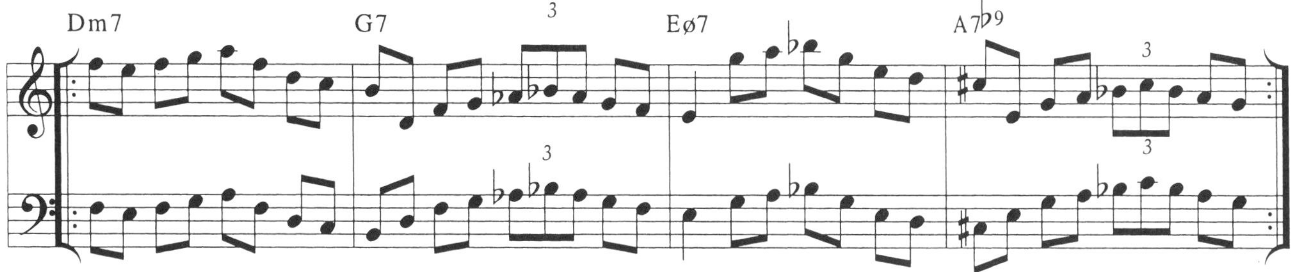

15.37 Outline no.2 cycle on turnaround progression: ii7 - V7 - iiø7/ii - V7/ii. Starting the exercise in the third measure creates another typical turnaround progression: iiø7/ii - V7/ii - ii7 - V7. The initial arpeggios extend beyond the 7th. A 5-3-2-1 minor pattern is used over the dominant chords a half-step above the root. (A♭ minor/G7, B♭ minor/A7)

15.38 Outline no.2 cycle on turnaround progression: ii7 - V7 - iiø7/ii - V7/ii. Starting the exercise in the third measure creates another typical turnaround progression: iiø7/ii - V7/ii - ii7 - V7. The initial arpeggios extend beyond the 7th. The CMAR quote is used over the dominants emphasizing the minor chord a half-step above the root of the dominant. (G♭ minor/F7, A♭ minor/G7).

15.39 Outline no.2 cycle on turnaround progression: ii7 - V7 - I - V7/ii. Starting the exercise in the third measure creates another typical turnaround progression: I - V7/ii - ii7 - V7. The initial arpeggios extend beyond the 7th.

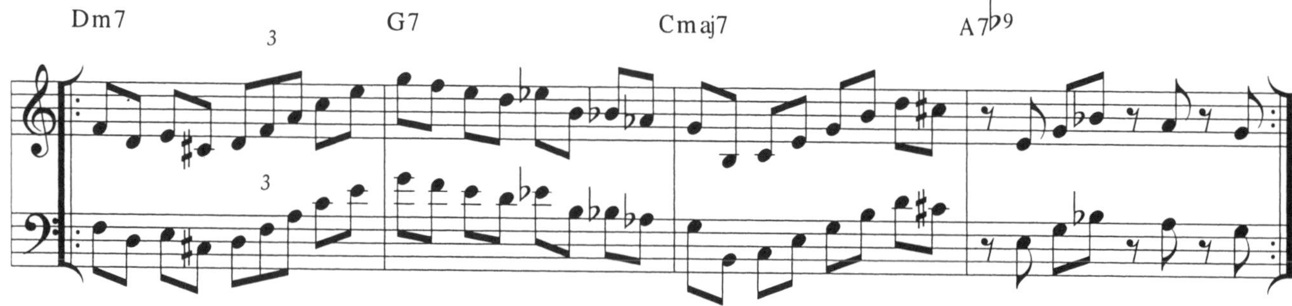

15.40 Outline no.1 in A minor. Delayed resolutions. The 3-5-7-9 arpeggio of the E7 chord spills over into the A minor measure.

15.41 **Outline no.1 in A minor. Similar to the previous exercise.**

15.42 **Outline no.1 in A minor. Similar to the previous two exercises.**

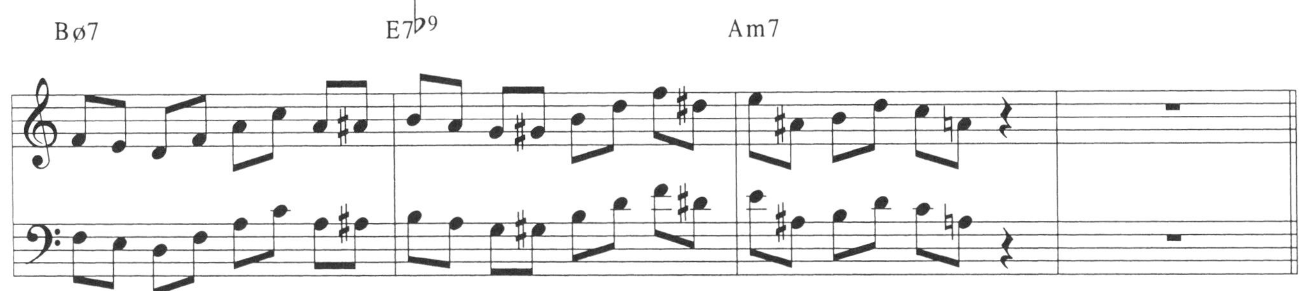

15.43 **Outline no.1 in A minor. Begins with chromatic approach from above and below the third of the iiø7 chord and includes a chromatic approach from above to the third of the tonic.**

15.44 **Outline no.1 in A minor. Only uses diatonic tones (which includes the leading tone, G♯)**

15.45 **Outline no.2 in D minor. Uses cyclical quadruplet pattern on iiø7 chord and inverted 3-5-7-9 arpeggio on V7 chord. The use of arpeggiated escape tones in the D minor measure gives more angularity to what would have been a simple 5-4-3-2-1 descending scale pattern (shown with circled notes).**

15.46 **Outline no.2 in D minor. Uses cyclical quadruplet pattern on iiø7 chord.**

15.47 **Outline no.3 in G minor.**

15.48 **The accents of the previous exercise create a series of dotted quarter notes superimposed over the quarter note pulse as shown below.**

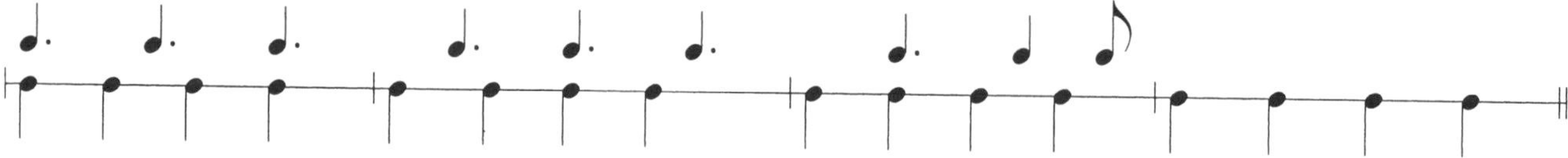

15.49 Outline no.2 in D minor. The initial arpeggio extends to the ninth delaying the resolution to the A7 chord. Note the use of what sounds like an E♭7 chord in the second half of the m.3. The E♭7 chord is the tritone dominant substitute for A7. (This tritone substitute as written below would in traditional music be called an augmented sixth chord: C♯ - E♭ - G - B♭.)

15.50 Outline no.1 in G minor. Note the use of a D♭ major 7 arpeggio over the Gø7, and the A♭ major fragments over the C7.

15.51 This exercise covers a lot of real estate. A broken chord pattern is used (as shown following the exercise). The addition of a leading tone to each pair of notes suggests the dotted quarter note rhythm as shown after exercise 15.47.

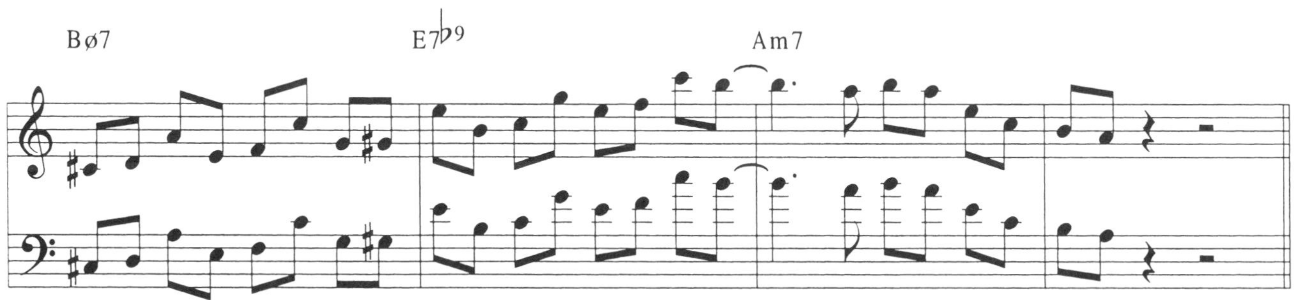

Basic structure of exercise 15.51

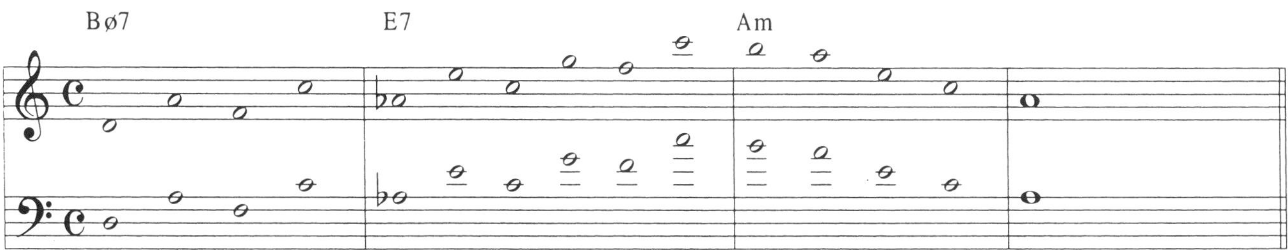

15.52 Outline no.1 in A minor utilizing leaps, chromatic approaches and encircling.

15.53 Outline no.3 in F minor with a several encircling patterns.

15.54 Outline no.2 with encircling patterns.

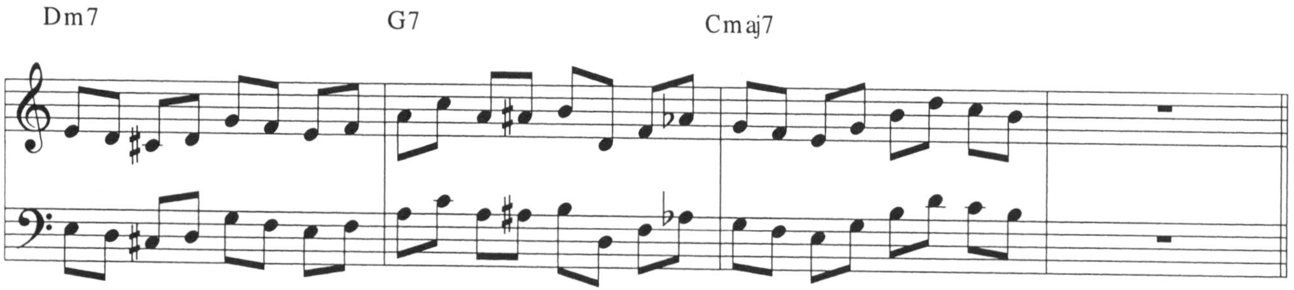

15.55 Outline no.2 with encircling patterns.

15.56 Outline no.1 with chromatic approaches and encircling patterns.

15.57 **Outline no.1 with chromatic approaches and encircling patterns.**

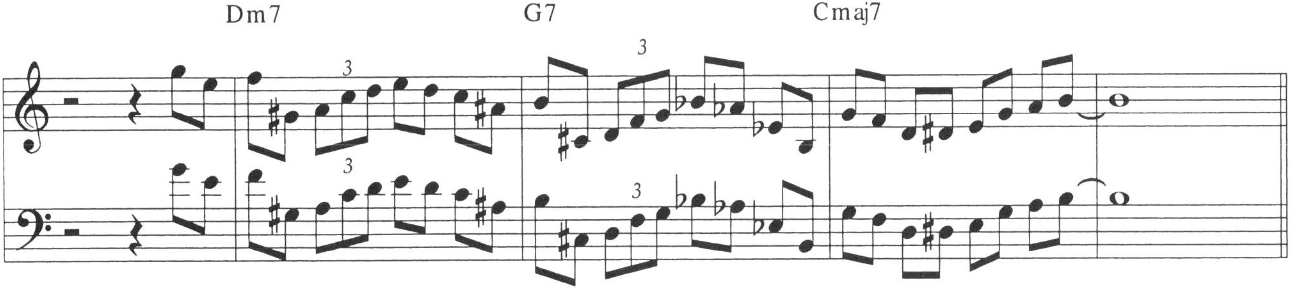

15.58 **Outline no.2. Note the deceptive resolution from Dm7 to G7. The C, the seventh of Dm7 is expected to resolve to the B, the third of G. Moving up to the C♯ defies the voice leading gravity and delays the resolution to B until beat three. Knowing the expected voice leading may help you create lines that do the unexpected.**

15.59 **Outline no.2. Deceptive resolutions to both G7 and Cmaj7.**

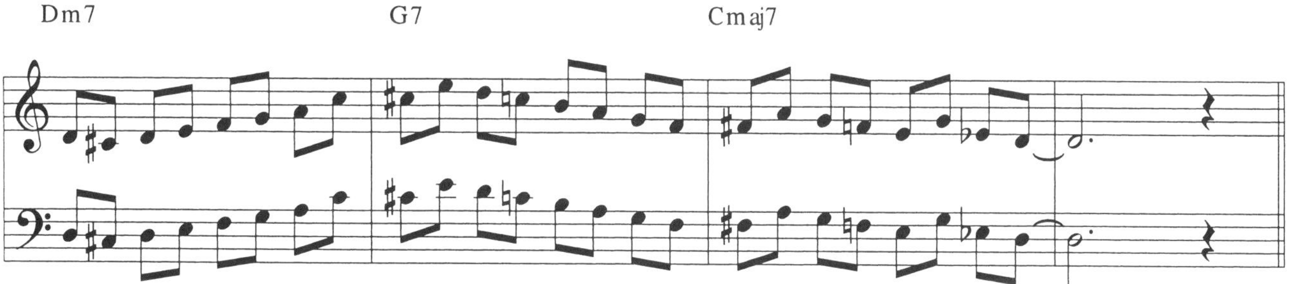

15.60 **Outline no.3 with leading tones, and chromatic encircling.**

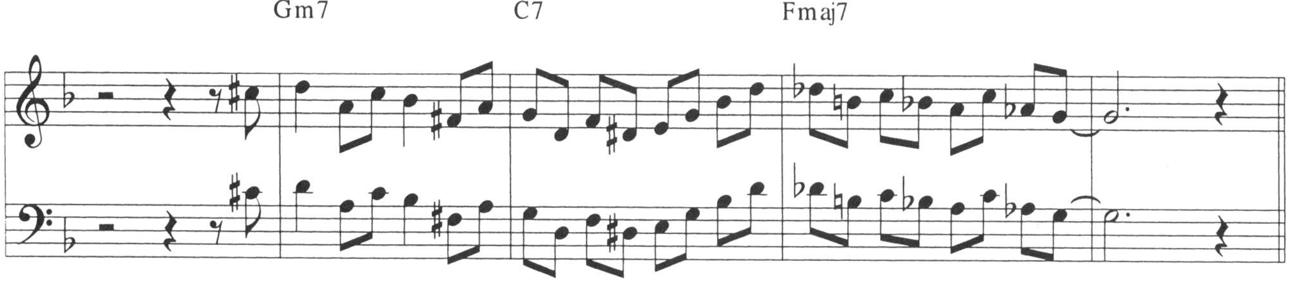

15.61 Outline no.3. Deceptive and delayed resolutions.

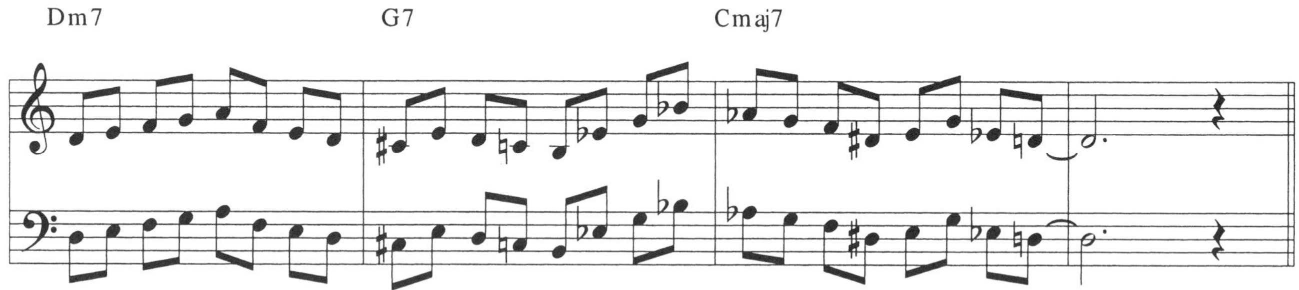

OUTLINES OVER LONGER PROGRESSIONS

15.62 Outline no.1 with various devices over iii7 - V7/ii - ii7 - V7 - I progression.

15.63 Outline no.2 with various devices over iii7 - V7/ii - ii7 - V7 - I progression.

15.64 Outline no.3 with various devices over iii7 - V7/ii - ii7 - V7 - I progression.

15.65 Outline no.3 with various devices over ii7 - V7 - I - V7/ii - ii7 - V7 - I progression.

15.66 **Outlines with various devices over ii7 - V7 - I - IV - iiø7/vi - V7/vi - vi progression.**

15.67 **Outline no.2 in m.1, outline no.2 in m.3, outline no.1 in mm.4-7.**

15.68 Outline no.3 with neighbor tones over iiø7/ii - V7/ii - ii7 - V7 - I progression.

15.69 Cycle emphasizing encircling and chromatic approaches over ii7 - V7 - I - V7/ii.

MORE ii7 - V7 - I & iiø7 - V7 - i EXERCISES

15.70 Outline no.1 with various devices in A minor.

15.71 Outline no.1 with various devices in F minor.

15.72 Outline no.2 with various devices in C minor. The upper extensions of the Dø7 chord suggests locrian ♮2, the sixth mode of F melodic minor. The line over the G7 suggests G superlocrian (7th mode of A♭ melodic minor) or the 3rd mode of E♭ major ♭6.

15.73 Outline no.2. The upper extensions of the Bø7 chord suggests locrian ♮2, the sixth mode of D melodic minor. The line over the E7 suggests E superlocrian (7th mode of F melodic minor) or the 3rd mode of C major ♭6.

15.74 In F minor. The A♮ suggests Gø7♯2; there is an A♭ melodic idea over the C7 and a CMAR quote over the F minor.

15.75 An A minor progression.

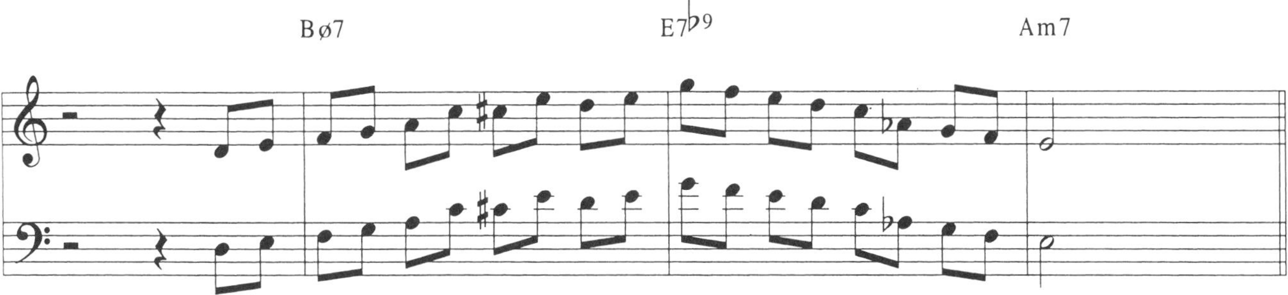

15.76 Upper extensions emphasized.

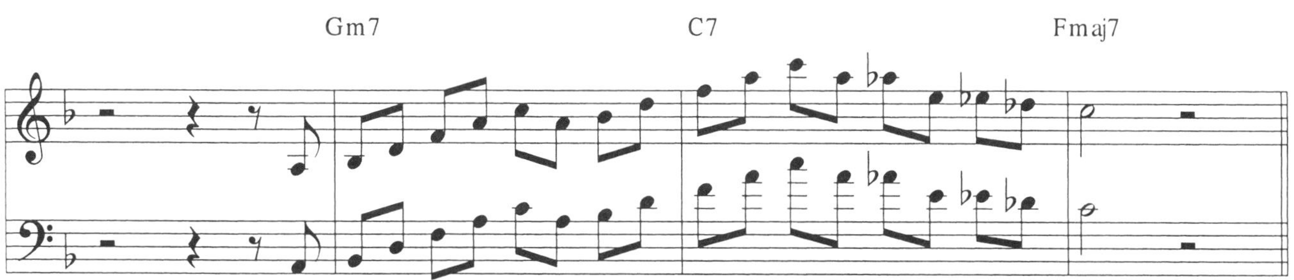

15.77 B♭maj7 implied over Eø7. Note the similarity to the previous exercise. The same material (B♭ major 7 arpeggio) is used for the previous ii7 in F major and the iiø7 in the relative D minor.

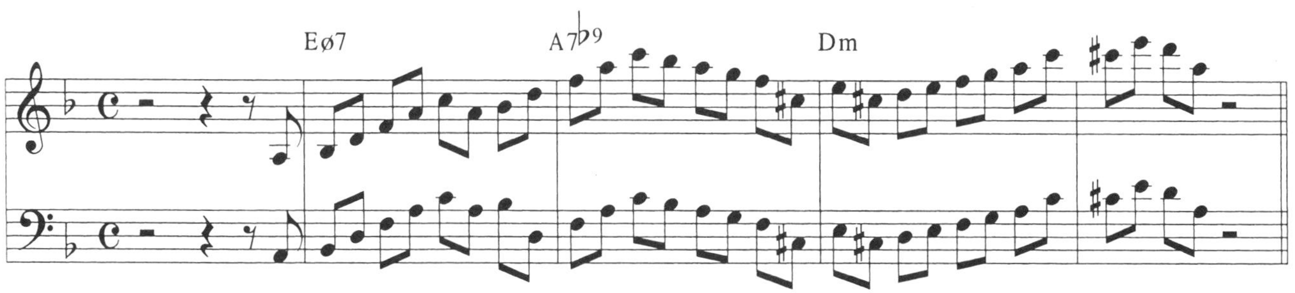

15.78 **Similar to the exercise 15.77, but shown in G minor**

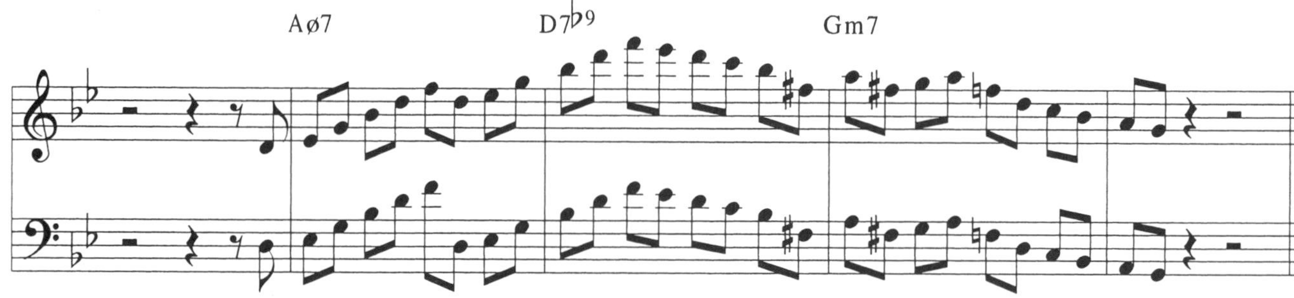

15.79 **Encircling ideas eventually lead to outline no.1 in the following exercise. The chord tones for F minor (C - A♭ - F) are encircled over the Dø7, and the C minor chord tones (G - E♭- C) are encircled in a similar fashion in the last measure.**

15.80 **Outline no.3 using encircling ideas over the Dm7 and sequenced over the Cmaj7.**

15.81 **Outline no.2. Variations of 1-2-3-5 patterns are used over the G7 and the C. A 5-3-2-1 E♭ over the G7 and a 3-5-2-1 C over the C.**

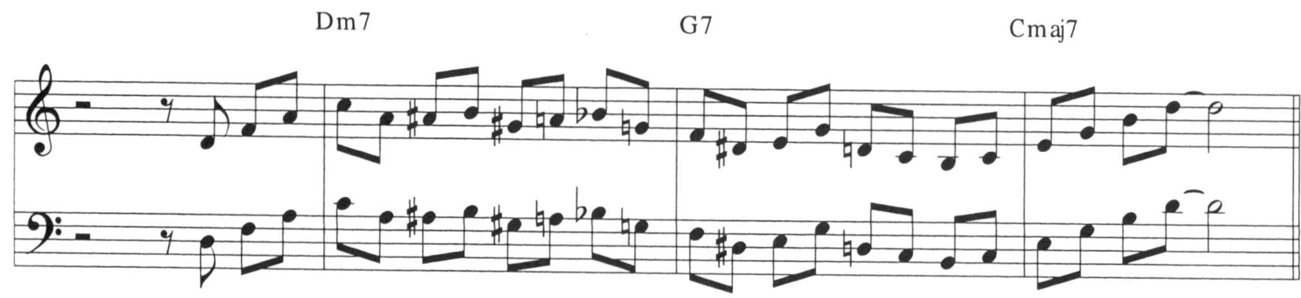

15.82 **Outline no.1 with chromatic approaches.**

15.83 **Outline no.2.**

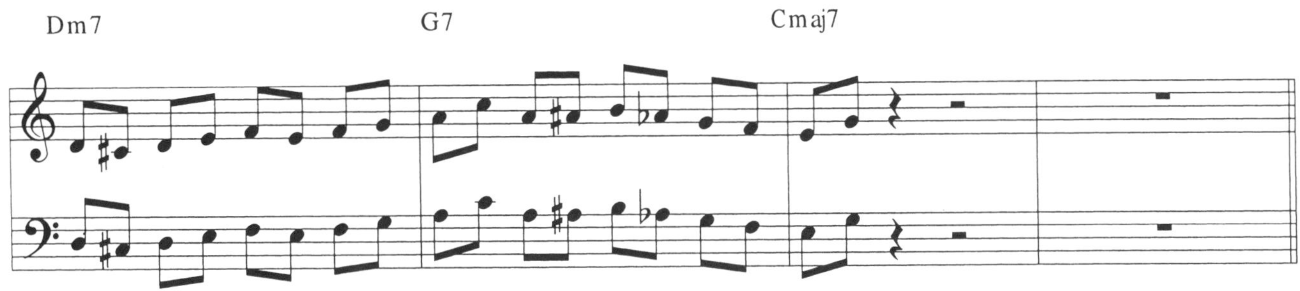

15.84 **Outline no.1.**

15.85 **Outline no.3 with encircling and chromatic approaches.**

15.86 Outline no.3 with encircling and chromatic approaches.

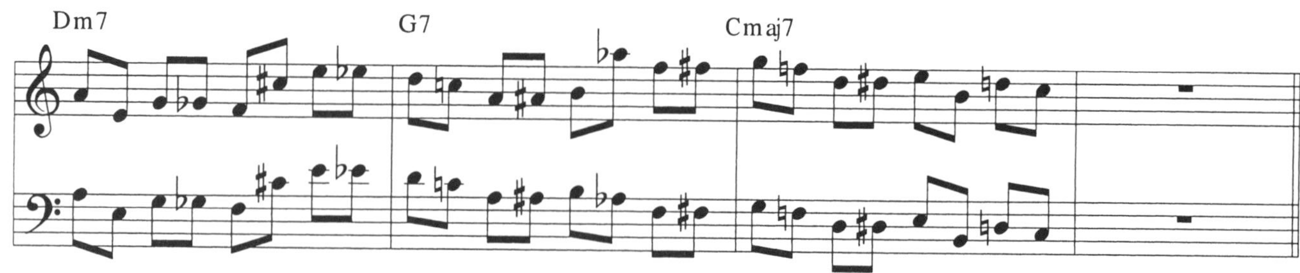

15.87 Outline no.2 with encircling and chromatic approaches.

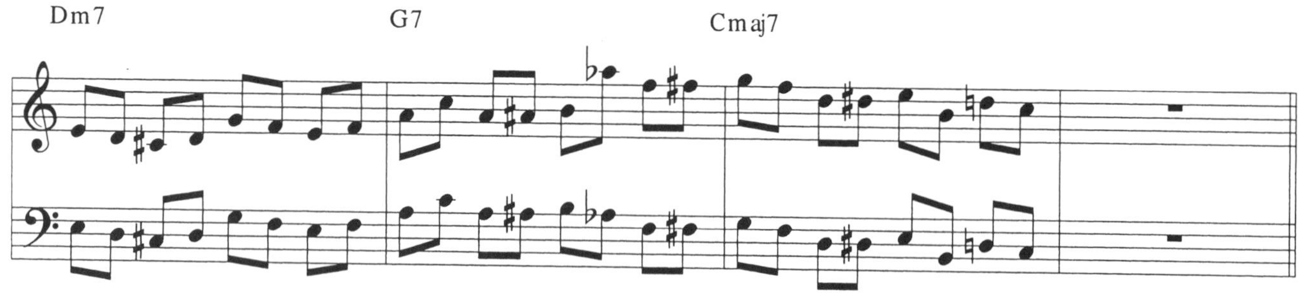

15.88 Outline no.1 with encircling and chromatic approaches.

15.89 Exercise emphasizing 9ths and 13ths over dominants.

15.90 Exercise emphasizing 9ths and 13ths over dominants.

15.91 Outline no.2 & no.3 3rd mode major ♭6 used over dominants.

15.92 Exercise emphasizing 9ths and 13ths over dominants.

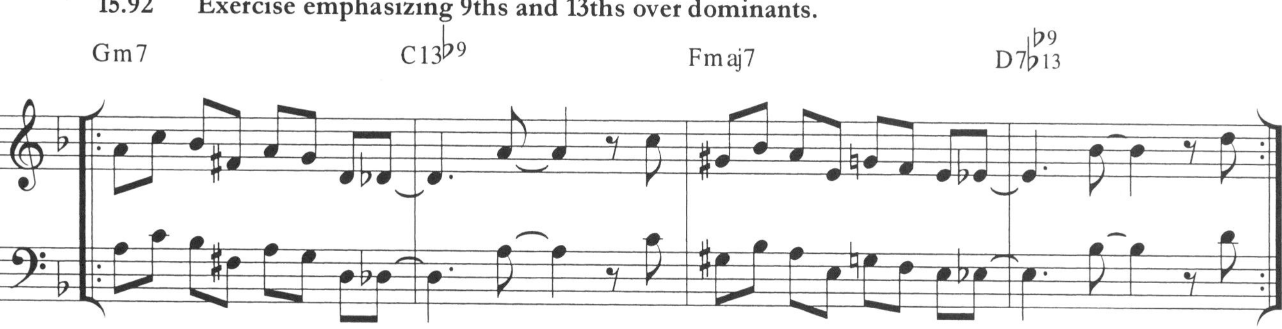

15.93 Exercise emphasizing 9ths and 13ths over dominants.

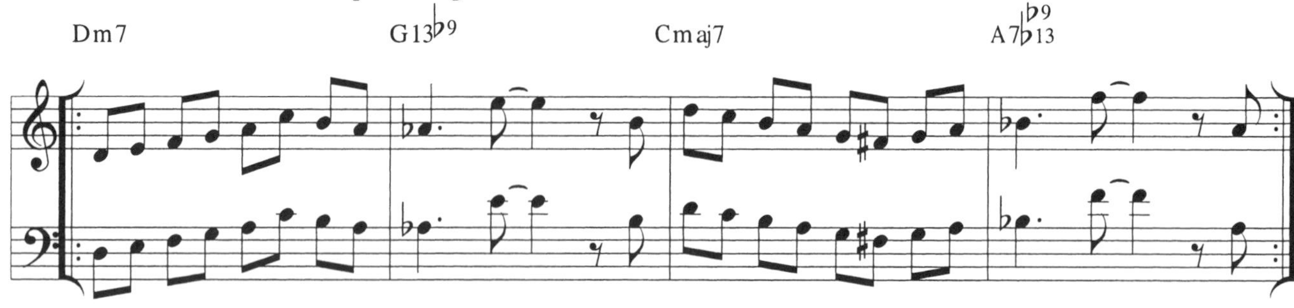

15.94 Exercise emphasizing 9ths and 13ths over dominants.

15.95 Outline no.1 emphasizing 9ths and 13ths with vii°7/iii superimposed over I.

15.96 Outline no.2 emphasizing 9ths and 13ths with vii°7/iii superimposed over I.

15.97 **Outline no.3 emphasizing 9ths and 13ths with vii°7/iii superimposed over I.**

15.98 **Outline no.3 with extensive chromatic elaboration.**

15.99 **Outline no.1 with extensive chromatic elaboration. The common chromatic approach is shown in boxes.**

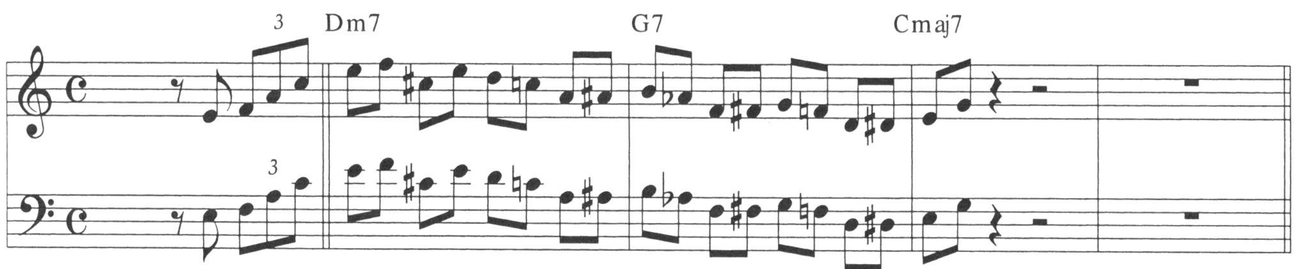

15.100 **Outline no.2 with neighbor tone encircling and a deceptive resolution at the Cmaj7.**

15.101 Outline no.1 with extensive chromatic elaboration.

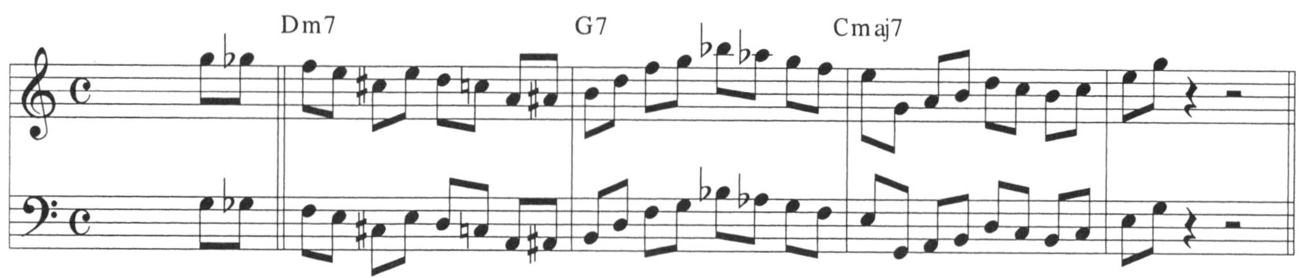

15.102 Outline no.2 with delayed resolution.

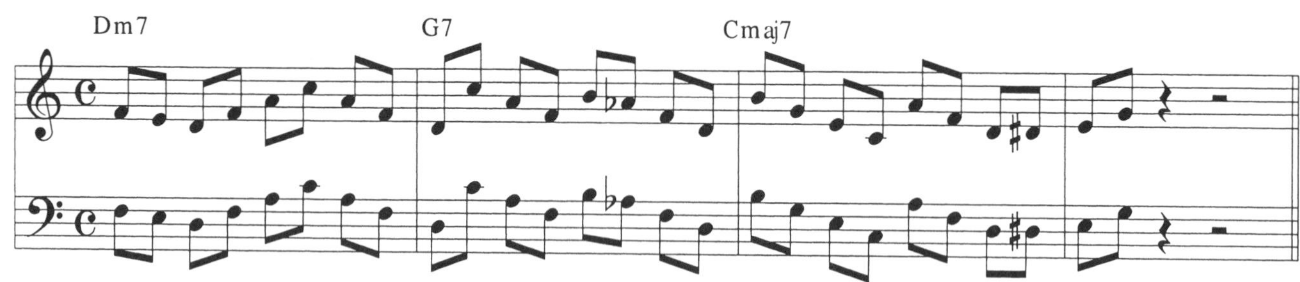

15.103 Outline no.3.

15.104 Outline no.3 using neighbor tone encircling.

15.105 Outline no.2 using lower neighbor tones

15.106 Outline no.1 with extensive chromaticism

DEVELOPING & PRACTICING OUTLINE EXERCISES

Exercises 15.107-15.114 take a step by step approach to using ideas and developing them into more involved and interesting lines. Exercises 15.115-15.125 take exercise 15.114 and break it down into manageable units in order to learn and apply in all twelve keys. These methods should be applied to any practice of the exercises in this book.

15.107 Begin with simple outline no.1 with added 3-5-7-9 arpeggios

15.108 Add chromatic approaches to the third of each chord and invert selected arpeggios

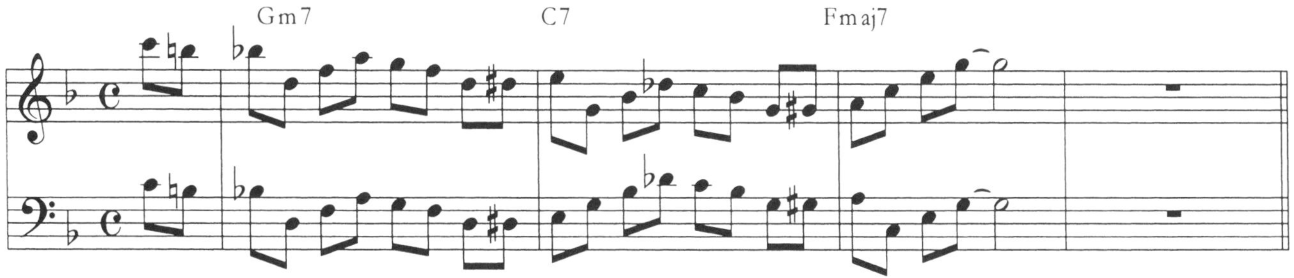

15.109 **Add double chromatic approach to the third of the ii7 chord and a bop cliché over the C7.**

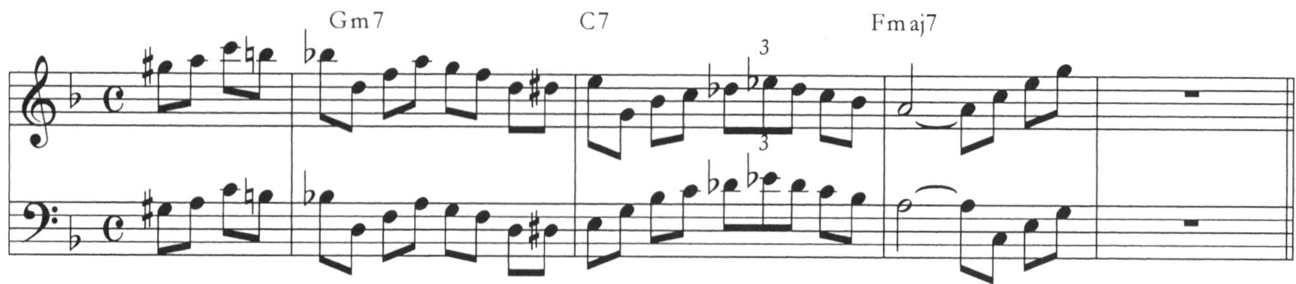

15.110 **Keep the bop cliché and use it with this outline no.2. The extra notes are diatonic passing tones.**

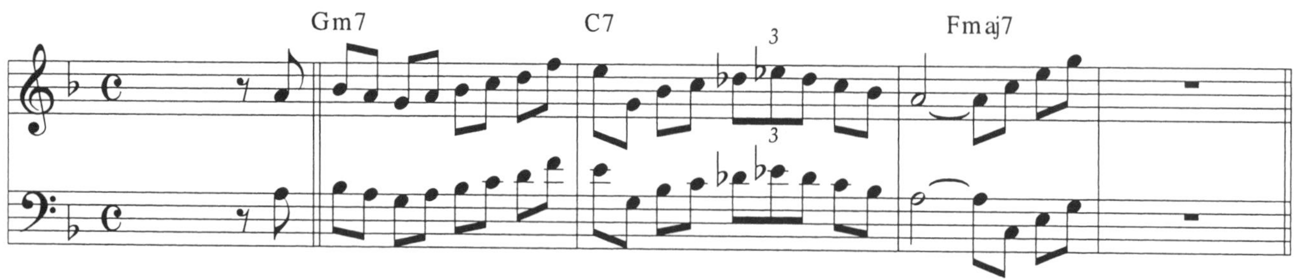

15.111 **Add the chromatic encircling to the first measure, a deceptive resolution on the C7, and another bop cliché over the Fmaj7 in this outline no.2 exercise.**

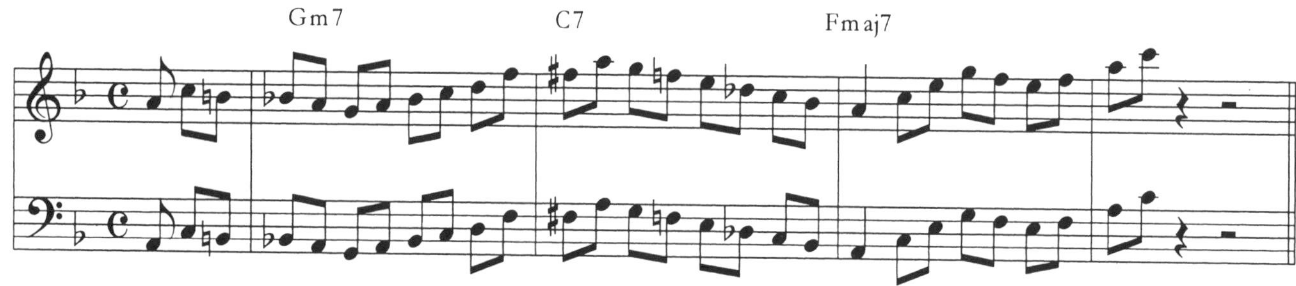

15.112 **Begin outline no.3 with a chromatic leading tone. The third of C7 (E) is approached chromatically from above and below (G-F♯-F-E & D-D♯-E) creating a chromatic wedge, and the tonic chord tones are encircled with upper and lower neighbor tones.**

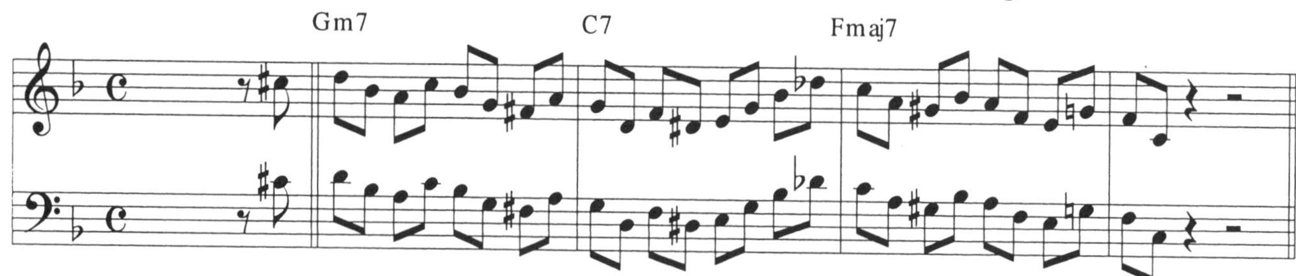

15.113 **The internal chromatic line (G-F♯-F-E) is emphasized in this outline no.3 exercise.**

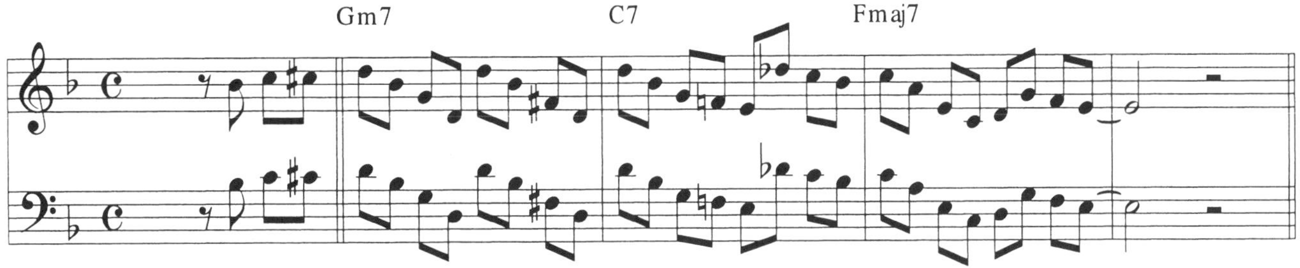

15.114 **Outline no.3 (or no. 1) with chromatic encircling, common chromatic approaches and bop cliché.**

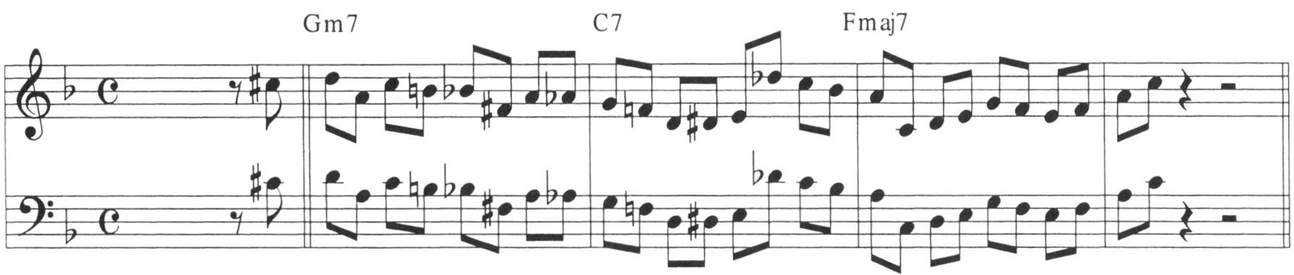

HOW TO LEARN EXERCISE 15.114 IN THIS & ALL MAJOR KEYS?

15.115 **Begin by being able to play the essential skeleton outline no.3 in this and all keys.**

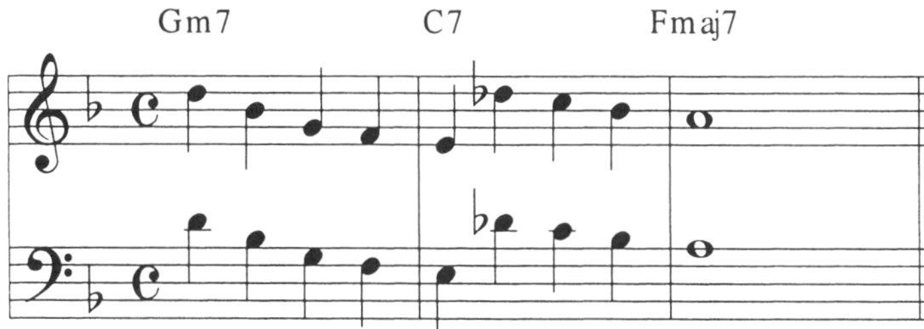

15.116 **Then add the chromatic pickup note for all keys.**

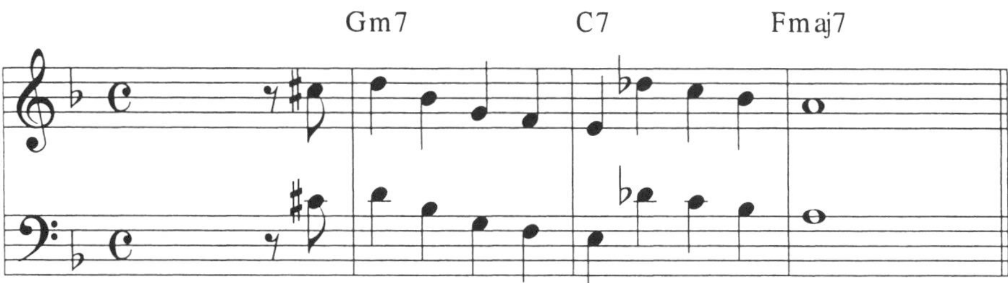

15.117 **Make sure you can play 5-3 with the shown chromatic approach for all ii7 chords.**

15.118 **Make sure you can play 3-1 with the shown chromatic approach for all ii7 chords.**

15.119 **Combine the two previous and play for all ii7 chords.**

15.120 **Now add the single chromatic pickup note for all ii7 chords.**

15.121 Practice this common chromatic approach to the third of all V7 chords.

15.122 Practice this common chromatic approach to the third of the V7 chord and the continuation of outline no.1 to the third of the I chord for all keys.

15.123 Isolate and practice just the tonic triad excerpt.

15.124 Practice just the first few beats.

15.125 **Playing the entire example should be easier after isolating and preparing each part.**

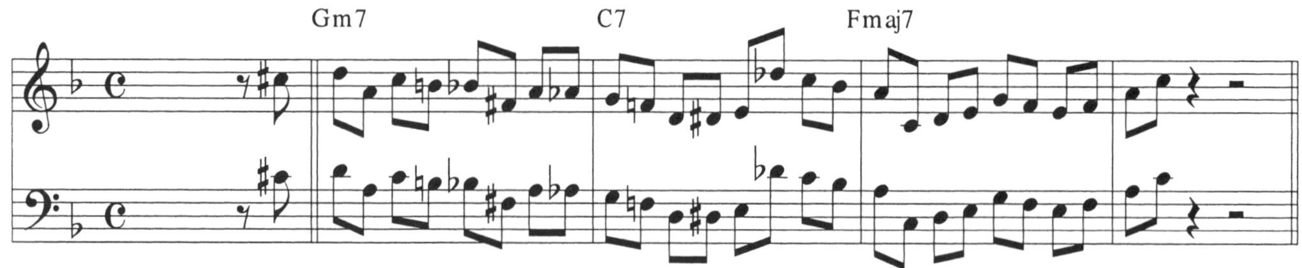

15.126 **Try creating your own exercises. Here is an outline no.1 idea that includes chromatic devices and 3-5-7-9 arpeggios.**

15.127 **Here is the previous exercise displaced. The arpeggios now occur on the downbeat of three and not the downbeat of one.**

EXERCISES WITH QUICKER HARMONIC RHYTHM

15.128 **Outline no.1 (3-5-2-1 G♭ minor pattern over F7)**

15.129 Outline no.2 (3-5-2-1 G♭ minor pattern over F7)

15.130 Outline no.3 (3-5-2-1 G♭ minor pattern over F7)

15.131 Outline no.3 (3-5-2-1 G♭ minor pattern over F7)

15.132 Outline no.3 with encircling, bop cliché and deceptive resolution

15.133 Outline no.1 in G minor

15.134 Outline no.2 in G minor

15.135 Outline no.3 in G minor

OUTLINES IN COMBINATIONS ELABORATED

Find the outlines in the following exercises. Identify the elaboration devices used. Exercise 15.136 includes chromatic encircling, extended tertian arpeggios, minor 1-2-3-5 patterns superimposed a half-step above the root of a dominant chord, common chromatic approaches, octave and rhythmic displacement applied to 3-5-7-9 arpeggios.

15.136 Outlines in combinations over ii7- V7 - I - V7/ii - ii7 - V7 - I progression.

15.137 Outlines in combinations over ii7- V7 - I - V7/ii - ii7 - V7 - I progression.

15.138 Outlines in combinations over iiø7/ii- V7/ii - ii7 - V7 - I progression.

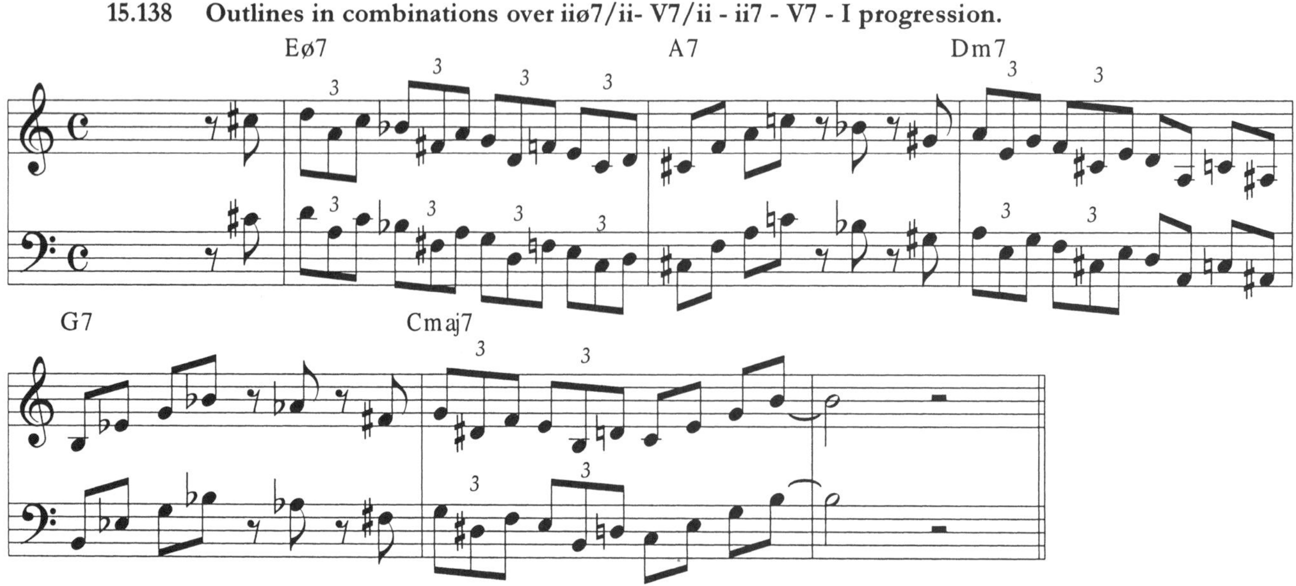

EXCERPTS FROM SOLO TRANSCRIPTION

From a live performance of Bert Ligon on piano.

15.139 Outline no.2

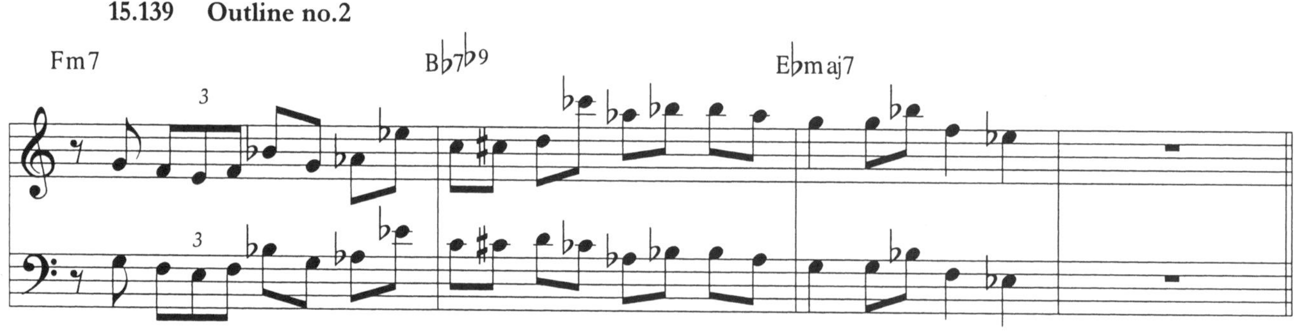

15.140 Outline no.1

15.141 Outline no.1

15.142 Outline no.2

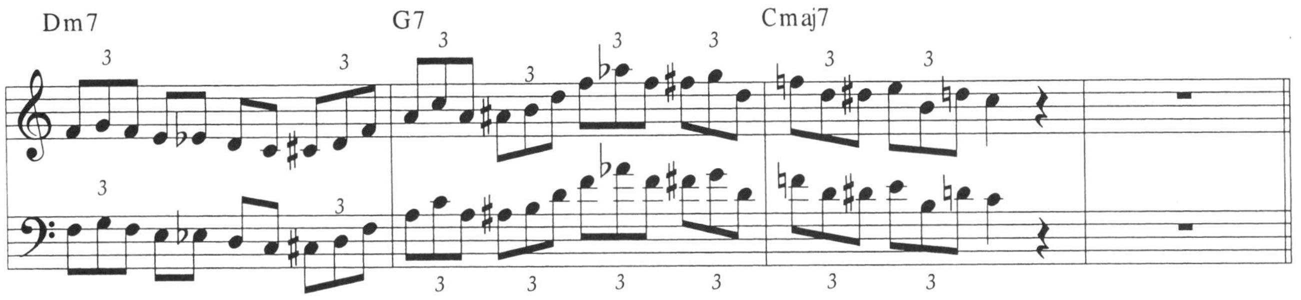

15.143 Outline no.3

15.144 Outline no.2

15.145 Outline no.1

15.146 Upper Extension Connections

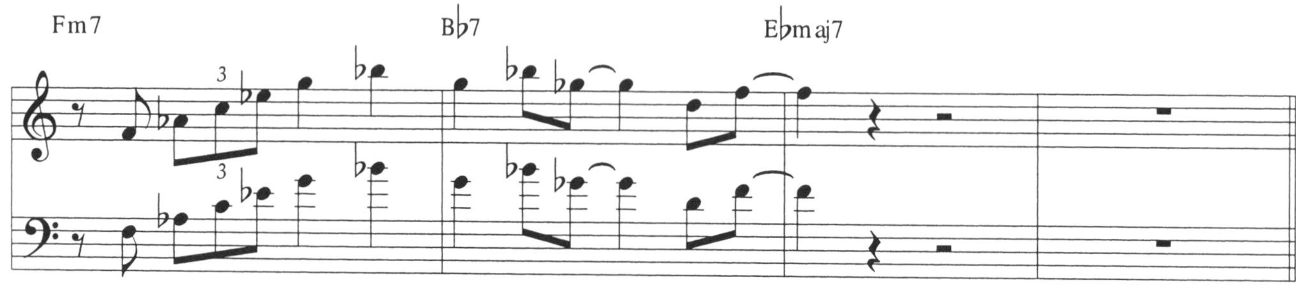

15.147 Outline no.2

15.148 Outline no.3

Douglas MacArthur once said "Chance favors the prepared man." This is true for the military and baseball, and it certainly is true for jazz improvisation. Students who wait for the muses to descend and land on their shoulders providing guidance, or those who hope to just play what they hear, will not have as much success as those students who prepare. Practice all things in all keys. The muses also favor the prepared musician.

> *"Chance favors the prepared man."*
> *—Douglas MacArthur*

XVI. APPLICATIONS & ETUDES

> ***There is no abstract art. You must always start with something. —Pablo Picasso***

It is almost impossible to create when staring at infinity. The best way to free yourself as an artist is paradoxically by limiting yourself. Making some initial decisions allows the creative side to begin making connections. An example of establishing limits would be deciding to improvise on a medium swing blues in B♭. Infinity has been narrowed down to a twelve measure form in a specific key with a specific rhythmic setting. The next decisions involve how you want to express your ideas in that particular setting: Do I play simple or complex rhythmic ideas? inside or against the chord? play the pretty notes or create tension? play in the low or high registers?

These are decisions that are made on the fly when improvising. In every phrase there are thousands of considerations for an improviser. How can you think of all these things when the quarter note is around 250 bpm and the changes are tricky? You can't. You have to practice enough to be able to make decisions intuitively. The intuition is trained by how your time is spent in the practice room. Learn from the field of sports. Tennis players drill certain shots thousands of times in order to be able to react to a 125 mph serve or a tricky cross-court shot. Baseball infielders repeatedly practice double play combinations, the wheel play, backing up other positions so that when these things must be executed in a few short seconds, they do not have to think: they react. They react from intuition trained from hours of repeating specific skills.

Yogi Berra once said "How can you think and hit at the same time?" The same could be said for improvising music. How can you think and play at the same time? Tony Gwynn, several time National League batting champion, one of the greatest hitters in baseball history does not have any more time to see the ball than anyone else, yet he has better success. Gwynn is one of those who pays close attention to details. He has broken down the individual elements that make up that fraction of a second that the entire body must move in synchronization to attempt to squarely hit with a round bat a round ball traveling in anything but a straight line at 80-100 mph. Gwynn feels like he needs to swing at a hundred balls per day to maintain muscle memory. It has been said that hitting is over coached and under trained, meaning there is too much theory and not enough humdrum repetition that builds up muscle memory. Is this not also true of jazz improvisation? So many students are able to name scales but have trouble creating meaningful music unless they have spent the hours it takes to build up that muscle memory.

You cannot improvise while trying to remember every possible combination of notes and rhythms you have ever learned. You must limit your choices. You may choose to move from one approach to another. You must learn to do it without thinking about it. This is achieved by thinking about it ahead of time, committing it to muscle memory by drilling one concept over and over, one concept at a time. There is a reason that school curriculum is organized with math at one hour, history at another; and a reason to divide books into chapters. Practice one thing at a time before trying to put it all together.

> ***"What survives every change of system is melody."***
> ***—Igor Stravinsky***
> ***"Melody is the very essence of music."***
> ***—Mozart***

LEARN THE MELODY

Always learn the melody to a tune before practicing anything else. Try playing the melody in all keys as an aid to memorization. Practice embellishing the melody and making it your own by using the melody or theme as your point of departure using rhythmic displacement and neighbor tone patterns.

AGENDAS

Any good story is a mixture of many elements, devices, moods and textures. The blues, or any piece of music should have the same mixture. A good solo would have a balance of harmonic specific elements like outlines and lines constructed from arpeggios, generalization with the joyful sounding major blues, and generalization with the sorrowful, down and dirty sounding minor blues. A way to practice mixing up the approaches is to use an agenda when you practice. On a piece of paper, sketch out a list of different approaches. Play each for a four measure phrase. For example, play the blues alternating between major and minor blues scales for each four measure phrase:

- Minor Blues Scale/Major Blues Scale/Minor Blues Scale
- Major Blues Scale/Minor Blues Scale/Major Blues Scale

The following two choruses of C blues are based on the simple agenda of alternating between minor and major blues scales.

Or try combinations like:

- Specific (outlines, arpeggios, chord specific material)/Major Blues Scale/Minor Blues Scale
- Minor Blues Scale/Specific/Major Blues Scale
- Specific/Minor Blues Scale/Specific

Other agenda items:

- Practice applying several different concepts to the same section of a piece.
- Create "improvisations" from a predetermined agenda and learn them as an etude.
- Practice improvising following the same agenda several times, but creating unique lines.

The variations are endless. Practicing this way should open up the door to more variety. Ultimately, strive for seamless construction and remember to tell a story.

Application of several concepts over a common progression, Part One

Several different approaches will be applied to the following progression. The progression can be found in music by Mozart and in many popular jazz vehicles.

Am7	Dm7	G7	Cmaj7	Fmaj7	Bø7	E7	Am
vi7	ii7	V7	I	IV	iiø7/vi	V7/vi	vi

16.1 Begin by locating 3rds and 7ths. Hear where and when the resolve to the next voice:

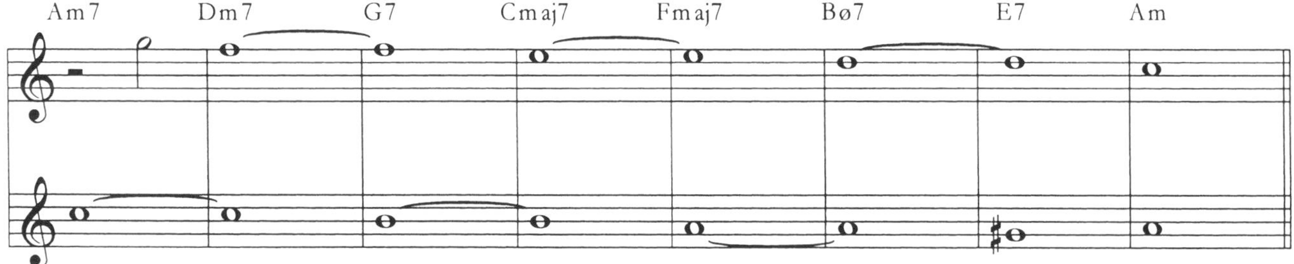

16.2 Create simple lines connecting the 3rds and 7ths:

16.3 **Surround each 3rd with its UNT and LNT:**

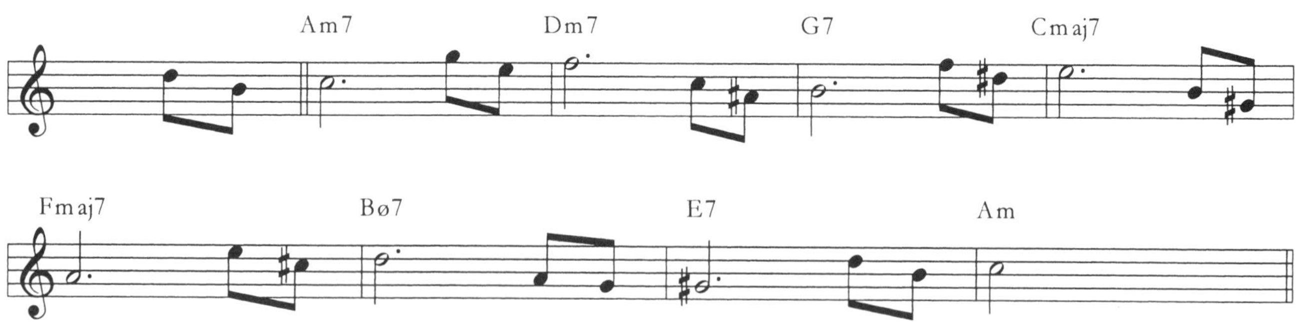

16.4 **Connect the 3rds using outline no. 1. Devices used below include diatonic scale motion, 8va displacement, and sequences:**

16.5 **Outline no. 1 used as framework using pivot tones, chromatic approaches to 3rd, 3-5-7-9 arpeggios, tones borrowed from minor, and delayed resolutions:**

16.6 **Outline no. 1 use as framework using chromatic approaches to 3rd, tones borrowed from minor, and 3-5-7-9 arpeggios:**

16.7 **Outline no. 1 with 3-5-7-9 arpeggios used as framework:**

16.8 **Highly chromatic using outline no. 1 as framework using chromatic approaches to 3rd and 3-5-7-9 arpeggios:**

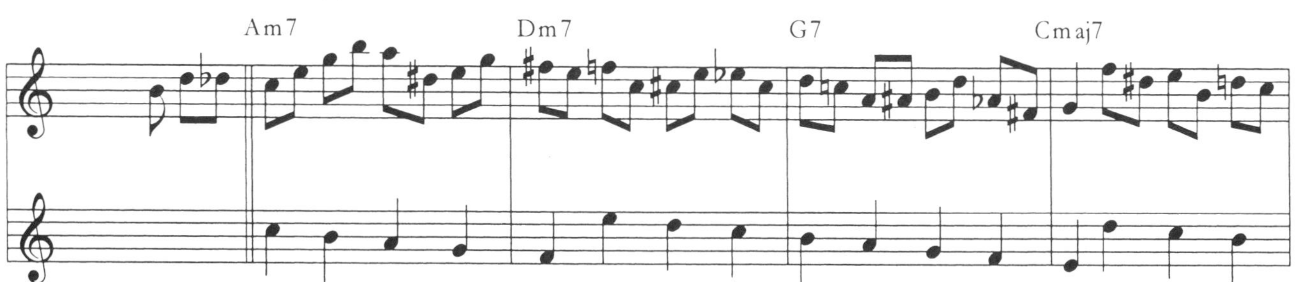

16.9 **Chromatic approaches added to outline no. 1 in waltz time. Notice how the chromatic approaches change where the 3rd occurs in the measure:**

16.10 **Chromatic approaches added to outline no. 1 in waltz time. Notice how the chromatic approaches change where the 3rd occurs in the measure:**

16.11 **Outline no. 2 used as framework using passing tones, chromatic approaches, sequences, and neighbor tones:**

16.12 Outline no. 2 used as framework using neighbor tone groups and chromatic approaches.

16.13 Outline no. 2 used as framework using chromatic passing tones and LNTs:

16.14 **Outline no. 3 used as framework. Outline no. 3 is followed by a 3-5-7-9 arpeggio using pivot tones, chromatic neighbors and chromatic passing tones:**

16.15 **Outline no. 3 used as framework. Each 3-5-7-9 arpeggio is followed by outline no. 3 using pivot tones, chromatic neighbor and chromatic passing tones. Notice the chromatic wedge in mm.2-3: D-C♯-C♮-B from above and A-A♯-B from below:**

16.16 **Adding harmonic and colorful substitutions. A secondary dominant has been added in m.1. The A7 points to Dm. B♭ minor over the A7 yields an A7♭13♯9. A♭ minor and E♭ major triads over the G7 create a G7♭13♯9♭9. A♭ major over the C7 creates a C7♭13♯9. The C and Fm patterns over the E7 are from Chapter 7, and create an E7♭13♯9:**

16.17 **Application of quartal patterns. The quartal chords over the G7 suggest G7♭13♯9♭9:**

16.18 **Application of quartal patterns:**

16.19 **Triadic superimposition from Chapter 8. The following triads were used: G over Am, C over Dm, D♭ & E♭ over G7 (yielding the altered tones ♭5, ♭9, ♭13 & ♯9, A major over the Bø7 yielding the ♮2, and C major over the E7 creating an E7♯9♭13:**

16.20 **Other harmonic substitutions. A chromatic ii7 – V7 (A♭m7 – D♭7) has been inserted in place of the G7. A ii7/IV – V7/IV (Gm7 – C7) has replaced the C major chord. The line begins with a neighbor tone group and is followed by an ascending Am7 arpeggio (A-C-E-G) which becomes outline no. 2 when it resolves to the F at the Dm. Descending arpeggios for the A♭m7 and Gm7 are used in mm.3-4, but elaborated with passing tones. The whole step pattern in m.4 suggests a half-whole diminished scale. The whole step diminished scale pattern returns over the E7:**

16.21 **A secondary dominant (A7) points to Dm. A symmetrical diminished pattern is used over the G7. Notes from the diminished scale are used again over the C7 acting as a V7 of F. Bø7 is replaced by a B7 (V7/iii). Arpeggios from the superlocrian scales are used for the B7 and E7 chords:**

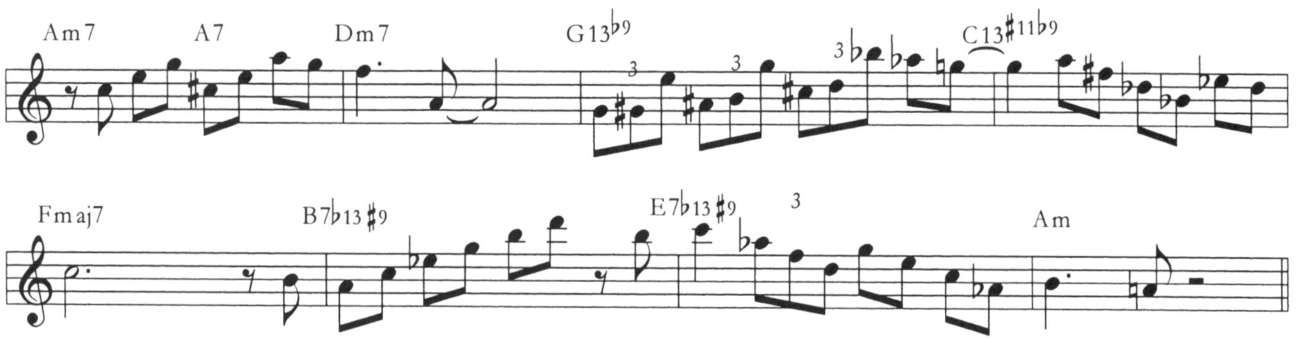

16.22 **Ascending scale patterns that begin with a neighbor tone group. A superlocrian sound is used for the G7, so the scale pattern is from A♭ minor. Gm7 - C7 replaces the C chord. A superlocrian sound is used for the E7, so the pattern is from F minor. In the last measure, the pattern is reversed—a descending scale follows a neighbor tone group:**

16.23 **Descending scale patterns that begin with a neighbor tone group. In the last measure, the pattern is reversed—an ascending scale follows a neighbor tone group:**

16.24 **Simple framework with chromatic approaches. The line is highly complicated, but at the heart of it is a simple framework that has been elaborated with chromatic approaches. This is not random chromaticism, but chromatic notes that point to the simplest of chord tones:**

16.25 Simple framework with chromatic approaches:

16.26 Extended tertian arpeggios. The arpeggio in m.3 over the G7 creates a G7 ♯9 ♭13. That measure may be understood as a tritone substitute, D♭9♯11, and the arpeggio would then be 3-5-7-9-♯11-13. The altered notes in the second half of m.4 create a C7 ♯9 ♭13, or a descending 9-7-5-3 arpeggio of the tritone substitute G♭7. The C♯ over the Bø7 is derived from locrian ♯2, the 6th mode of D melodic minor. The notes for the E7 chord are from E superlocrian, the 7th mode of F melodic minor:

16.27 Augmented scales can provide exotic flavor:

Later in this chapter are two completely different etudes based on this progression.

Application of several concepts over a common progression, Part Two

The following progression occurs frequently in jazz tunes. Exercises 16.28-16.45 will apply different individual concepts and exercises from the previous chapters to the same progression, one concept at a time. The basic progression is:

Eø7	A7	Dø7	G7	Cø7	F7	B♭
iiø7/iii	V7/iii	iiø7/ii	V7/ii	iiø7/i	V7/i	I

An exhaustive examination of possibilities over one specific area of a tune will better prepare one for making spontaneous musical choices.

Chapter 8 discussed the superimposition of major triads over other chords. The formula for exercise 16.28 is:

D/Eø7 = Eø7♮2
F/A7 = A7♯9♯13
C/Dø7 = Dø7♮2
E♭/G7 = G7♯9♯13
B♭/Cø7 = Cø7♮2
D♭/F7 = F7♯9♭13
F/B♭ = B♭ maj7.

16.28 Major triad superimposition:

Minor triads may also be superimposed over each chord. The formula for exercise 16.2 is: Gm/E = Eø7; B♭m/A7 = A7 ♭9♭13; Fm/D = Dø7; A♭m/G7 = G7 ♭9♭13; E♭m/C = Cø7; F♯m/F7 = F7 ♭9♭13; and Dm/B♭ = B♭ maj7.

16.29 Minor triad superimposition:

16.30 Quartal triad superimposition over all the chords in this progression:

16.31 More quartal triad superimposition:

16.32 Superimposition of minor 1-2-3-5 patterns over all the chords:

16.33 Superimposition of major and minor 1-2-3-5 patterns over all the chords:

The simple triads superimposed over the chords in the progression may be elaborated using neighbor tones (NT). In exercise 16.34 m.1, a Gm triad is used over an Eø7 chord. The D is preceded by a leading tone, B♭ is preceded by LNT & UNT, and G is preceded by LNT, UNT and a chromatic passing tone. M.2 uses only outline no.1 as a balance to the previous chromaticism. This idea is sequenced through the rest of the progression.

16.34 Triad superimposition with NT elaboration:

16.35 Outline no.1 sequenced through the progression:

The first two chords could be voiced with these extended tertian voicings and then sequenced through the rest of the progression.

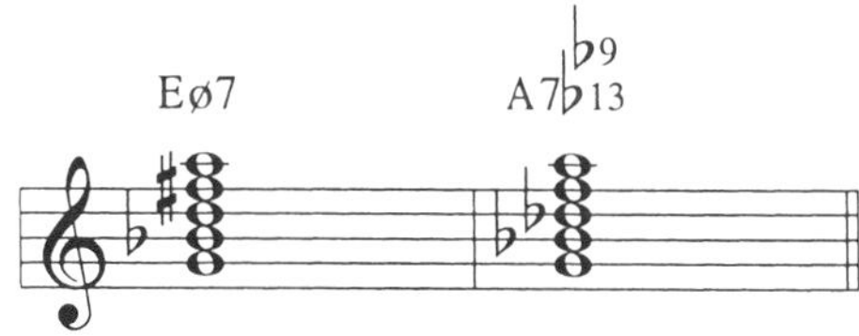

16.36 Lines created following extended tertian voicings:

16.37 Lines created following extended tertian voicings:

16.38 Lines created following extended tertian voicings:

Outline no.3 with elaborations could be applied to the progression. B♭ is followed by its LNT & UNT and returns to B♭; G is followed by its LNT & UNT and returns to G before continuing down to the E - D - C♯. this line is sequenced through the progression.

16.39 Outline no.3 sequenced through the progression:

16.40 CMAR quote sequenced through the progression:

16.41 ***Gone But not Forgotten*** **quote sequenced through the progression:**

Here is a three note symmetrical grouping of half-step - perfect fourth derived from the diminished scale and sequenced up in minor thirds:

16.42 **Three note symmetrical grouping sequenced through the progression:**

Here is another three note symmetrical grouping of whole-step - major third derived from the diminished scale and sequenced down in minor thirds:

16.43 Three note symmetrical grouping sequenced through the progression:

16.44 Diminished scale idea emphasizing each chord tone preceded by its leading tone sequenced through the progression.

16.45 This exercise using modes of melodic minor and follows voice leading using wide ranges.

The next agenda item may be to combine some of the above items integrating two or more ideas over this eight measure progression. Can you think of other individual approaches to practice for this passage?

Application of several concepts over a common progression, Part Three

After the blues, "rhythm changes" (a harmonic progression similar to *I Got Rhythm*) may be the most commonly played jazz progression. The "rhythm changes" bridge is a cycle of dominant chords lasting two measures each. Each of these dominant chords can be colored using any combination of dominant scales, and each may be preceded by a ii7 chord.

16.46 Inserting a ii7 chord before each dominant and connecting using outline no. 1:

16.47 Using outlines no. 2 and no. 3 to connect the chords:

16.48 **Inserting a ii7 chord preceding each dominant and using outline no. 2.**

16.49 **Inserting a ii7 chord preceding each dominant and using outline no. 3. Be sure to bop (accent) the top of the line to bring out the dotted quarter rhythm in the last three measures.**

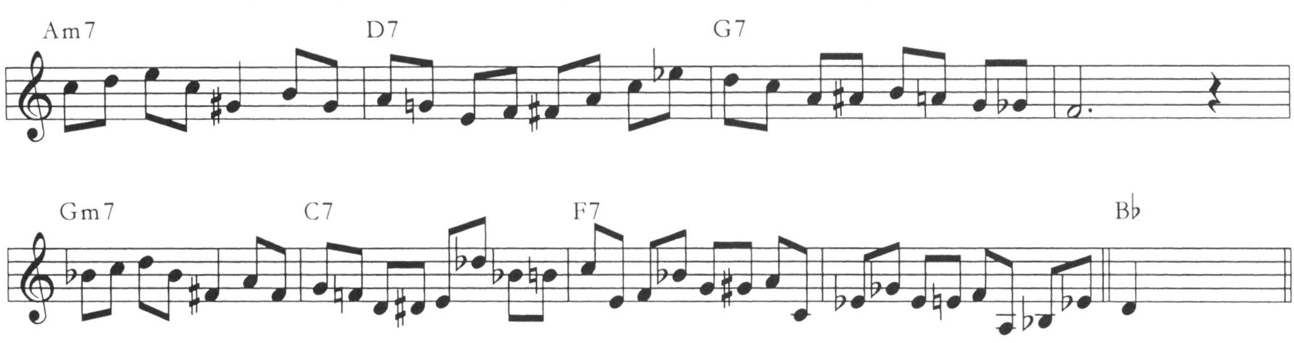

16.50 **Since the A section is in B♭, using Aø7 to precede D7 smoothes the connection to the bridge. This line sequences outline no. 3, uses 3-5-7-9 arpeggios and NT patterns.**

16.51 **Using modes of melodic minor. An E♭ melodic minor is used over the D7 creating a superlocrian mode. D melodic minor over the G7 creates a Lydian dominant. D♭ melodic minor is used over the C7, then C melodic minor and F♯ melodic minor over the F7 chord.**

16.52 **Arpeggios from A melodic minor are used over the D7, from D melodic minor over the G7, from G melodic minor over the C7; and C melodic minor and then F♯ melodic minor over the F7 chord.**

16.53 **Arpeggios from A melodic minor are used over the D7, from A♭ melodic minor over the G7, from G melodic minor over the C7; and from F♯ melodic minor over the F7 chord. The G7 chord could be understood as a D♭9♯11, and the F7 chord as a C♭9♯11, both tritone substitutions.**

16.54 **The symmetrical half-whole diminished scale is used for this series.**

16.55 **A mixture of conventional dominant sounds and more colorful substitutions. E♭ melodic minor is used over the D7 chord. A G9 is followed by a G7 with alterations. It may be easier to understand this chord as a D♭7 tritone substitution chord. A C9 is followed by a C7 with alterations that correspond with the G♭7 tritone substitute chord. An F♯ melodic minor is used over the F7 chord.**

16.56 **Quartal patterns are applied over these dominant chords. Notes from an F minor pentatonic are imposed over the D7, yielding the altered notes: ♯9, ♭9, ♭13, and ♭5. These notes are found in the superlocrian scale, the 7th mode of E♭ melodic minor. A quartal pattern over the G7 chord is sequenced a tritone away. As an answer to the D7 sound, an E♭ minor pentatonic scale is used over the C7. The first quartal pattern over the F7 is derived from the diminished scale and produces the ♮13, ♭9, ♯11, and ♯9. The last quartal idea over the F7 is from superlocrian, the 7th mode of F♯ melodic minor.**

16.57 **The Am pattern over the D7 is sequenced a tritone away (E♭ minor) creating an altered D7 chord. The 3-5-7-9 arpeggio of G9 is sequenced a tritone away suggested a D♭9 or a G7♭9♭13. Both of those ideas are sequenced over the C7 and F7 chords.**

16.58 Begins with outline no. 1, followed by outline no. 2. Half-whole diminished scale used for C7. Outline no. 1 returns over the Cm7 and F7 superlocrian is used in the last measure.

The next agenda item may be to combine some of the above items integrating two or more ideas over this eight measure progression. Can you think of other individual approaches to practice for this passage?

ETUDES ON STANDARD PROGRESSIONS

The following etude was based on a popular jazz harmonic progression and was created following the agenda shown below. Each four measure phrase has a different approach. Creating agendas like this will help you avoid running the same old lines and the same old ideas one right after the other. Practicing by following an agenda that forces you to change approaches will help your ability to shift gears and directions in real life improvisation. When creating the agendas, keep in mind the contrast between one idea and the next. After a period of harmonic specific lines, a bluesy generalization may be welcome. After a blistering note filled passage, some silence or restful simple lines may be welcome. It may be easier at first to make these assessments sitting in the practice room looking at a list than reacting in a live setting with a loud drummer and a non-responsive reed. Deliberately thinking through these choices will help train your ear and instincts to make those decisions live on the bandstand.

Agenda for Etude No. 1

- Paraphrasing the melody & outline no.1 with chromatic approaches to thirds
- Generalization - blues/pentatonic sequence
- Outline no .2 sequence
- Outline no. 2 sequence continues
- Blues/pentatonic idea with rhythmic displacement
- Outline no. 3 sequence
- Outline no. 2 & outline no. 3
- Bluesy ending

The following etude is broken down into individual four measure phrases to illustrate the agenda concepts but is meant to be played with the phrases connected in a thirty-two measure form.

ETUDE No. 1

- Paraphrasing the melody & outline no.1 with chromatic approaches to thirds

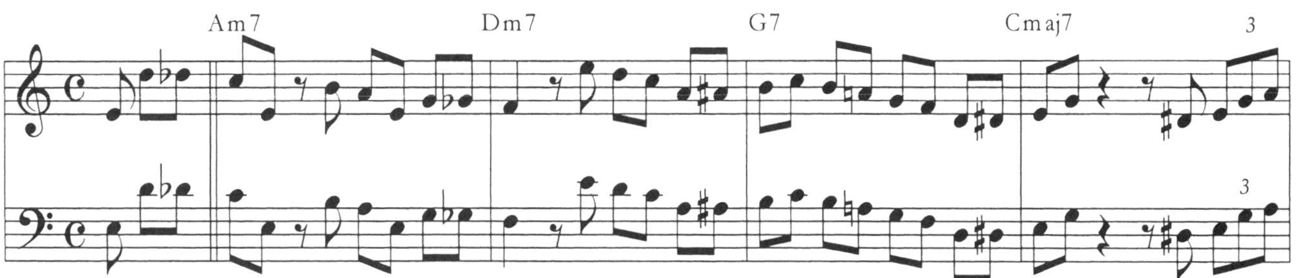

- Generalization - blues/pentatonic sequence

- Outline no.2 sequence

- Outline no.2 sequence continued

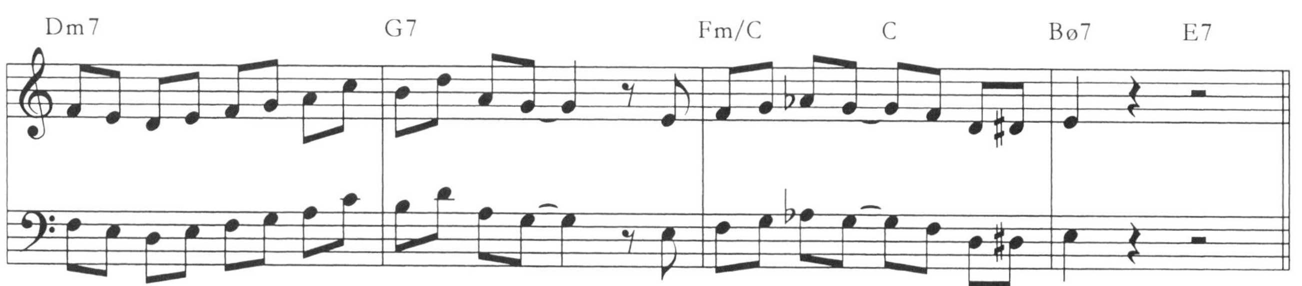

- Blues/pentatonic idea with rhythmic displacement

- Outline no. 3 sequence

- Outline no.2 & outline no.3

- Bluesy ending

Etude No. 2 is based on the same progress as Etude No. 1, but focuses more on colorful substitutions.

Agenda for Etude No. 2

- Upper extensions, secondary dominants, tritone subs, altered dominants.
- voice leading (C♯-C♮). Secondary dominant A7=E♭9
- extended arpeggio, half-whole diminished, locrian ♯2
- Blues Generalization
- Triad superimposition (G/Am – C/Dm – D♭/G – D/C)
- Simple arpeggio sequence
- Compound melody. Top line = E - E – F♯ - F♮ – E. Bottom line = A -A♭ - B - B♭ - A
- Chromatic voice leading continues

ETUDE No. 2

- Upper extensions, secondary dominants, tritone subs, altered dominants.

- Voice leading (C♯-C♮). Secondary dominant A7=E♭9

- Extended arpeggio, half-whole diminished, locrian ♯2

- Blues Generalization

- Triad superimposition (G/Am – C/Dm – D♭/G – D/C)

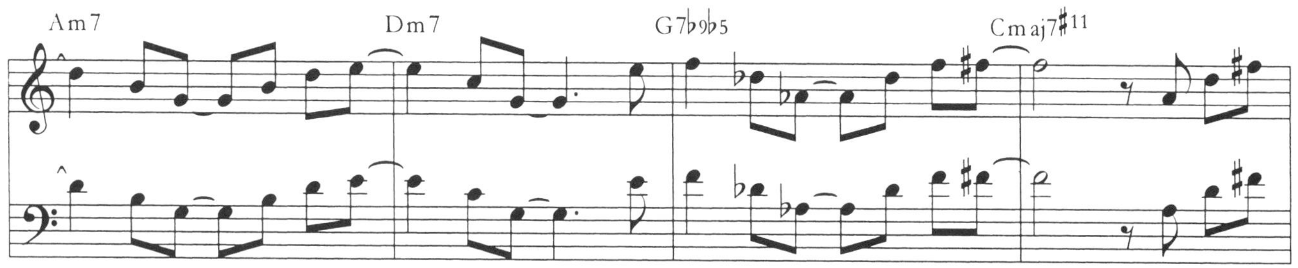

- Simple arpeggio sequence

- Compound melody. Top line = E - E – F♯ - F♮ – E. Bottom line = A -A♭ - B - B♭ – A

- Chromatic voice leading continued

Etude no. 3 is based on another popular jazz harmonic progression and uses specific approaches for each of the nine four measure phrases.

Agenda for Etude No. 3

- mm.1-4: 3-5-7-9 arpeggios.
- mm.5-6 outline no.1 including 3-5-7-9 arpeggio in m.6. /mm.7-8: bop cliché.
- mm.9-12 neighbor tones encircling triad notes.
- mm.13-16 neighbor tones continue.
- mm.17: extended tertian arpeggio 1-3-5-7-9-11/mm.18: E♭ melodic minor idea over D7 leading to 3-5-7-9 arpeggio over Gmaj7 in m.19.
- major and minor triads and 1-2-3-5 patterns over F♯ø7 chord in m.21 (E/F♯ø7 & Am/F♯ø7), and B7 chord in m.22 (Cm/B7 & G/B7)./mm.24: C♯m *Cry me a River* quote over C7.
- mm.25-32: compound melody, outline no.1 connects mm.28-29.
- mm.33-34: A♭ major blues line.
- m.36: Two triads tritone apart superimposed over C7 (C/C7 & G♭/C7).

The following etude is also broken down into individual four measure phrases to illustrate the agenda concepts but is meant to be played with the phrases connected in a thirty-six measure form.

ETUDE No. 3

- mm.1-4: 3-5-7-9 arpeggios.

- mm.5-6 outline no.1 including 3-5-7-9 arpeggio in m.6. /mm.7-8: bop cliché.

- mm.9-12 neighbor tones encircling triad notes.

- mm.13-16 neighbor tones continue.

- mm.17: extended tertian arpeggio 1-3-5-7-9-11/mm.18: E♭ melodic minor idea over D7 leading to 3-5-7-9 arpeggio over Gmaj7 in m.19.

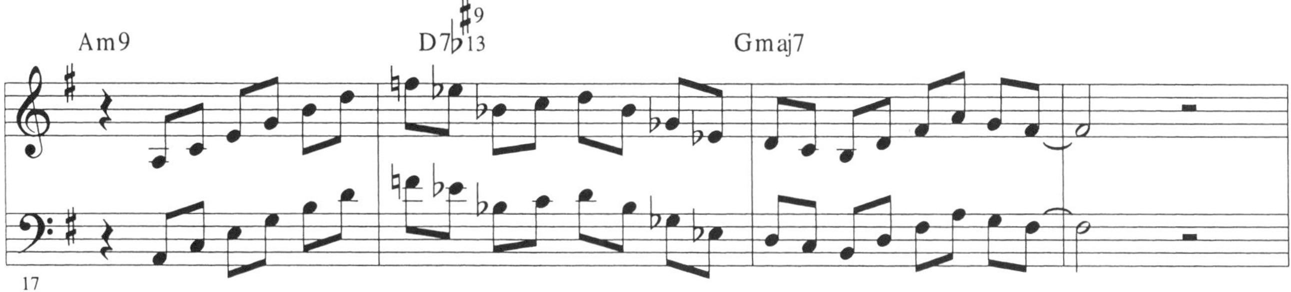

- major and minor triads and 1-2-3-5 patterns over F♯ø7 chord in m.21 (E/F♯ø7 & Am/F♯ø7), and B7 chord in m.22 (Cm/B7 & G/B7)./mm.24: C♯m CMAR quote over C7.

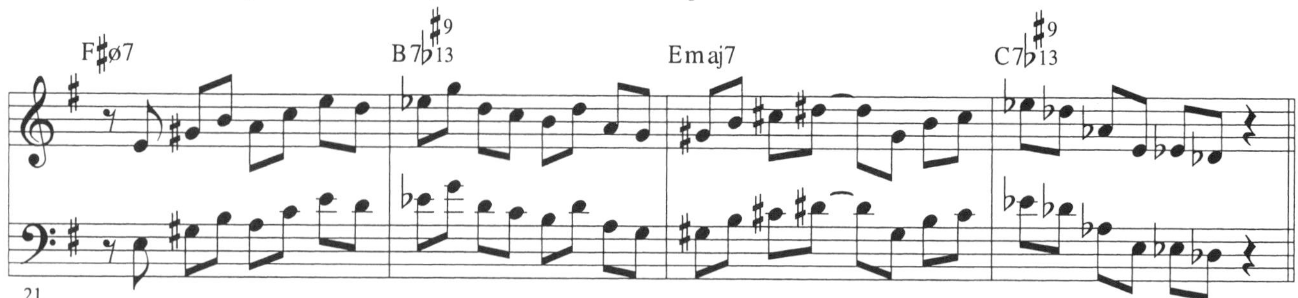

- mm.25-32: compound melody, outline no.1 connects mm.28-29.

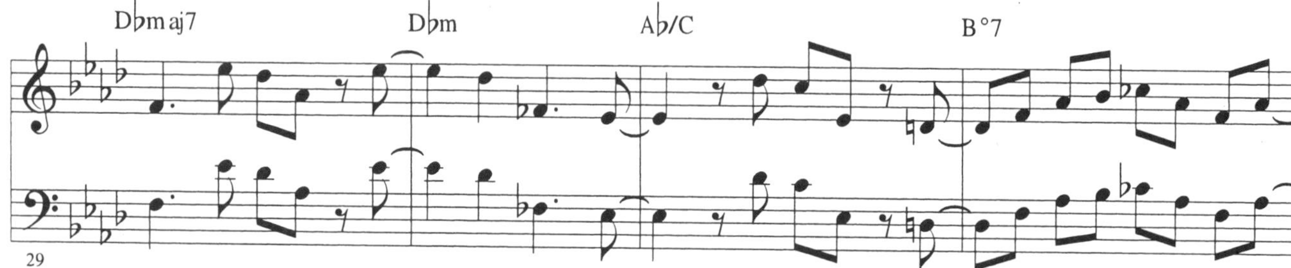

- mm.33-34: A♭ major blues line.
- m.36: Two triads tritone apart superimposed over C7 (C/C7 & G♭/C7).

BLUES ETUDES

Blues Etude No. 1: Following guide tone line:

Blues Etude No. 2: Extended using mixed elements:

continued on following pages:

F
B♭7
F
F7
13
B♭7
F
D7
17
Gm7
C7
F
Gm7 C7
21
F
B♭7
F
F7
25
B♭7
F
D7
29
Gm7
C7
F
Gm7 C7
33

F
B♭7
F
F7
37
B♭7
F
D7
41
Gm7
C7
F
Gm7
C7
45

This next blues chorus follows the guide tone lines suggested by the harmony. The A is approached with an arpeggio and chromatic passing tones. Outline no.1 is used to connect mm.3-5 and mm.9-10.

Blues Etude No. 3: Following guide tone line:

Often a harmonic progression is generalized with just the tonic triad for melodic material. The blues chorus below is limited to notes from the F triad (major and minor) with embellishments.

Blues Etude No. 4: Tonic triad generalization:

The major blues scale can be used as a way of generalizing the blues harmony. The major blues scale is just the major triad with some embellishing tones. The following blues chorus is limited to notes from the major blues scale.

Blues Etude No. 5: Major blues scale:

The minor blues scale can be used as a way of generalizing the blues harmony. The minor blues scale is just the minor triad with some embellishing tones. The following blues chorus is limited to notes from the minor blues scale.

Blues Etude No. 6: Minor blues scale:

The following example is harmonically specific. It is not limited to any one triad or blues scale. Attention is paid to each harmonic area. Arpeggios are clear and specific devices and can be found in mm. 1, 2, 3, 6, 8, 9, 11, and 12. Outlines are also clear and specific (sevenths resolve to thirds keeping counterpoint with the bass) and can be found in mm. 1-2, m.4, and m. 8-10.

Blues Etude No. 7: Harmonic specific using outlines & 3-5-7-9 arpeggios:

MORE ETUDES ON STANDARD PROGRESSIONS

Etude no. 4 is based on another popular progression primarily using the ii7 - V7 - I - IV - iiø7/vi - V7/vi - vi progression.

Agenda for Etude no.4:

Chorus I

- Outline no.1/guide tones
- Blues generalization/outline no.1
- Outline no.2/outline no.3
- Outline no.3 sequenced
- Guide tones/3-5-7-9 arpeggio
- Guide tones sequenced/arpeggio
- Arpeggio/Outline no.3 sequence
- Blues generalization

Chorus II

- Bb triad & scale generalization
- Bb triad & scale generalization
- 1-2-3-5 pattern superimposition
- Sequence continued
- M7 interval motive
- M7 interval sequence continues
- Outline no.1/guide tones
- G minor generalization

Etude No. 4 Chorus I

Etude No. 4 continued

Etude No. 4 continued

Etude no. 5 is based on another popular progression and was created using primarily the outline exercises from chapter 15 transposed to the appropriate keys. The exact exercise from which the lines came are shown in parentheses above each phrase.

Etude No. 5 Outlines exercises from chapter 15 used as agenda

Gmaj7

Gm7

Aø7 (15.41) D7 Bø7 (15.42) E7

Am7 (15.22) D7 Gmaj7

Cm7 (15.93) F7 B♭maj7 G7 (15.101)

Cm7 F7 B♭maj7

Etude No. 5 continued

Etude no. 6 is based on the same progression as Etude no.5 and was created using primarily the outline exercises from chapter 15 transposed to the appropriate keys. The exact exercise from which the lines came are shown in parentheses above each phrase.

Etude No. 6 Outlines exercises from chapter 15 used as agenda

Etude No. 6 continued

Here is one last etude for the book. You should invent more etudes. Using methods illustrated here, you could create a new "improvisation" every week as an etude. Put new ideas you want to learn into musical settings and work until you can play them and make them swing.

Etude No. 7 Mixture of Elements over Standard Progression

Etude No. 7 continued

Look for the following items included in Etude No. 7:

1. Quote from classic jazz tune
2. CMAR quote sequenced
3. Outline no.3
4. Outline no.2
5. Upper extension of tritone substitute dominant G♭9♯11 (♭7-9-♯11-13)
6. Outline no.3 or no.1
7. F♯ triad over B♭7
8. G minor triad over E♭ major 7
9. F triad over Dm7
10. E triad over G7
11. G triad over C major 7
12. *Gone but not Forgotten* quote
13. E triad over D7
14. E♭ triad over D♭7
15. Outline no.1
16. Outline no.1
17. Outline no.3 sequence
18. Dm7 arpeggio followed by blues triadic generalization

CODA

I encourage you to create your own etudes and exercises and hope that the information in this book has helped stir and inspire your imagination. Remember that music is a lifelong mission, not a puzzle to be solved in a day, week or year. This book includes a considerable amount of information about the materials of improvisation, but a great deal is left out. The most important part is left out and that is the key to putting all this to musical use. The key must come from you making decisions on what to practice, what you want to hear, and what you want to play. The next book to buy is one filled with blank staff paper.

Sometimes as a musician, or a living human being, you may become discouraged and find yourself in a creative rut. It happens to all of us, great musicians included. Just keep playing and practicing and enjoy the process of developing as an artist.

Some closing thoughts regarding the arts:

"The arts cannot thrive except where men are free to be themselves and to be in charge of the discipline of their own energies and ardors. The conditions for democracy and for the arts are one and the same. What we call liberty in politics results in freedom in the arts. A world turned into a stereotype, a society converted into a regiment, a life translated into a routine make it difficult for either art or artists to survive. Crush individuality in society and you crush art as well. Nourish the conditions of a free life and you nourish the arts, too."
—Franklin D. Roosevelt, 1939

"We start out playing by ear, learning everything we can, and finally ending up playing by ear again."
—Lee Konitz

"It gets to the point where the player, if he's going to be any kind of serious player, teaches himself."
—Bill Evans

"You have to know 400 notes that you can play, then pick the right four."
"It's not the note you play that's the wrong note — it's the note you play afterwards that makes it right or wrong."
"There are no wrong notes in jazz: only notes in the wrong places."
—Miles Davis

Jazz Theory and Technique

COMPREHENSIVE TECHNIQUE FOR JAZZ MUSICIANS – 2ND EDITION

by Bert Ligon

This book is an essential anthology of technical, compositional, and theoretical exercises, with lots of musical examples.

00030455 All Instruments $29.95

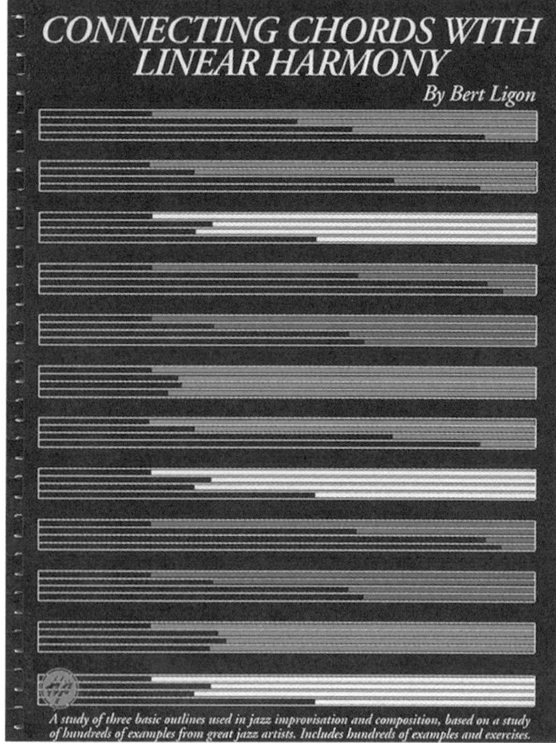

CONNECTING CHORDS WITH LINEAR HARMONY

by Bert Ligon

A study of three basic outlines used in jazz improv and composition, based on a study of hundreds of examples from great jazz artists.

00841077 . . . .$35.00

JAZZ THEORY RESOURCES

by Bert Ligon

Volume I includes: review of basic theory, rhythm in jazz performance, basic tonal materials, triadic generalization, diatonic harmonic progressions and harmonic analysis, substitutions and turnarounds, common melodic outlines, and an overview of voicings.

Volume II includes: modes and modal frameworks, quartal harmony, other scales and colors, extended tertian structures and triadic superimposition, pentatonic applications, coloring "outside" the lines and beyond, analysis, and expanding harmonic vocabulary. Appendices on chord/scale relationships, elaborations of static harmony, endings, composing tips, and theory applications are also included.

00030458 Volume 1 . . . .$39.95
00030459 Volume 2 . . . .$29.95

FOR MORE INFORMATION, SEE YOUR LOCAL MUSIC DEALER, OR WRITE TO:

7777 W. BLUEMOUND RD. P.O. BOX 13819 MILWAUKEE, WI 53213

Prices, contents, and availability subject to change without notice.